The Changing
Wealth of Nations

E N V I R O N M E N T
A N D
D E V E L O P M E N T

◑

A fundamental element of sustainable development is environmental sustainability. Hence, this series was created in 2007 to cover current and emerging issues in order to promote debate and broaden the understanding of environmental challenges as integral to achieving equitable and sustained economic growth. The series will draw on analysis and practical experience from across the World Bank and from client countries. The manuscripts chosen for publication will be central to the implementation of the World Bank's Environment Strategy, and relevant to the development community, policy makers, and academia. Topics addressed in this series will include environmental health, natural resources management, strategic environmental assessment, policy instruments, and environmental institutions, among others.

Titles in this series:

The Changing Wealth of Nations: Measuring Sustainable Development in the New Millennium

Convenient Solutions to an Inconvenient Truth: Ecosystem-Based Approaches to Climate Change

Environmental Flows in Water Resources Policies, Plans, and Projects: Findings and Recommendations

Environmental Health and Child Survival: Epidemiology, Economics, and Experiences

International Trade and Climate Change: Economic, Legal, and Institutional Perspectives

Poverty and the Environment: Understanding Linkages at the Household Level

Strategic Environmental Assessment for Policies: An Instrument for Good Governance

Strategic Environmental Assessment in Policy and Sector Reform: Conceptual Model and Operational Guidance

The Changing Wealth of Nations

*Measuring Sustainable
Development in the
New Millennium*

THE WORLD BANK
Washington, DC

© 2011 The International Bank for Reconstruction
and Development / The World Bank
1818 H Street NW
Washington DC 20433
Telephone: 202-473-1000
Internet: www.worldbank.org

1 2 3 4 13 12 11 10

This volume is a product of the staff of the International Bank for
Reconstruction and Development / The World Bank. The findings,
interpretations, and conclusions expressed in this volume do not
necessarily reflect the views of the Executive Directors of The World
Bank or the governments they represent.

The World Bank does not guarantee the accuracy of the data
included in this work. The boundaries, colors, denominations, and
other information shown on any map in this work do not imply any
judgement on the part of The World Bank concerning the legal status of
any territory or the endorsement or acceptance of such boundaries.

ISBN: 978-0-8213-8488-6
eISBN: 978-0-8213-8554-8
DOI: 10.1596/978-0-8213-8488-6

Library of Congress Cataloging-in-Publication Data
The changing wealth of nations : measuring sustainable development in
the new millennium.
    p. cm. — (Environment and development)
  Includes bibliographical references and index.
  ISBN 978-0-8213-8488-6 — ISBN 978-0-8213-8554-8 (electronic)
1. Economic indicators. 2. Sustainable development.
I. World Bank.
  HC59.15.C434 2010
  338.9'27—dc22

                                                              2010034836

Cover photos: Kirk Hamilton/World Bank (outer circle);
    Scott Wallace/World Bank (inner circle)
Cover design: Naylor Design

C O N T E N T S

Boxes

Figures

Tables

Foreword

"What is not measured is not managed" is one of the truisms of management science, and it points to a weakness in the indicators we use to gauge development progress. As this book demonstrates, natural resources account for over 20 percent of the wealth of developing nations. Yet indicators like the growth rate of gross domestic product (GDP), used by ministries of finance and development everywhere, do not account for the depletion of those natural resources.

Not only are natural resources an important share of national wealth, but the composition of natural wealth varies widely across developing countries and regions. Some countries are blessed with mineral and energy resources which can generate significant revenues for governments but which may also distort development by providing "easy money." Some countries are rich in crop and pasture lands, which places a premium on protecting soil fertility and managing the water resources which underpin productive use of the land. Other countries have magnificent forests, as well as wild lands with abundant biodiversity, which can draw ecotourists to visit from all over the world. Without sound management, this natural patrimony is at risk.

This book is about development and measuring development progress. While precise definitions may vary, development is, at heart, a process of building wealth—the produced, natural, human, and institutional capital which is the source of income and wellbeing. A key finding is that it is intangible wealth—human and institutional capital—which dominates the wealth of all countries, rising as a share of the total as countries climb the development ladder. The accounting of wealth in over 100 countries over the decade from 1995 to 2005 points to the important progress that has been made in developing countries.

The first chapter of the book ends by suggesting that "how we measure development will drive how we do development." We invite the reader to join us in an exciting endeavor—taking a truly comprehensive approach to development by building the wealth of nations.

INGER ANDERSEN
Vice President and Head of Network
Sustainable Development Network
The World Bank

OTAVIANO CANUTO
Vice President and Head of Network
Poverty Reduction and Economic Management Network
The World Bank

Acknowledgments

The Changing Wealth of Nations has been written by a team including Glenn-Marie Lange, Kirk Hamilton, Giovanni Ruta, Lopa Chakraborti, Deval Desai, Bram Edens, Susana Ferreira, Barbara Fraumeni, Michael Jarvis, William Kingsmill, and Haizheng Li. Research assistance was provided by Justin Ram. The contributions of Xiaolin Ren and Jana Stoever to the development of the database are gratefully acknowledged.

The report received insightful comments from the peer reviewers, Giles Atkinson, Jan Böjo, Richard Damania, and Marian Delos Angeles.

We are grateful to colleagues inside and outside the World Bank who provided useful feedback. Our thanks go to Milan Brahmbhatt, Julia Bucknall, Kevin Carey, Charles di Leva, Marianne Fay, Michael Levitsky, Eduardo Ley, Ian Noble, Per Ryden, Apurva Sanghi, Susanne Scheierling, Jon Strand, Mike Toman, Dominique van der Mennsbrugghe, and Jeff Vincent.

Finally, we are indebted to the late Professor David Pearce, the father of much of the economics of sustainable development, John O'Connor, who led the first work on wealth accounting at the World Bank, and three individuals—John Dixon, Partha Dasgupta, and Karl-Goran Mäler—who have contributed not only to theory and practice, but have also tirelessly championed the cause of applying environmental economics to development problems through their writing and teaching across the developing world.

The financial support of the Government of Sweden is acknowledged with gratitude.

Abbreviations

$/tCO$_2$	dollars per ton of carbon dioxide
$2005	constant 2005 U.S. dollars
ANS	adjusted net saving
CAIT	Climate Analysis Indicators Tool
CDIAC	Carbon Dioxide Information Analysis Center
CEA	Country Environmental Analysis
CEM	Country Economic Memorandum
CO_2	carbon dioxide
CO_2D	CO_2 damages
CW	crop wealth
Depr	depreciation
ED	energy depletion
EE	education expenditure
EITI	Extractive Industries Transparency Initiative
EU	European Union
FAO	Food and Agriculture Organization
FAOSTAT	Food and Agriculture Organization database
GDP	gross domestic product
GHG	greenhouse gas
Global FRA	*Global Forest Resources Assessment* (of the FAO)
GNI	gross national income
GNS	gross national savings
GTAP	Global Trade Analysis Project
IEA	International Energy Agency
IMF	International Monetary Fund
IPCC	Intergovernmental Panel on Climate Change
J-F	Jorgenson-Fraumeni
LMDI	logarithmic mean Divisia index
MD	mineral depletion
NFD	net forest depletion
NGO	nongovernmental organization
NNI	net national income
NNS	net national savings
NPV	net present value

OECD	Organisation for Economic Co-operation and Development
PIM	Perpetual Inventory Method
PM	particulate matter
PMD	particulate matter damages
ppmv	parts per million by volume
PV	present value
SCC	social cost of carbon
SEEA	System of Integrated Environmental and Economic Accounting
SNA	System of National Accounts
UN	United Nations
UNCTAD	United Nations Conference on Trade and Development
UNECE	United Nations Economic Commission for Europe
UNESCO	United Nations Educational, Scientific, and Cultural Organization
UNSD	United Nations Statistics Division
USGS	U.S. Geological Survey
WDI	*World Development Indicators*
WDR	*World Development Report*
WTP	willingness to pay

Note: Dollar amounts are U.S. dollars unless otherwise indicated.

P A R T   1

Changes in Wealth, 1995 to 2005

CHAPTER 1

Introduction and Main Findings: The Changing Wealth of Nations

PERHAPS THE EARLIEST ASSESSMENT OF THE WEALTH OF nations was the *Domesday Book,* prepared at the command of William the Conqueror in 1085–86. According to the *Anglo-Saxon Chronicle,* the book aimed to record "what, or how much, each man had, who was an occupier of land in England, either in land or in stock, and how much money it were worth."

William's goal in measuring the wealth of England was fiscal. He needed to know the value of crown lands in the conquered territory, as well as the value of individual landholdings that could be subject to taxation. Our goals in this book are both more modest and more ambitious than those of William the Conqueror: more modest because we will not present accounts at the level of individual property holdings, and more ambitious because we set forth broad wealth accounts for over 120 countries for the years 1995, 2000, and 2005.

When we pose the question of "how much money it were worth" for assets such as land, we are inevitably asking a question about the future: what is the flow of rents (or economic profits) that this asset can sustain in the future? This concern with futurity is, we argue, the principal reason to build wealth accounts. If we extend this concept to comprehensive wealth—produced capital; natural capital; and human, social, and institutional capital—then measuring changes in wealth permits us to measure the *sustainability* of development. This is an urgent concern today in the poorest developing countries, as we will show.

More generally, measuring changes in real, comprehensive wealth provides an indication to governments of whether policy, broadly conceived, is producing increases in both current and future well-being—what economists would term "social welfare."[1] It certainly could be argued that the fundamental duty of government is to ensure that its policies lead to increases in social welfare.

Today, wealth accounts are an integral part of the System of National Accounts (SNA), which provides the basis for the measurement of economic progress used by ministries of finance around the world (European Commission et al. 2009).[2] However, wealth accounts are not nearly as widely implemented as are the measures of production and income. The traditional indicator of economic progress is growth in gross domestic product (GDP), a broad measure of the value of production occurring within a nation's borders. The problem with GDP growth as an indicator, however, is that it treats both the production of goods and services and the value of asset liquidation as part of the product of the nation. Thus, a country could grow its GDP by depleting stocks of forests and minerals, for example, but this growth would not be sustainable.

This book extends and builds upon *Where Is the Wealth of Nations? Measuring Capital for the 21st Century* (World Bank 2006), which reported comprehensive wealth accounts for more than 120 countries. As in that book, we conceive of development as a process of building and managing a portfolio of assets. The challenge of development is to manage not just the total volume of assets—how much to save versus how much to consume—but also the composition of the asset portfolio, that is, how much to invest in different types of capital, including the institutions and governance that constitute social capital.

The Changing Wealth of Nations adds several new components to the previous work. Most important, because wealth accounts are now available over a 10-year period, 1995 to 2005, it is possible to go beyond a snapshot of wealth at a point in time and provide the first intertemporal assessment of global, regional, and country performance in building wealth and achieving sustainable development.[3]

In this book we take a comprehensive approach to measuring wealth, presenting accounts for the following categories of assets:

- *Total wealth:* The measure of total (or comprehensive) wealth is built upon the intuitive notion that current wealth must constrain future consumption. Chapter 5 presents the theory underpinning this assumption and the methods used to estimate total wealth.
- *Produced capital:* This comprises machinery, structures, and equipment.[4]
- *Natural capital:* This comprises agricultural land, protected areas, forests, minerals, and energy.
- *Intangible capital:* This asset is measured as a residual, the difference between total wealth and produced and natural capital. It implicitly includes measures of human, social, and institutional capital, which includes factors such as

the rule of law and governance that contribute to an efficient economy. Net foreign financial assets, the balance of a country's total financial assets and financial liabilities, are generally included as part of intangible capital in this book (with the exception of chapter 5, in which theoretical concerns are tightly linked to empirical estimation methods).

The book is divided into two parts. The first part provides the big picture of changes in wealth by income group and geographic region, with a focus on natural capital because it is especially important for low-income developing countries. The second part presents case studies that illustrate particular aspects of wealth accounting, including accounting for climate change, the role of intangible capital in growth and development, measuring human capital, and the use of wealth accounting to improve transparency and governance in resource-rich economies. The final chapter reports on the implementation of wealth accounting by countries. The appendixes provide the full wealth accounts for individual countries and for aggregations by income group and geographic region.

How Does Wealth Change with Development?

Where Is the Wealth of Nations? established the links between development outcomes and the level and composition of comprehensive wealth. Some of the important insights from that volume, based on wealth accounts for 2000, continue to apply in 2005 and, indeed, across the decade from 1995 to 2005. In chapter 2 of this volume, we begin by analyzing patterns of wealth and changes in per capita wealth for countries grouped by income category. Grouping countries by income is useful because it reveals the direct links between wealth, income, and development. Among income groups, trends for low-income countries are of particular interest because of the concentration of the world's poor in these countries. Developing countries must make decisions about (a) how much to invest versus how much to consume and (b) what mix of assets to invest in. The middle-income countries are important because they shed light on this process of wealth creation during the transition from low to high income. High-income countries provide insight into the volume and composition of wealth in those countries that have achieved high material standards of living. We then look more closely at developing countries, grouping them by geographic region because of the importance of shared geographic and historical features.

Between 1995 and 2005, global wealth increased in per capita terms by 17 percent in constant 2005 U.S. dollars.[5] Wealth grew fastest in the lower-middle-income countries, which are dominated by the economy of China; per capita wealth in this group increased by nearly 50 percent. High-income countries in the Organisation for Economic Co-operation and Development (OECD) continue to hold most of the world's wealth (82 percent), but there have been slight gains by low- and middle-income countries. The world's poorest countries, accounting for 10 percent of the global population, hold less than 1 percent of global wealth (table 1.1).

Intangible wealth is the largest single component of wealth in all income groups, and the fastest growing one as well. Whether one compares wealth across different income groups for a single year or looks at a single income group over time, the comprehensive wealth accounts tell a clear story about the relationship between development and wealth: development entails building total wealth, but also changing the composition of wealth. Most countries start out with relatively high dependence on natural capital—agricultural land, subsoil assets, and/or forests. They use these assets to build more wealth, especially produced capital and intangible (human and institutional) capital.

This relationship between development and capital is clearly seen in the lower-middle-income countries, where the economy of China dominates. As figure 1.1 shows, per capita wealth has increased dramatically, and just as important, the composition has changed markedly. The share of natural capital fell from 34 percent in 1995 to 25 percent in 2005 (although, as chapter 2 shows, the level of natural capital per person actually increased by nearly $1,100), while the shares of produced capital and intangible capital increased strongly.

The rapid growth of intangible capital is due partly to increased educational attainment in most countries, but a significant part of the increase in intangible capital results from improvements in institutions, governance, and other factors that contribute to better, more efficient use of all of a country's capital—produced, natural, and human. The study of China in chapter 6 shows that rapid economic change and the transition to a market-oriented economy offered people opportunities to realize much higher returns for a given level of educational attainment.

Although wealth is dominated by intangible capital, in low-income countries natural capital constitutes a large share of comprehensive wealth, larger than produced capital. In upper-middle-income countries, natural capital is only slightly less than produced capital, 15 percent and 16 percent, respectively. The high dependence of low-income countries on natural capital and the important role of natural capital in building wealth suggest that it should receive close attention.

For countries dependent on nonrenewable natural capital, transforming natural capital into other forms of wealth is the path to sustainable development. Where natural capital is potentially renewable, such as forest land, appropriate property rights and management regimes are essential if the country is to develop sustainably rather than deplete its natural capital, ending up poorer than before.

Furthermore, natural capital warrants special focus in the wealth management of all countries, even those where its share in wealth is small, because of

TABLE 1.1
Wealth and Per Capita Wealth by Type of Capital and Income Group, 1995 and 2005

Income Group	1995					2005				
	Total Wealth (US$ billions)	Per Capita Wealth (US$)	Intangible Capital (%)	Produced Capital (%)	Natural Capital (%)	Total Wealth (US$ billions)	Per Capita Wealth (US$)	Intangible Capital (%)	Produced Capital (%)	Natural Capital (%)
Low income	2,447	5,290	48	12	41	3,597	6,138	57	13	30
Lower middle income	33,950	11,330	45	21	34	58,023	16,903	51	24	25
Upper middle income	36,794	73,540	68	17	15	47,183	81,354	69	16	15
High income OECD	421,641	478,445	80	18	2	551,964	588,315	81	17	2
World	504,548	103,311	76	18	6	673,593	120,475	77	18	5

Source: Authors' calculations based on World Bank data.
Note: Figures are based on the set of countries for which wealth accounts are available from 1995 to 2005. Data in this table do not include high-income oil exporters.

several characteristics that set it apart from most produced and intangible capital. Natural capital is the source of many ecosystem services, provided as externalities without market prices; hence, these services are often undervalued and vulnerable to threats. Many forms of natural capital are nonrenewable, or renewable only under restricted management regimes. Losses and degradation of natural capital may lead to irreversible changes in the provision of ecosystem services and biodiversity, and the potential for substitution is limited (for example, in the case of the ozone layer). Some natural "bads" (atmospheric carbon dioxide [CO_2] for example) are global in scope and provenance and are both nonrival and nonexcludable; only cooperative solutions can deal with the problem.

As chapter 2 shows, among the developing countries, all geographic regions have increased their per capita wealth, but the gains appear smallest in

FIGURE 1.1
Changing Volume and Composition of Wealth in Lower-Middle-Income Countries, 1995-2005

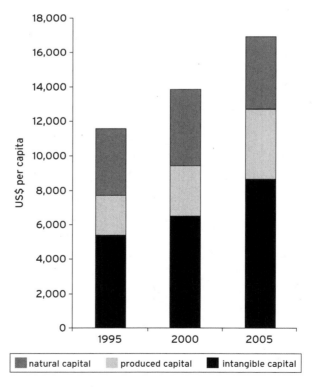

Source: Authors' calculations based on World Bank data.

Sub-Saharan Africa: only 4 percent between 1995 and 2005. If we look more closely at this region, however, we find two sharply distinct stories. One story is about a handful of countries, led by resource-rich Nigeria, that experienced steep declines in per capita wealth and dragged down performance for the entire region relative to the rest of the world. The other story, however, is about the success in increasing per capita wealth achieved by nearly two-thirds of African countries over the decade. This second group was led by the largest African economy, South Africa, but also includes others such as Botswana, Burkina Faso, Ethiopia, Ghana, Mozambique, and Uganda. For the region as a whole, the successful countries were able to offset the decline in per capita wealth in the underperformers.

Most of the increase in per capita wealth in all regions resulted from the growth of intangible capital—improvements in human capital, institutions, and technology that support more efficient use of produced and natural capital. But natural capital remains an important asset. Agricultural land dominates the natural capital of Asia, Latin America, and Sub-Saharan Africa, while subsoil assets account for more than 60 percent of the natural capital of Europe and Central Asia and the Middle East and North Africa. Forest land is particularly important in Latin America. Both Sub-Saharan Africa and South Asia experienced a decline in natural capital from 1995 to 2005, which is worrying given the continued dependence of so many people on agriculture.

Harnessing Natural Capital for Development

The Hartwick rule (Hartwick 1977; Solow 1986) provides a simple rule of thumb for sustainable development in countries that depend on nonrenewable natural resources. The Hartwick rule holds that consumption can be maintained—the definition of sustainable development—if the rents from nonrenewable resources are continuously invested rather than used for consumption. But, in fact, many resource-rich developing countries do not reinvest the rents. So here we pose a counterfactual question: "What would total capital be if, each year since 1980, countries had invested all the resource rent in produced capital?"[6] The hypothetical capital stock is then compared to actual produced capital to see (a) whether countries followed the Hartwick rule, and (b) if they did not, how much richer they could have been if they had followed the rule.

The consequences of not investing resource rents in productive assets were highlighted in *Where Is the Wealth of Nations?* through the analysis of the "Hartwick rule counterfactual." We update these figures to 2005 to show what is foregone when resource-rich countries do not reinvest resource rents from nonrenewable natural capital.

Figure 1.2 shows the results of the Hartwick rule counterfactual for five resource-rich countries. In 2005, Trinidad and Tobago had accumulated $20,021

FIGURE 1.2
Produced Capital Per Capita, Actual and Hypothetical, in Five Resource-Rich Countries, 2005

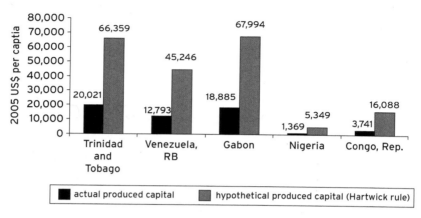

Source: Authors' calculations based on World Bank data.
Note: Actual capital is the amount the country accumulated in 2005. Hypothetical produced capital is the amount the country could have accumulated if it had followed the Hartwick rule and reinvested all resource rents since 1980.

per capita in manufactured capital. If it had followed the Hartwick rule and reinvested all the resource rents from oil and gas, it would have accumulated more than three times as much manufactured capital: $66,359 per capita. The situation is similar in the other four resource-rich countries shown in the figure: if rents had been reinvested, these countries would have accumulated far greater amounts of produced capital per person, substantially adding to the productive base of their economies.

Figure 1.3 shows the same information for a large number of countries in which rents on nonrenewable resources constitute at least 1 percent of gross national income. The horizontal axis shows the share of resource rents in GDP, while the vertical axis shows how much more produced capital a country would have if it had reinvested all its resource rents. Countries falling at or below the zero line have produced capital that meets or exceeds the Hartwick rule. Those above the zero line have not reinvested rents; if they had, they would have greater wealth in 2005.

Among the countries in figure 1.3 are a subset of resource-rich countries, defined as those in which resource rents account for at least 5 percent of GDP. A few of these countries have followed the Hartwick rule. Countries like Mexico (MEX) or Peru (PER) have largely compensated for depletion of minerals by investing in produced capital, so their hypothetical capital is not much different from their actual capital accumulation. Countries like Malaysia (MYS) and

FIGURE 1.3
Resource Abundance and Capital Accumulation: Where Has the Hartwick Rule Been Applied?

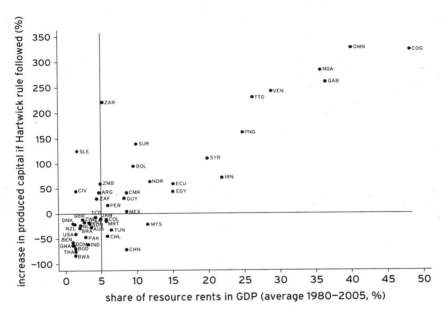

Source: Authors' calculations based on World Bank data.
Note: Resource abundance is indicated by the share of resource rents in GDP. Capital accumulation shows the increase in produced capital a country could have achieved if it had reinvested all the rent. See World Bank (2006) for further explanation of the approach. Country names per ISO 3166-1 alpha-3.

China (CHN) have invested far more than the Hartwick rule requires. However, many resource-rich countries have not followed the Hartwick rule. In fact, the greater the dependence on mineral rents, the greater the gap between actual produced capital and hypothetical capital. All countries in which rents account for 15 percent or more of GDP have underinvested.

Extending and Deepening Wealth Accounts

This introductory chapter has presented some key analytical insights derived from the wealth accounts for 1995, 2000, and 2005, regarding how wealth changes with development and how natural capital can drive development. These insights preview results that are presented in more detail in chapter 2, which examines the composition of and trends in total wealth and its components over the decade. We now turn to the main messages of the remaining chapters of the book.

Decomposing Changes in Natural Wealth from 1995 to 2005

Having described the changing composition of capital, we would also like to understand the driving forces behind this change. We focus on natural capital both because of the importance of natural capital to developing countries and because we have concrete, independent measures for detailed components of this type of wealth to support this analysis.

Changes in the value of natural capital can result from many factors, some related to the price or returns to an asset and some related to the physical quantity of an asset. For example, the value of total agricultural land in a country may increase when more land is brought under cultivation (a quantity effect) or when the net price of crops produced on a given amount of land increases (price effect). Similarly, the value of subsoil assets may increase with rising world market prices (price effect) or an increase in proven reserves (quantity effect). Obviously, many of these factors change simultaneously and it is not easy to sort out the relative importance of each one.

A technique called decomposition analysis, applied in chapter 3, is used to determine the relative importance of different factors that change the value of natural capital over time. We found that price changes played a significant role in many regions. Declining agricultural land value in Sub-Saharan Africa and South Asia has been driven mainly by declining prices for crop and livestock products.[7] The decline was partly offset by increases in production and yields, but the price effect has dominated in these regions. By contrast, in East Asia and the Pacific as well as Latin America and the Caribbean, there was a net increase in agricultural land values because the decline in prices was more than offset by increases in crop production area, crop yields, and livestock production. Forest land has been particularly important to wealth creation in Latin America and the Caribbean, mainly because of the increase in timber prices. The effect is particularly important in Brazil.

In other regions, the rising value of subsoil assets played a major role in changing the value of natural capital. While the expanding volume of reserves contributed, the most important factor was the sharp increase in unit rents for subsoil assets. Worldwide, 71 percent of the growth in subsoil asset values can be explained by increases in unit rents. In developing countries, unit rent increases contributed 65 percent of the increase in subsoil asset values.

Greenhouse Gas Emissions and the Wealth of Nations

Damages from greenhouse gas emissions will have an impact on future well-being and on the sustainability of individual countries and the world. The high level of global concern with climate change demands that we start to look at greenhouse gas emissions from a wealth-accounting perspective.[8] Annual country emissions of greenhouse gases are closely monitored, and estimates of the shares of the stock of atmospheric CO_2 by country, based on emissions from 1850 to 2006, are now available from the Climate Analysis Indicators Tool (CAIT) database.

In chapter 4, we calculate the economic value of the stock of CO_2 attributable to countries by applying an estimate of the social cost of carbon to cumulative CO_2 emissions by country, adjusted for the (slow) decay of CO_2 in the atmosphere over time. In per capita terms, this value is particularly large in high-income countries, while it is large as a share of total wealth in many developing countries, particularly in the transition economies of Eastern Europe and Central Asia.

To bring these CO_2 values formally into the national accounting and wealth framework, there would have to be agreement about property rights, the principles of international law to apply, and the ethics of imposing either climate damages or the costs of climate mitigation on developing countries. These stocks of carbon "depreciate" according to physical laws, unlike financial obligations that can be discharged by increased savings. Accordingly, as argued in *World Development Report 2010*, the development process itself must be transformed, because high-carbon growth is no longer sustainable (World Bank 2010b). Achieving this transformation must also accord with the "common but differentiated responsibilities" of all countries embodied in the United Nations Framework Convention on Climate Change.

Understanding the Intangible: The Importance of Human and Social Capital

Intangible capital encompasses human, social, and institutional capital, and other unaccounted-for factors that contribute to human well-being. It makes up a large share of total wealth, an estimated 60–80 percent, in most countries. However, unless we understand more about the composition of intangible wealth, governments may be tempted to conclude that a wide range of public expenditures are somehow yielding intangible benefits. *Where Is the Wealth of Nations?* showed that education and the rule of law accounted for most of the intangible capital (World Bank 2006). Using the more extensive database afforded by country wealth accounts for three time periods and new data on net foreign financial assets, this book is able to clarify the composition and contribution of intangible capital to development.

Chapter 5 presents two key findings in this regard:

- Human capital is the most important component of intangible wealth for all countries and especially for high-income countries. In developing countries, human capital dominates intangible wealth, but the quality of institutions and the legacy of geography and history are also strong factors.
- Intangible capital is the *only* statistically significant factor of production in high-income OECD countries. This suggests that in these economies all of

the potential constituents of intangible capital—the quantity and quality of human capital, the constituents of total factor productivity (closely linked to technological change), and institutional quality broadly conceived—may be the key drivers of production and growth.

This analysis holds clear policy implications for developing-country governments. It is no surprise that investments in human capital are an important part of the development process. But strengthening institutions and developing the capacity to generate and use knowledge—the precursors to total factor productivity growth—will also be strongly wealth-enhancing. Finally, our growth accounting analysis shows that governments also need to ensure that complementary investments in infrastructure and natural resource management will support these investments in intangible capital, and vice versa.

Human Capital Accounting in China

Delving more deeply into human capital accounting, chapter 6 reports a case study for China, based on country-specific data (Li et al. 2009), to explore the relation between economic development and human capital. The Chinese case provides an important contribution to our understanding of the global importance of human capital. First, China is the most populous country in the world. Second, it has undergone very rapid economic and demographic changes (due, for example, to the one-child policy, migration, and urbanization), accompanied by the rapid expansion of education during the course of economic development. Human capital accounts support better assessment of the contribution of human capital to growth and development.

Global evidence indicates that the share of human capital in total wealth increases as national income increases, and that is certainly the case for China. Between 1985 and 2007 both total and per capita human capital grew rapidly in China, especially after 1995, when annual growth averaged 9.6 percent. Growth of human capital has been driven mainly by increases in educational attainment and the higher returns to education offered by a market-driven economy, rather than by population growth, as evidenced by the rapidly increasing value of per capita human capital. A gender gap exists for total human capital, and on a per capita basis the gap between male and female human capital has increased somewhat since 1985.

In 1985 the rural population held 60 percent of China's total human capital, but by 2007 the situation was reversed and a large urban-rural gap has developed since then. This is in part the result of urbanization and large-scale rural-urban migration, as well as higher educational attainment of the urban population and the higher returns to education in urban areas where the modern economy is concentrated. On a per capita basis, there is also a significant gap: by 2007 per capita human capital in urban areas was twice that of the rural population.

The Challenge Facing Resource-Rich Countries: Transforming Natural Wealth into the Capital Needed for Growth and Development

Natural capital constitutes a major component of wealth and is a principal source of income for many developing countries. Nonrenewable resources, the subsoil assets, present a particular challenge: the revenue stream represents a one-time opportunity to finance rapid development and poverty reduction. Evidence has shown that the economic performance of less-developed countries has often been inversely related to their natural resource wealth, a phenomenon known as the "resource curse."[9] However, this relationship is not deterministic; some countries such as Chile and Botswana have done well with their natural capital. As described in chapter 7, having the right policy matters.

The development challenge for resource-rich economies is to transform nonrenewable natural capital into other forms of productive wealth so that once the extractive resources (oil, gas, and minerals) are exhausted, there are other income-generating assets to take their place. Mining is not sustainable, but the revenue from the extractive sector can be invested in other forms of wealth—infrastructure, human capital, renewable natural capital, and strengthening institutions (social capital)—to build economies that are sustainable. To achieve this transformation requires getting policy right in three areas:

- Promoting efficient resource extraction in order to maximize resource rent generated
- A system of taxes and royalties that enables government to recover rent
- A clear policy for investment of resource rent in productive assets

The last point is especially important: for sustainable economic development, income from nonrenewable resources must be reinvested, not used to fund consumption. Comprehensive wealth accounts can strengthen and underpin endeavors like the Extractive Industries Transparency Initiative (EITI) to promote greater accountability in resource-rich countries through transparency about the full economic consequences of revenue (mis)management.

Mainstreaming Wealth Accounting in Country Statistical Systems

In addition to the work by the World Bank reported in this volume, a considerable amount of work on wealth accounting has been done by other institutions and individual scholars over the last two decades. Considering only work carried out by official statistical offices, wealth accounting has been institutionalized in more than 30 countries, 16 of which compile at least one type of asset account on a regular basis. The majority of countries focus on mineral and energy assets, but some countries, notably Australia and Norway, construct comprehensive accounts for natural capital. Chapter 8 provides a detailed description of this work.

Along with the study by Hamilton and Clemens (1999) at the World Bank, substantial theoretical advances in comprehensive wealth accounting for sustainable development have been achieved by Kenneth Arrow, Partha Dasgupta, and Karl-Göran Mäler (e.g., Arrow, Dasgupta, and Mäler 2003; Dasgupta and Mäler 2000, 2004). National statistical offices, the academic community, and nongovernmental organizations (NGOs) have produced a large body of empirical work on natural capital accounting at the national, regional, and local levels. Taken together, these studies have deepened our knowledge of wealth accounting and clarified issues related to it.

At the same time there has been considerable effort over the past 20 years to develop statistical methodology for environmental accounting (a broad framework that includes natural capital accounting) under the aegis of the United Nations (UN) Statistical Commission. The Commission established the London Group on Environmental Accounting and later a high-level body, the UN Committee of Experts on Environmental Accounting, to develop methodological guidelines. In 2003 the *Handbook of National Accounting: Integrated Environmental and Economic Accounting*, commonly referred to as the SEEA, was produced (United Nations et al. 2003). This manual is currently under revision and will become part of the statistical standard, like the System of National Accounts that establishes methodology for national accounts.

Further support for the comprehensive wealth approach to sustainable development is provided in the recent report by Stiglitz, Sen, and Fitoussi (2009). The report proposes ways to modify and extend conventional national accounts in order to provide a more accurate and useful guide for policy. An important component of the proposed changes, to better reflect sustainability of economies, is comprehensive wealth. The Stiglitz-Sen-Fitoussi report recommends the compilation of accounts for each category of asset reported in this book, and changes in the assets, which correspond to the components of adjusted net saving.

The Agenda for Future Work on Natural Wealth

Constructing detailed wealth accounts for 152 countries on a regular basis that are comparable both across countries and over time is a daunting task. We drew on a large number of databases compiled by national and international agencies.[10] Specific natural resources are included in the accounts when they meet two criteria: (a) reliable data on price and volume are available on a regular basis, not from occasional or one-off studies, and (b) data are available for a large number of countries, if not for all. There are some natural resources where the available data do not meet these criteria, notably fisheries, certain minerals, and certain water services such as hydropower. As a result, the value of natural capital is underestimated, and for specific countries this omission can be significant.

In addition, some components of natural capital, the regulating ecosystem services and environmental damages, do not appear explicitly in the wealth accounts. Many of these services are already included in the value of agricultural land, but because they are only implicit, supporting what we value indirectly, their values are hidden. For example, the value of natural pollinators or groundwater is incorporated in the value of agricultural land. Fully accounting for the value of these ecosystem services would not add to the wealth of nations but would change the composition, for example by shifting part of the asset value from agricultural land to groundwater or forests. This information is useful for management of natural resources, because if policy makers are unaware that services critical to agriculture are provided by forests or wetlands, they may make decisions about forests that inadvertently reduce the productivity and value of agricultural land.

But the land accounts—focusing on agricultural land, which is most important for developing countries and can be most readily measured—are not complete. We are missing ecosystem services associated with other types of land, notably residential and commercial land, but also other public land that is not under protected status.[11] For these properties, the aesthetic amenity services provided by natural landscapes can be very important, especially in high-income countries where people are willing to pay high prices for lakeside or beachfront homes, for example. If the value of these ecosystem services were included in the natural capital accounts, it would likely increase the share of natural capital in total wealth, especially in high-income countries.

The missing natural capital, treatment of ecosystem services, substitutability among different types of capital, and implications for the wealth accounts are discussed in more detail in the chapter annex. Filling the gaps in concepts, methods, and data, particularly for natural capital, constitutes an important agenda for improving the coverage and usefulness of wealth accounting.

Summing Up

The work reported in this book offers lessons about how countries can develop sustainably. The analysis of wealth accounts over the decade from 1995 to 2005 shows development to be a process of building wealth. Furthermore, in this process, the composition of wealth shifts away from natural capital and toward produced capital and, increasingly, intangible capital. The important role of the changing composition of wealth in the development process points to the need for *comprehensive* wealth accounting.

Intangible capital dominates the wealth accounts of all countries. Investing in human capital is important in this process, but building good institutions and governance is equally important because this provides the basis for more efficient use of, and higher economic returns to, all forms of capital.

For developing countries, where natural capital is a large share of comprehensive wealth, sound management of natural capital to build wealth is critical.

However, even when a country's share of comprehensive wealth is small, it is essential to focus on management of natural capital because it differs in key ways from produced and intangible capital. Natural capital can provide a wide range of local and global public goods. Many forms of natural capital are nonrenewable, or renewable only under certain management regimes. Losses of natural capital may lead to irreversible changes, and the potential for substitution is often limited. While produced and intangible capital share these characteristics to some degree—for example, provision of public goods, and limited substitutability—the danger of irreversible change is far less than for natural capital. If produced capital is damaged or destroyed, it can usually be replaced.

Box 1.1 looks in more detail at the issue raised at the beginning of this chapter: if our concern is with increasing social welfare—the sum of present and future well-being—then we need to shift our focus from measuring output to measuring wealth and its changes over time. In this book we document how this can change our perspective on the process of development by emphasizing the shifting roles of natural, produced, and intangible capital as countries grow and develop.

If we wish truly to understand economic development, then simple backward-looking indicators of output growth, such as GDP growth rates, will not suffice. Countries need to know where they are going, in addition to where they have been. To what extent have economic actors—households, firms, and governments—increased the wealth of nations by saving and investing for the future? To what extent have institutional reform, technical progress, and investment in human capital accelerated the process of development? These questions have particular force and urgency in developing countries, where, our numbers show, many of the most resource-intensive economies are actually consuming wealth, and where the potential value of human capital is constrained by the quality of institutions and governance. How we measure development will drive how we do development.

BOX 1.1
Measures of Economic Performance: Wealth or Production?

The key to increasing standards of living lies in building national wealth, which requires investment and national savings to finance this investment. We have examined wealth accounts at three points over a decade; savings/investment is the dynamic behavior that explains how an economy moves from one point to the next. The companion to total or comprehensive wealth is adjusted net saving (ANS), also called genuine saving, defined as national net saving adjusted for the value of resource depletion and environmental degradation and credited

(continued)

for education expenditures (a proxy for investment in human capital). Since wealth changes through saving and investment, ANS measures the change in a country's national wealth. The rule for interpreting ANS is simple: if ANS is negative, then we are running down our capital stocks and future well-being will suffer; if ANS is positive, then we are adding to wealth and future well-being.

While wealth is typically a large number that changes slowly, ANS is an incremental measure and can change rapidly. Thus, ANS provides an early warning signal if an economy is on a downward path. Furthermore, ANS is very policy-sensitive: if government decides to spend more on education or enacts policies to increase private sector investment, the results will show up immediately in ANS. Small, negative ANS may not produce changes that are immediately noticeable, but if it is sustained over time, wealth and well-being will eventually decline. ANS for Sub-Saharan Africa, shown in the figure below as a percentage of gross national income (GNI), clearly shows an unsustainable trend since 1994–although, as noted earlier, this trend is driven mainly by a small handful of resource-rich states, particularly oil producers.

While ANS is theoretically sound and relatively easy to implement, national saving is not an important indicator in the macroeconomic toolkit. The concept of accounting for depletion and degradation of natural capital is widely recognized, but countries have far more often experimented

Adjusted Net Saving in Sub-Saharan Africa as a Percentage of Gross National Income

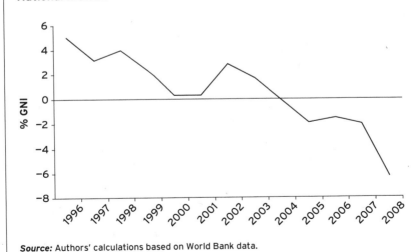

Source: Authors' calculations based on World Bank data.

(continued)

BOX 1.1 (*continued*)

with adjustments to conventional macroeconomic aggregates such as GDP or net national income (NNI), subtracting depletion and degradation of natural capital. Even the three countries that regularly compile wealth accounts, Norway, Australia, and Mexico, compile adjusted NNI or related indicators rather than ANS (see chapter 8). The major reason for this seems to be that macroeconomists most often focus on measures of output (GDP) rather than on well-being, a distinction that the landmark report by Stiglitz, Sen, and Fitoussi (2009) makes very clear.

The information used to calculate ANS can also be used to adjust net national income, but the interpretation of the latter is less clear. The next figure shows NNI for Sub-Saharan Africa after adjusting for depletion and degradation. Adjusted NNI typically follows a trend line over time at a lower level than NNI, but adjusted NNI alone does not tell us whether growth is sustainable or not. However, if we add consumption to the graph, as seen in the figure, the interpretation becomes clear: a gap arises between consumption and adjusted NNI that becomes especially pronounced after 2004. This gap between consumption and adjusted NNI shows that Sub-Saharan Africa is consuming more than its current (net) income. It can only do this by liquidating its capital, which will leave its citizens poorer and with less capacity to generate income in the years to come. This gap is closely related to ANS, lacking only the adjustment to reflect investment in human capital.

Consumption and Adjusted Net National Income in Sub-Saharan Africa, 1990–2008

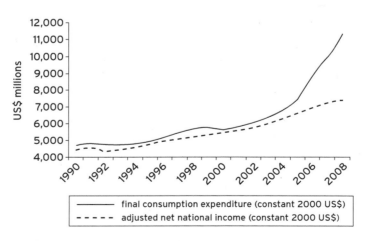

Source: Adapted from Hamilton and Ley 2010.

Annex: Missing Natural Capital and Ecosystem Services

In this annex we discuss missing natural capital and ecosystem services. We identify obstacles to measurement and the likely impact of those omissions on measures of wealth.

Missing Natural Resources: Minerals, Fisheries, and Water

Minerals

The wealth accounts include four energy resources and 10 major metals and minerals. Because of a lack of data, the accounts omit a number of mineral resources, such as diamonds, uranium, and lithium, even though they are extremely important for specific countries. Information about the volume and value of annual production is generally available, but information about reserves and the costs of production—needed to calculate asset values—is not. As a result, the value of natural capital is underestimated, and for certain countries this omission can be significant.

Fisheries

Fisheries are not included in the wealth accounts because of a lack of information about fish stocks and uncertainty about their future.[12] But this omission probably has a smaller impact on global and country wealth accounts than the omission of minerals. The key issue here is management. Poor management is seen in the economics of fishing and in the depleted state of the world's fisheries (FAO 2009).

Under current management, most commercial fishing operates with high net losses and is kept going only by extensive subsidies (Milazzo 1998; World Bank and FAO 2009). There are notable exceptions to this, such as fisheries in Iceland, New Zealand, and Namibia, where better management allows substantial rents to be generated. But in the majority of cases, very little if any rent is produced. Subsistence and small-scale fishing in developing countries often operates under open-access conditions that tend to erode resource rents. So the majority of fisheries have little or no economic value under current management.

Water

Water resources encompass a wide array of services, from drinking water and agricultural water to hydroelectric power and wetland services. Hydropower is one of the "missing" resources in the natural capital accounts. Among the countries that construct asset accounts for natural capital (discussed in chapter 8), only Norway includes hydropower in its wealth accounts. In a case study of the Lao People's Democratic Republic, the World Bank estimated hydropower as part of the country's wealth accounts (World Bank 2010c). But there is not sufficient information across countries to include hydropower in the wealth accounts at this time.

The largest use of water is as an input to agriculture, and in most instances agricultural water does not have a market price.[13] Growing reliance on shared, international water resources and depletion of groundwater are major concerns and warrant close monitoring. The value of groundwater is incorporated in the value of agricultural land, but it is not explicit in the natural capital accounts. The value of other water resources may not be fully reflected in land values.

Wetland ecosystem services and the recreational value of water bodies are at least partly captured in land and produced capital, which includes residential and recreational properties, but the values are likely to be underestimated as described in the section below on ecosystem services. Water poses an especially difficult challenge for wealth accounting because the values are highly site-specific. There have been many case studies of the value of water services, but they are not readily scaled up to the national level.[14]

Pollution and Damages to Human Health

Adjusted net saving includes a measure of the human health damage from particulate air pollution. The corresponding capital asset affected by pollution is human capital, which is part of intangible capital in the wealth accounts. Pollution damage is implicitly included in the intangible component of total wealth.

Ecosystem Services

The Millennium Ecosystem Assessment (2003) classified all ecosystem services into four broad categories: provisioning, cultural and recreational, regulating, and supporting services. Provisioning and cultural/recreational services are mostly those that we use directly and recognize an economic value for, such as food, fiber, timber, and tourism. Most of the provisioning services (with the exception of fisheries and some water services) are included explicitly in the wealth accounts in the form of agricultural land and forest land values that produce food, fiber, timber, nontimber forest products, and so on.

Regulating and supporting services have value because they contribute indirectly to the production of goods and services that have economic values. For example, pollination services or groundwater services are valuable as inputs to agriculture. Many of these services are already included in the value of land assets, but because they are only implicit, supporting what we value indirectly, their values are hidden. For example, the value of natural pollinators or groundwater is incorporated in the value of agricultural land.

One "missing ecosystem service" likely to be of great economic significance, particularly in high-income countries, is the aesthetic service provided by natural landscapes, embodied in nonagricultural land values.[15] People are willing to pay high prices for residences and, to some extent, for commercial properties in areas of great aesthetic beauty, such as lakefront, coastal, or woodland settings. Case studies have quantified the value of a home with beachfront, for example, compared to one farther from the shore. The value of this important service of natural capital is not included in the comprehensive wealth accounts due to a lack of data. If this value were included, it would likely increase the share of natural capital in total wealth, especially in high-income countries.

Public goods, such as carbon storage and biodiversity, pose special challenges and are not well represented in the wealth accounts. The wealth accounts include an estimated value for protected areas, but it is certainly an underestimate. Protected areas provide many local and global ecosystem services, but these are largely nonmarket services that are difficult to measure. As with many other ecosystem services, the values are highly site-specific, and case studies do not provide values that can readily be scaled up to a national level. Given these severe data limitations, the wealth accounts apply what is a lower bound on the value of protected areas: the opportunity cost of an alternative land use, namely, agricultural use. This is certainly an underestimate because it does not include other ecosystem services that protected areas may provide, such as tourism, which is often far more economically valuable than the agricultural alternative, and biodiversity, whose value we do not know. This is a priority issue for future work.

Substitutability among Different Types of Capital

Comprehensive wealth accounting combines all forms of wealth into a single measure that assumes a very high degree of substitutability among different forms of capital. Such a measure does not convey the very real limits to substitutability, impending thresholds for natural capital, or possible irreversibilities and catastrophic events. Given the poor state of many of the world's ecosystems, these are serious concerns (Millennium Ecosystem Assessment 2003). In addition, economic sustainability is not the same as human well-being. Although the value of comprehensive wealth may be similar for countries, the well-being of citizens may be quite different, due to factors such as cultural capital that cannot be incorporated in economic values. A major review of current measures of economic performance such as GDP by Stiglitz, Sen, and Fitoussi (2009) discusses these issues; despite the limitations, the report recommends comprehensive wealth as one useful indicator of economic performance.

Notes

1 Strictly speaking, social welfare is equal to the present discounted value of current and future well-being. The link between change in real, comprehensive wealth and change in social welfare has been established in a large body of theoretical work by such authors as Hamilton and Clemens (1999), Dasgupta and Mäler (2000), and Asheim and Weitzman (2001). The theory has been tested empirically by Ferreira and Vincent (2005) and Ferreira, Hamilton, and Vincent (2008).

2 Note, however, that the SNA measure of wealth is much narrower than what is presented here, because the asset boundary includes only produced assets and natural assets that are subject to property rights. The expansion of the asset boundary for natural capital is discussed in the *Handbook of National Accounting: Integrated Environmental and Economic Accounting*, which is currently undergoing revision (United Nations et al. 2003).

3 Net financial assets are not available for all countries. The information assists in the analysis of intangible capital in chapter 5 and is reported in the appendixes.

4 Note that urban land is estimated as a simple markup of the value of produced capital. It is generally reported as part of produced capital in the aggregates presented in this book.

5 Throughout the book, all wealth figures are reported in constant 2005 U.S. dollar prices. It is important to keep in mind that when we compare wealth across countries, we are using nominal market exchange rates. Because of this, wealth does not reflect the purchasing power of the income generated by wealth in a given country. To get an idea of the purchasing power of wealth, we would have to use purchasing power parity (PPP) exchange rates, which are often used to compare GDP across countries. Consequently, the wealth accounts are most appropriate for making comparisons across broad income groups and for looking at a country's wealth over time—its volume and composition— but are less useful for making comparisons between individual countries.

6 In principle, the rents could be invested in human capital or renewable natural capital, but it is easiest to demonstrate the Hartwick counterfactual by assuming that all rents go into produced capital.

7 This has clearly changed since the rapid increase in food prices in recent years.

8 The release of the Stern review on the economics of climate change (Stern 2006), the fourth assessment report of the Intergovernmental Panel on Climate Change (IPCC 2007), and *World Development Report 2010* on development and climate change (World Bank 2010b) has significantly raised the profile of climate change as a development issue.

9 The resource curse is attributed to several factors, some related to macroeconomic management and some to political economy and governance. For a review of the resource curse literature, see Frankel (2010) and Humphreys, Sachs, and Stiglitz (2007).

10 See appendix A for description of the data and methods.

11 An estimate of urban land is included under produced capital.

12 Even accurate information about fish catch and its value is not readily available (World Bank 2010a).

13 Water is either abstracted without charge by the user or provided at a cost that does not represent value.

14 Issues regarding the valuation of water for wealth accounting are discussed in the United Nations final draft handbook on water accounting (UNSD 2006).

15 Even land classified as agricultural may be simultaneously used for recreation. The additional aesthetic and recreational values are not reflected in the value of agricultural land, which is based on the value of agricultural production. This missing value may be particularly important in some developed countries.

References

The *Anglo-Saxon Chronicle*. 2005. Trans. James Ingram. Ed. James H. Ford. El Paso: El Paso Norte Press.

Arrow, K., P. Dasgupta, and K-G. Mäler. 2003. "Evaluating Projects and Assessing Sustainable Development in Imperfect Economies." *Environmental and Resource Economics* 26 (4): 647–85.

Asheim, Geir B., and Martin L. Weitzman. 2001. "Does NNP Growth Indicate Welfare Improvement?" *Economics Letters* 73 (2): 233–39.

Dasgupta, P., and K.-G. Mäler. 2000. "Net National Product, Wealth, and Social Well-Being." *Environment and Development Economics* 5: 69–93.

———, eds. 2004. *The Economics of Non-Convex Ecosystems*. Dordrecht, Netherlands: Kluwer Academic Publishers.

European Commission, International Monetary Fund, Organisation for Economic Co-operation and Development, United Nations, and World Bank. 2009. *System of National Accounts 2008*. New York: United Nations.

FAO (Food and Agricultural Organization). 2009. *The State of World Fisheries and Aquaculture 2008*. Rome: FAO Fisheries and Aquaculture Department.

Ferreira, S., K. Hamilton, and J. Vincent. 2008. "Comprehensive Wealth and Future Consumption: Accounting for Population Growth." *World Bank Economic Review* 22: 233–48.

Ferreira, S., and J. Vincent. 2005. "Genuine Savings: Leading Indicator of Sustainable Development?" *Economic Development and Cultural Change* 53: 737–54.

Frankel, Jeffrey A. 2010. "The Natural Resource Curse: A Survey." NBER Working Paper 15836, National Bureau of Economic Research, Cambridge, MA. http://www.nber.org/papers/w15836.

Hamilton, K., and M. Clemens. 1999. "Genuine Savings Rates in Developing Countries." *World Bank Economic Review* 13 (2): 333–56.

Hamilton, K., and E. Ley. 2010. "Measuring National Income and Growth in Resource-Rich, Income-Poor Countries." Economic Premise 28. http://siteresources.worldbank.org/INTPREMNET/Resources/EP28.pdf.

Hartwick, John M. 1977. "Intergenerational Equity and the Investing of Rents from Exhaustible Resources." *American Economic Review* 66: 972–74.

Humphreys, Macartan, Jeffrey Sachs, and Joseph Stiglitz, eds. 2007. *Escaping the Resource Curse*. New York: Columbia University Press.

IPCC (Intergovernmental Panel on Climate Change). 2007. *IPCC Fourth Assessment Report: Climate Change 2007*. Geneva: IPCC.

Li, Haizheng, Barbara M. Fraumeni, Zhiqiang Liu, and Xiaojun Wang. 2009. "Human Capital in China." NBER Working Paper 15500, National Bureau of Economic Research, Cambridge, MA.

Milazzo, M. 1998. "Subsidies in World Fisheries: A Re-examination." World Bank Technical Paper 406, World Bank, Washington, DC.

Millennium Ecosystem Assessment. 2003. *Ecosystems and Human Well-being: A Framework for Assessment.* Washington, DC: Island Press.

Solow, R. 1986. "On the Intergenerational Allocation of Natural Resources." *Scandinavian Journal of Economics* 88 (1): 141–49.

Stern, Nicholas. 2006. *The Economics of Climate Change: The Stern Review.* Prepared for the U.K. Government. New York: Cambridge University Press.

Stiglitz, Joseph E., Amartya Sen, and Jean-Paul Fitoussi. 2009. *Report by the Commission on the Measurement of Economic Performance and Social Progress.* Paris: Commission on the Measurement of Economic Performance and Social Progress.

United Nations, European Commission, International Monetary Fund, Organisation for Economic Co-operation and Development, and World Bank. 2003. *Handbook of National Accounting: Integrated Environmental and Economic Accounting 2003.* New York: United Nations. http://unstats.un.org/unsd/envaccounting/seea.asp.

UNSD (United Nations Statistics Division). 2006. "System of Environmental-Economic Accounting for Water." Final draft.

World Bank. 2006. *Where Is the Wealth of Nations? Measuring Capital for the 21st Century.* Washington, DC: World Bank. http://unstats.un.org/unsd/envaccounting/SEEAWDraft Manual.pdf.

———. 2010a. *The Hidden Harvests: The Global Contribution of Capture Fisheries.* Washington, DC: World Bank.

———. 2010b. *World Development Report 2010: Development and Climate Change.* Washington, DC: World Bank.

———. 2010c. "Lao PDR Development Report: Natural Resource Management for Sustainable Development." World Bank, Washington, DC.

World Bank and FAO (Food and Agriculture Organization). 2009. *The Sunken Billions: The Economic Justification for Fisheries Reform.* Washington, DC: World Bank.

C H A P T E R   2

Wealth and Changes in Wealth, 1995-2005

THIS CHAPTER TELLS THE STORY OF WEALTH AND HOW IT
changes over time, drawing out lessons for development. We start by comparing
comprehensive wealth over several widely spaced intervals to understand how
the volume and composition of wealth change with development and population growth. We then turn to adjusted net saving to understand better the
process of building wealth on an annual basis. These two measures provide
related ways of analyzing changes in social welfare and complementary information for policy makers seeking to guide their country on a path of sustainable
development.

Changing Global Wealth

Global wealth reached $673,593 billion in 2005 (table 2.1).[1] Intangible capital was
the largest single component in all regions, and its share increases in importance
with rising income, from 57 percent of total wealth in low-income countries to
81 percent in high-income countries. We see a symmetrical decline in the importance of natural capital as income rises, from 30 percent in low-income countries
to 2 percent in high-income countries. But does this apparent relationship between
the composition of wealth and income, seen when comparing different regions

at a point in time, really hold for a given income group as it develops over time? To answer that question, we look at our wealth accounts from 1995 to 2005.[2]

Global wealth increased by 34 percent over the decade (table 2.2). All income groups increased their capital between 1995 and 2005, and there has been little change in the distribution of wealth over time. The majority of global wealth is concentrated in high-income countries of the Organisation for Economic Co-operation and Development (OECD), although its share declined slightly from 84 percent to 82 percent. Low- and middle-income countries saw their combined share grow from 14 percent to 17 percent; despite rapid accumulation of wealth, their share of wealth is still far less than their share of world population, which was 81 percent in 2005. The poorest countries, accounting for 10 percent of global population, held only 1 percent of global wealth.

TABLE 2.1
Total Wealth and Shares by Type of Asset and Income Group, 2005

Income Group	Total Wealth (US$ billions)	Intangible Capital (%)	Produced Capital (%)	Natural Capital (%)
Low income	3,597	57	13	30
Lower middle income	58,023	51	24	25
Upper middle income	47,183	69	16	15
High income OECD	551,964	81	17	2
World	673,593	77	18	5

Source: Authors' calculations based on World Bank data.
Note: Figures are based on the set of countries for which wealth accounts are available from 1995 to 2005, as described in annex 2.1. High-income oil exporters are not shown.

TABLE 2.2
Total Wealth and Population, with Shares by Income Group, 1995–2005

Income Group	Total Wealth (world total in constant 2005 US$ billions)			Population (world total in millions)		
	1995	2000	2005	1995	2000	2005
Low income (%)	<1	1	1	9	10	10
Lower middle income (%)	7	7	9	61	61	61
Upper middle income (%)	7	7	7	10	10	10
High income OECD (%)	84	83	82	18	17	17
World	504,548	590,121	673,593	4,884	5,247	5,591

Source: Authors' calculations based on World Bank data.
Note: Figures are based on the set of countries for which wealth accounts are available from 1995 to 2005, as described in annex 2.1. High-income oil exporters are not shown. Percentages may not total to 100 percent due to rounding.

Changing Composition of Wealth

For the world as a whole, most of the new wealth created between 1995 and 2005 ($169,045 billion) consisted of intangible capital (80 percent), followed by produced capital (16 percent) and a relatively small amount of natural capital (4 percent) (figure 2.1).

How has the composition of wealth changed over time? For the world as a whole, where high-income countries dominate trends in wealth, there is virtu- ally no change in composition over time. This reflects the virtually unchanged composition of capital in high-income countries, where intangible wealth already accounts for at least 80 percent of total wealth (table 2.3). However, a different dynamic is observed in low-income and lower-middle-income countries, where there was a large decline in the share of natural capital and a corresponding increase in produced and intangible capital.

Among low-income countries, natural capital accounts for 30 percent of total wealth in 2005, down from 41 percent in 1995, and among the lower-middle- income countries, natural capital declined from 34 percent to 25 percent of

FIGURE 2.1
Additions to Wealth by Type of Asset and Income Group, 1995-2005

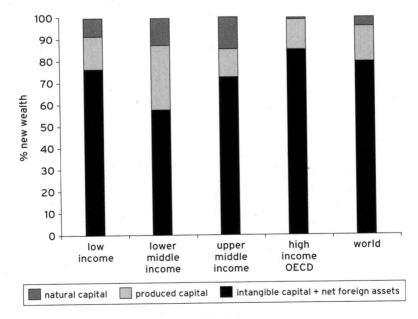

Source: Authors' calculations based on World Bank data.
Note: Figures are based on the set of countries for which wealth accounts are available from 1995 to 2005, as described in annex 2.1.

TABLE 2.3
Total Wealth and Shares by Type of Asset and Income Group, 1995 and 2005

Income Group	1995				2005			
	Total Wealth (US$ billions)	Intangible Capital (%)	Produced Capital (%)	Natural Capital (%)	Total Wealth (US$ billions)	Intangible Capital (%)	Produced Capital (%)	Natural Capital (%)
Low income	2,447	48	12	41	3,597	57	13	30
Lower middle income	33,950	45	21	34	58,023	51	24	25
Upper middle income	36,794	68	17	15	47,183	69	16	15
High income OECD	421,641	80	18	2	551,964	81	17	2
World	504,548	76	18	6	673,593	77	18	5

Source: Authors' calculations based on World Bank data.
Note: Figures are based on the set of countries for which wealth accounts are available from 1995 to 2005, as described in annex 2.1. High-income oil exporters are not shown.

wealth. Even in upper-middle-income countries, natural capital still accounts for 15 percent of wealth. The continued importance of natural capital in low- and middle-income countries suggests that management of natural resources, especially agricultural land, must be a key part of development strategies. In high-income OECD countries, natural capital has remained at only 2 percent of wealth. But its small share does not mean that natural capital is unimportant in these countries. Even at only 2 percent of the total, the value of natural capital in high-income countries ($10,367 billion) is still more than nine times that in low-income countries ($1,094 billion).[3]

Changing Wealth Per Capita

In economies where the population is growing, and especially in developing countries that aspire to higher material standards of living for their citizens, sustainable development requires not just increasing wealth but also increasing *per capita* wealth. This requires sufficient accumulation of capital to overcome the "population dilution effect," whereby more and more people must share the benefits from a fixed amount of wealth, reducing the share each one receives. If wealth increases only enough to keep per capita wealth constant over time, there will be no sustainable increase in average social welfare. If wealth increases, but not enough to compensate for population growth, average social welfare will decline. Only when per capita wealth increases will average social welfare grow.

Between 1995 and 2005, global wealth grew rapidly (by 34 percent), but population also grew rapidly, so that the net increase in per capita wealth was only 17 percent over the period (figure 2.2, table 2.4). Per capita wealth grew fastest, by 49 percent, in lower-middle-income countries, a group dominated by China's economy. Per capita wealth in high-income OECD countries continued to increase rapidly, widening the gap between them and many developing countries.

Generally, the share of produced capital in total wealth is relatively similar across all income groups, a phenomenon noted in *Where Is the Wealth of Nations?* (World Bank 2006). The exception to this trend occurs in the lower-middle-income countries, which have a share of produced capital, 24 percent, that is a third higher than the global average of 18 percent. China is the largest economy in this group, large enough to determine the trends for this set of countries. China has invested heavily in produced capital to expand its manufacturing base, and this trend is reflected in the wealth accounts for the entire group of lower-middle-income countries. India, the second-largest economy in this group, has also invested heavily in produced capital, although not as much as China.

The relationship between economic development and the changing composition of wealth over time can be seen most clearly in this same group of lower-middle-income countries. From 1995 to 2005, the share of natural capital declined while produced capital and intangible capital increased (figure 2.3). The changing relative shares of capital suggest a development process in which economic growth takes place in manufacturing and later services, sectors that require large amounts of human capital.

FIGURE 2.2
Growth in Per Capita Wealth, 1995-2005

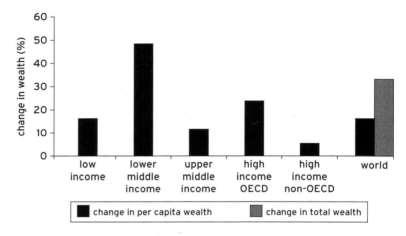

Source: Authors' calculations based on World Bank data.
Note: Figures are based on the set of countries for which wealth accounts are available from 1995 to 2005, as described in annex 2.1.

TABLE 2.4
Total Wealth Per Capita, 1995-2005
constant 2005 US$

Income Group	1995	2000	2005	Change from 1995 to 2005 (%)
Low income	5,290	5,672	6,138	16
Lower middle income	11,330	13,686	16,903	49
Upper middle income	73,540	77,986	81,354	11
High income OECD	478,445	538,364	588,315	23
High income non-OECD	225,664	232,583	236,504	5
World	103,311	112,474	120,475	17

Source: Authors' calculations based on World Bank data.
Note: Figures are based on the set of countries for which wealth accounts are available from 1995 to 2005, as described in annex 2.1.

FIGURE 2.3
Changing Composition of Wealth in Lower-Middle-Income Countries, 1995-2005

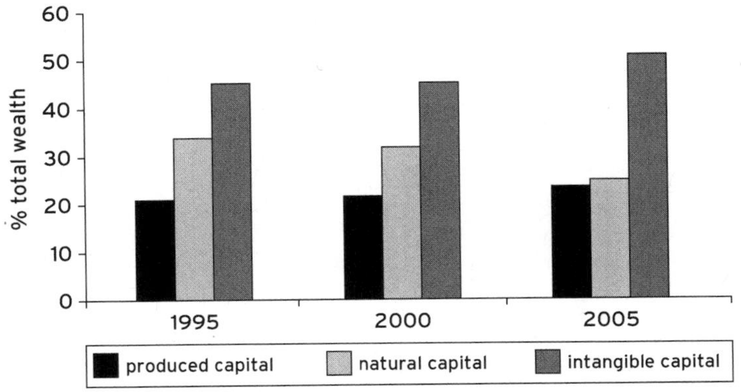

Source: Authors' calculations based on World Bank data.

Wealth Creation in Developing Countries

Analysis by geographic region can provide additional insight into wealth creation because of the importance of shared geographic and historical features. Our set of countries includes the low- and middle-income countries, organized by geographic region, and continues to include only those countries for which wealth accounts are available from 1995 to 2005. But we make an exception for Europe and Central Asia, as information for most countries in this region was only available from 2000. So, in the results discussed below, we include the comparison of wealth accounts in Europe and Central Asia from 2000 to 2005, while results for the other regions compare wealth in 1995 and 2005.

Among developing countries, wealth creation, both total and per capita, was highest in East Asia, followed by South Asia (figure 2.4). Surprisingly, total wealth creation in Sub-Saharan Africa was relatively high—higher than in either Latin America or Europe and Central Asia. However, on a per capita basis those two regions both outperformed Sub-Saharan Africa. In both, the smaller increase in total wealth supported an increase in per capita wealth because their populations grew more slowly than the population of Sub-Saharan Africa.

Looking more closely at Sub-Saharan Africa, we find that the regional results do not necessarily reflect the trends for most African countries. In this region, 27 countries increased per capita wealth between 1995 and 2005, including South Africa but also Botswana, Burkina Faso, Ethiopia, Ghana, Mozambique, Uganda, and many others. A much smaller number of countries, 12, saw per capita wealth decline. The latter group includes several whose poor performance is no surprise, such as the Democratic Republic of Congo, Nigeria, and Zimbabwe.

FIGURE 2.4
Change in Wealth and Per Capita Wealth in Developing Countries, 1995-2005

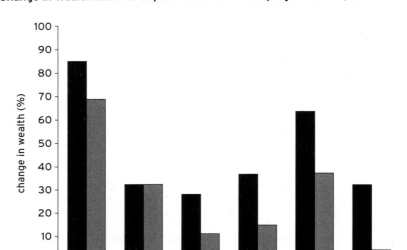

Source: Authors' calculations based on World Bank data.
Note: Changes for Europe and Central Asia are for 2000 to 2005 due to lack of data for 1995.

Sub-Saharan Africa is dominated by two economies: Nigeria and South Africa. Wealth in Nigeria declined by 15 percent, while South Africa—the larger of the two—increased per capita wealth by 13 percent from 1995 to 2005. The increase in per capita wealth in South Africa, and in most other Sub-Saharan African countries,[4] offset the decline in Nigeria and raised per capita wealth for all of Sub-Saharan Africa by 4 percent. Indeed, the growth of per capita wealth in Sub-Saharan Africa was quite high in many countries and more similar to that observed in other regions.

Intangible capital accounted for most of the growth in all regions except the Middle East and North Africa, where natural capital, mainly subsoil assets, accounted for 56 percent of additional wealth (figure 2.5).[5] Natural capital declined in both South Asia and Sub-Saharan Africa. In South Asia, large increases in produced and intangible capital more than compensated for the decline in natural capital, so total wealth per capita increased by 38 percent. In Sub-Saharan Africa, by contrast, the increase in intangible and produced capital was much smaller, raising wealth per capita by only 4 percent over the decade, as noted above. Again, performance for the region as a whole is greatly affected

FIGURE 2.5
Changes in Wealth in Developing Countries by Type of Asset, 1995-2005

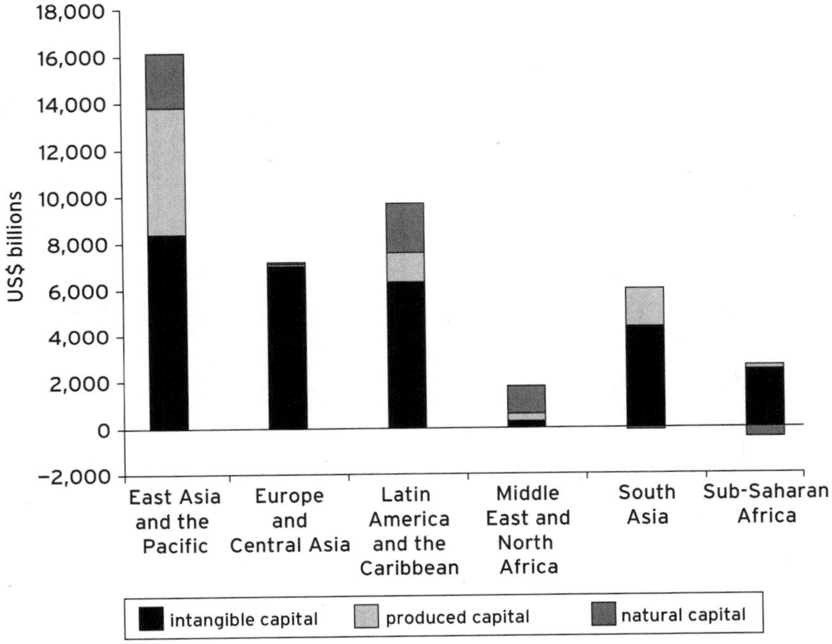

Source: Authors' calculations based on World Bank data.
Note: Changes for Europe and Central Asia are for 2000 to 2005 due to lack of data for 1995.

by Nigeria and a few other countries; the majority of countries in Sub-Saharan Africa did much better than the regional average would suggest over the decade.

The Europe and Central Asia region appears to be an unusual case where wealth creation was almost entirely due to intangible capital. However, the story becomes more complex when one looks at natural capital for the region in more detail. Over the period 2000 to 2005[6] there was a substantial increase in subsoil assets, mainly oil and gas, but this gain was almost completely offset by a loss of value for agricultural land, forest land, and protected areas. The resulting net contribution of natural capital to a change in wealth was near zero (for details, see chapter 3 and annex 3.2).

The importance of natural capital for developing countries, and the complex dynamics of changing value over time, suggests a closer look at natural capital (table 2.5).

Subsoil assets dominate the natural capital of two regions: Middle East and North Africa and Europe and Central Asia. Forests are most important in Latin America, and agricultural land is most important in the other regions.

TABLE 2.5
Composition of Natural Capital in Developing Regions, 2005

Region	Per Capita Wealth (US$ billions)				Components of Natural Capital (%)			
	Total Wealth	Intangible Capital	Produced Capital	Natural Capital	Crop Land	Pasture Land	Forest and Protected Areas	Subsoil Assets
East Asia and the Pacific	20,669	10,390	5,878	4,401	55	6	16	23
Europe and Central Asia	72,744	45,140	13,357	15,330	14	11	13	62
Latin America and the Caribbean	79,194	54,870	12,261	12,063	33	10	27	30
Middle East and North Africa	28,992	12,160	6,937	9,895	20	8	2	69
South Asia	10,441	5,978	1,826	2,637	49	25	13	13
Sub-Saharan Africa	13,888	8,291	1,911	3,686	35	13	17	36

Source: Authors' calculations based on World Bank data. Percentages may not sum to 100 percent due to rounding.

Natural capital is important in both South Asia and Sub-Saharan Africa, accounting for 25 percent and 28 percent, respectively, of total capital in 2005. The decline in per capita natural capital in both these regions was almost entirely due to a decline in agricultural land value and, to a lesser extent in Sub-Saharan Africa, forest land (reasons for this are discussed in the next chapter). This is indeed a worrisome trend given the dependence of large numbers of people on agriculture for their livelihood.

Savings and Changes in Wealth

The key to increasing standards of living lies in building national wealth, which requires investment and national savings to finance this investment. We have looked at per capita comprehensive wealth for three points in time between 1995 and 2005; savings/investment is the dynamic behavior that drives wealth changes from one point to the next. These dynamics are captured by adjusted net saving (ANS), or genuine savings, defined as gross national savings adjusted for the annual changes in the volume of all forms of capital. Since wealth changes through saving and investment, ANS measures the annual change in a country's national wealth.

This discussion suggests that there are two ways of measuring a change in wealth: calculating ANS or comparing comprehensive wealth between two time periods. In theory they are very similar. The major difference is that comprehensive wealth includes capital gains—changes in the real prices of assets over time. But as currently implemented on a global scale, ANS differs from changes in comprehensive wealth because we do not have adequate data to measure changes in all types of capital on an annual basis. ANS is measured as net national savings minus the value of environmental degradation, depletion of subsoil assets, and deforestation, and credited for education expenditures (figure 2.6). Two important assets are missing: agricultural land and parts of intangible capital (box 2.1).

Comprehensive wealth offers two advantages over ANS: it includes all assets and it can be used to monitor how per capita wealth is changing over time, not just total wealth. But we cannot provide comprehensive wealth each year because some of the assets it includes—those excluded from ANS—are difficult to measure meaningfully on an annual basis in many countries, as described in box 2.1. Hence, comprehensive wealth provides a medium- to long-term indicator that is more comprehensive than ANS, but ANS provides policy makers immediate feedback on an annual basis about the direction the economy is headed and possible changes they may need to make. Furthermore, ANS includes most of the assets that policy makers can influence directly and for which the results can be directly measured. A policy maker looking at an ANS of -10 percent of gross national income (GNI) would be certain the country was on an unsustainable path if all assets were included. However, to the extent that we have unmeasured assets, the

FIGURE 2.6
Calculating Adjusted Net Saving for Sub-Saharan Africa, 2008

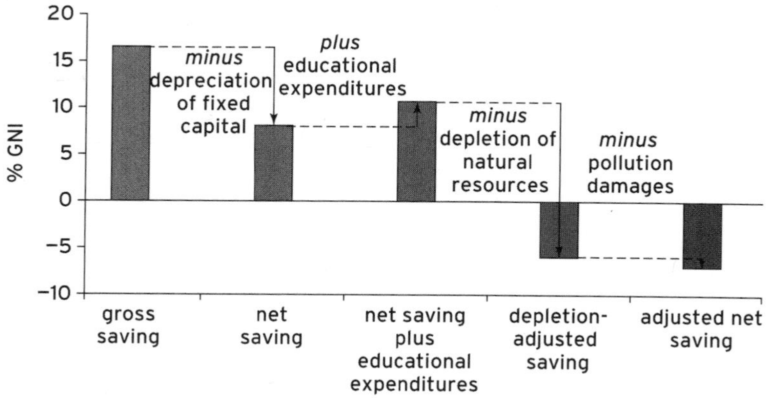

Source: Authors' calculations based on World Bank data.

BOX 2.1
Adjusted Net Saving and Missing Capital

Intangible capital, the largest component of wealth, is measured as a residual. In chapter 5, we report on work to identify the components of intangible capital, but we are far from having the ability to independently measure these components. ANS includes a measure of additions to human capital, the largest component of intangible wealth. But it is measured from the cost side, by expenditures on education, rather than as the value of the asset created, that is, the net present value of returns to education.

Regarding *agricultural land*, changes may only become apparent over a period of time longer than a year. Holding world market prices constant, agricultural productivity in a given year results from a combination of factors, mainly soil quality, annual weather, technology, and management decisions. Because all these factors fluctuate from year to year, their long-term implications for the value of agricultural land are hard to determine. When the calculation is done at the country level, with access to much more information, it may be possible (although difficult) to estimate these changes.

policy maker would have to assume that unmeasured wealth increased by at least 10 percent of GNI before concluding that the economy was on a sustainable path. ANS, therefore, puts a bound around what is necessary to achieve sustainability.

ANS can be a particularly useful indicator for resource-rich countries, those where resource rents are at least 5 percent of GNI. For these countries, transforming nonrenewable natural capital into other forms of wealth is a major development challenge. The rule for interpreting ANS is simple and clear: if ANS is negative, then we are running down our capital stocks and reducing future social welfare; if ANS is positive, then we are adding to wealth and future well-being. Figure 2.7 shows the performance of resource-rich countries, measured by the importance of resource rents in GNI. Positive ANS occurs in countries like Botswana and China, where mineral depletion is offset by investment in other types of capital. Those countries with negative ANS, below the zero ANS line, such as Angola and Uzbekistan, are depleting their natural capital without replacing it and are becoming poorer over time.

Figure 2.8 shows ANS for six developing-country regions. While there is marked volatility from year to year, two trends are clear: the upward trend of East and South Asia, where per capita wealth is increasing rapidly, and the downward trend of Sub-Saharan Africa, where per capita wealth barely changed between 1995 and 2005 (although, as noted earlier, this African trend is dominated by figures for Nigeria and a handful of other countries, particularly oil-exporting countries).

FIGURE 2.7
Adjusted Net Saving in Resource-Rich Countries, 2008

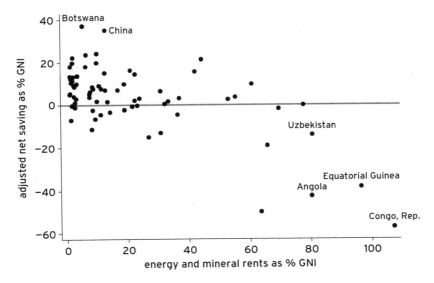

Source: Authors' calculations based on World Bank data.

FIGURE 2.8
Adjusted Net Saving for Developing-Country Regions, 1975-2008

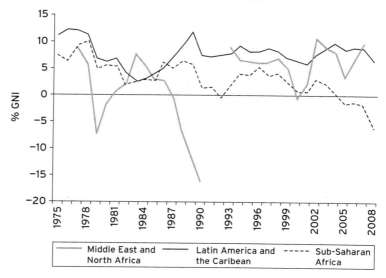

A. Middle East and North Africa, Latin America
and the Caribbean, and Sub-Saharan Africa

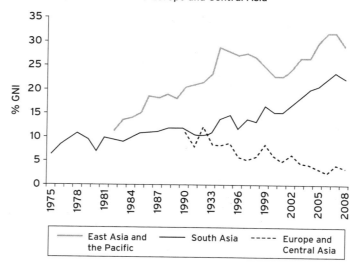

B. East Asia and the Pacific, South Asia,
and Europe and Central Asia

Source: Authors' calculations based on World Bank data.

Population Growth and the Adjusted Net Saving Gap

ANS captures change in total wealth, but for development, we are concerned with per capita wealth in order to maintain the standard of living for each person. So when population is growing, wealth must increase just to maintain the same amount of productive capital and income-generating potential per person. If ANS is negative, it is clearly an indication that wealth is declining. When ANS is positive, on the other hand, the signal for development is less clear. If ANS is high enough to maintain per capita wealth, then the economy is on a sustainable path; but if ANS is not sufficient, then the economy will not be able to maintain the same standard of living for its growing population.

Using the comprehensive wealth accounts, we can calculate the amount by which ANS must increase each year simply to keep per capita wealth intact. This amount is called the "Malthusian term." If we subtract the Malthusian term from ANS, the remaining savings (divided by population) is the amount by which per capita wealth increases. For example, countries as diverse as Gabon, Algeria, República Bolivariana de Venezuela, the United States, and New Zealand have had positive ANS but a decline in per capita wealth because savings has not been sufficient to compensate for population growth. In Gabon, for example, despite positive ANS of $393 in 2008, population growth caused per capita wealth to decline by $641 (see appendix E).

Figure 2.9 shows ANS adjusted for population growth scattered against the rate of population growth in 2005. The downward trend suggests that higher population growth rates are associated with lower per capita wealth accumulation, but it is notable that some countries had positive per capita wealth creation even at high rates of population growth. At the lower right-hand side, where ANS adjusted for population growth is extremely negative, we see countries that already had negative total ANS, like Angola and the Republic of Congo. Surprisingly, Uganda appears here as well. In the previous section, where we discussed changes in comprehensive wealth, Uganda appeared as one of the countries that had increased per capita wealth. Its negative performance under ANS reflects the fact that ANS does not include agricultural land and intangible capital—forms of capital that increased significantly in value in Uganda between 1995 and 2005. If they had been included, the population-adjusted ANS would have been positive.

The adjusted net saving gap measures, as a percentage of GNI, the difference between actual ANS and the amount necessary to maintain per capita wealth. Appendix E reports the adjusted net saving gap for more than 150 countries. For example, the ANS gap for Algeria is 2.3 percent of GNI. So, for wealth per capita to at least stay constant, saving in Algeria should increase from the current rate of 12.2 percent to 15.5 percent. The savings gap for the United States and New Zealand is 2 percent.

FIGURE 2.9
Population-Adjusted ANS and Population Growth Rates in Developing Countries, 2005

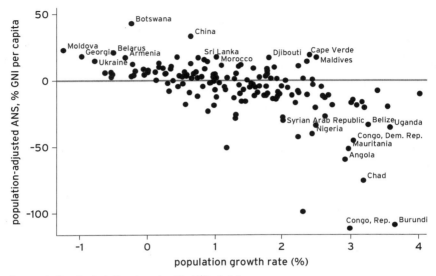

Source: Authors' calculations based on World Bank data.
Note: Population-adjusted ANS is per capita ANS minus the Malthusian term (the amount by which total wealth would have to increase in order to maintain constant per capita wealth). It is presented as a percentage of per capita GNI.

Conclusions

The decade from 1995 to 2005 saw a large increase in global wealth, with intangible capital—already the largest share of global wealth—accounting for nearly 80 percent of the change. Whether looking at changes across income groups at a single point in time, or at changes for a single income group over time, the wealth accounts confirm that development is a process of building wealth and shifting its composition from natural capital to produced and intangible capital. The large disparity in wealth has persisted, although the distribution of wealth shifted slightly in favor of low- and middle-income countries, whose share increased from 14 percent to 17 percent.

In most developing countries, wealth creation is dominated by intangible capital—increases in human capital, improvements in institutions and governance, and technological changes that support more efficient use of produced and natural capital and higher levels of consumption. At the global level, the share of natural capital in total wealth is small and declined in all income groups over the period. But natural capital remains important for low-income and lower-middle-income countries, where it accounts for 30 and 25 percent of wealth respectively in 2005. Agricultural land is the most important form of natural capital in most developing countries (aside from oil producers) and remains the basis of livelihoods for the majority of their people. Good management of agricultural land is therefore a priority for these countries.

Total wealth grew rapidly over the decade, outpacing population growth, so that per capita wealth increased 17 percent. Asian countries, mainly China and India, saw phenomenal growth in per capita wealth, nearly 70 percent. Sub-Saharan Africa accumulated a great deal of wealth, but high population growth kept per capita wealth increases very low, around 4 percent over the decade. The low growth of per capita wealth in Sub-Saharan Africa was strongly affected by the poor performance of a handful of resource-rich countries, led by Nigeria, where per capita wealth declined. Per capita wealth in many other Sub-Saharan African countries increased, led by intangible capital and the resulting improvements in efficiency of produced and natural capital.

Adjusted net saving provides a window on the dynamic process by which wealth grows over time. Most resource-rich countries had positive ANS in 2008, indicating that depletion is being offset by other forms of capital. But nine of these countries had ANS of −15 to −60 percent of GNI. While there may be gains in unmeasured capital, it is extremely unlikely that it would be sufficient to fully offset this loss.

Looking at regional ANS from 1975 to 2008, clear trends emerge, with ANS (as well as per capita wealth) increasing in Asia and ANS declining in Sub-Saharan Africa. In both instances, a few countries dominate the trend: the stellar performance of China and, more recently, India drives the positive trends in Asia, and the poor performance of Nigeria and a handful of other countries outweighs the positive performance of many other African countries.

Finally, adjusting ANS for the population effect—the amount of additional capital necessary to maintain per capita wealth for a growing population—shows that even countries with positive ANS may fail to maintain per capita wealth. The adjusted net saving gap is not just a phenomenon of developing countries, although arguably it is more critical in such countries because of the very low level of per capita wealth with which they start. Even developed countries such as the United States and New Zealand have had positive ANS but a decline in per capita wealth because saving has not been sufficient to compensate for population growth.

Annex 2.1: Countries Excluded from the Analysis of Changes in Wealth

The world wealth database for 1995 included 124 countries; over time, data for 28 additional countries became available and country coverage for 2000 and 2005 expanded to 152 countries. The 28 countries without data for 1995 are listed in box 2.2. Most of these missing countries (18) are in Europe and Central Asia.

Our analysis of wealth by income class is based on the restricted set of 124 countries for which we have data for all three years. In the analysis of developing countries by geographic region, however, we include Europe and Central Asia but analyze change in wealth between 2000 and 2005 only.

BOX 2A.1
Countries with Wealth Accounts in 2005 but Not in 1995

Albania*	Kyrgyz Republic*	Russian Federation*
Angola	Lao PDR	Slovak Republic
Armenia*	Latvia*	Tajikistan*
Azerbaijan*	Liberia	Turkey*
Belarus*	Lithuania*	Ukraine*
Bulgaria*	Macedonia, FYR*	Uzbekistan*
Cape Verde	Maldives	Vanuatu
Croatia	Moldova*	Vietnam
Czech Republic	Poland*	
Georgia*	Romania*	

* Countries in the Europe and Central Asia region.

Annex 2.2: Per Capita Wealth, 1995 and 2005, and Changes in Per Capita Wealth and Population, 1995-2005, by Region and Income Group

TABLE 2A.1
Per Capita Wealth by Region and Income Group, 1995
constant 2005 US$

Region/Income Group	Population (millions)	Total Wealth	Intangible Capital	Produced Capital	Natural Capital	Crop Land	Pasture Land	Forest/ Timber	Forest/ Nontimber	Protected Areas	Oil	Natural Gas	Hard Coal	Soft Coal	Minerals
East Asia and the Pacific	1,553	12,225	5,996	2,985	3,243	2,181	148	222	46	168	229	64	143	1	41
Europe and Central Asia[a]	409	55,135	26,784	13,125	15,226	3,349	2,748	453	991	2,137	2,450	2,876	132	12	79
Latin America and the Caribbean	459	71,536	49,458	11,556	10,523	4,013	1,561	809	379	1,063	2,116	246	3	0	333
Middle East and North Africa	203	25,015	12,628	5,912	6,475	1,962	838	64	21	125	2,763	680	2	0	20
South Asia	1,211	7,592	3,235	1,127	3,230	1,744	971	84	20	246	49	31	70	2	13
Sub-Saharan Africa	534	13,295	5,912	1,989	5,393	2,023	1,329	564	249	288	776	25	61	0	78
Low income	463	5,290	2,519	623	2,148	1,009	412	310	152	217	5	11	1	0	31
Lower middle income	2,997	11,330	5,128	2,331	3,870	2,187	583	220	56	206	429	60	102	1	28
Upper middle income	500	73,540	50,212	12,578	10,750	3,595	2,128	661	343	1,016	2,143	435	66	0	362
High income OECD	881	478,445	382,491	85,496	10,458	2,605	2,711	1,213	359	2,254	684	453	13	7	160
High income non-OECD	43	225,664	122,821	48,613	54,230	1,261	559	19	15	5,735	43,344	3,294	0	0	3
World[b]	4,884	103,311	78,632	18,634	6,045	2,287	1,109	451	149	708	989	193	72	2	86

Source: Authors' calculations based on World Bank data.
a. Figures for Europe and Central Asia are for 2000; data not available for most Europe and Central Asia countries in 1995.
b. World figures are for those countries for which we have wealth data.

TABLE 2A.2
Per Capita Wealth by Region and Income Group, 2005
constant 2005 US$

Region/Income Group	Population (millions)	Total Wealth	Intangible Capital	Produced Capital	Natural Capital	Crop Land	Pasture Land	Forest/ Timber	Forest/ Nontimber	Protected Areas	Oil	Natural Gas	Hard Coal	Soft Coal	Minerals
East Asia and the Pacific	1,707	20,669	10,390	5,878	4,401	2,424	277	374	56	272	334	251	302	1	109
Europe and Central Asia	408	72,744	44,057	13,357	15,330	2,146	1,624	239	519	1,241	4,249	4,789	318	39	167
Latin America and the Caribbean	531	79,194	54,870	12,261	12,063	4,025	1,225	1,711	386	1,120	2,477	416	16	0	687
Middle East and North Africa	240	28,992	12,160	6,937	9,895	1,977	837	56	29	155	4,400	2,395	2	0	44
South Asia	1,440	10,441	5,978	1,826	2,637	1,288	663	171	18	161	82	107	109	2	37
Sub-Saharan Africa	681	13,888	8,291	1,911	3,686	1,298	463	237	191	182	1,028	102	117	0	70
Low income	586	6,138	3,484	788	1,866	879	369	200	139	165	43	50	1	0	20
Lower middle income	3,433	16,903	8,550	4,088	4,265	1,997	500	323	53	255	634	232	196	2	73
Upper middle income	580	81,354	56,327	13,190	11,837	3,649	1,139	1,278	346	829	2,684	1,070	151	0	691
High income OECD	938	588,315	477,730	99,536	11,049	2,176	2,263	632	480	2,528	1,234	1,279	164	22	272
High income non-OECD	54	236,504	118,382	48,915	69,206	735	592	10	32	4,331	55,128	8,378	0	0	0
World[a]	5,591	120,475	92,770	21,137	6,568	2,069	849	458	164	726	1,414	555	163	5	164

Source: Authors' calculations based on World Bank data.
a. World figures are for those countries for which we have wealth data.

Changes in Per Capita Wealth and Population, 1995-2005
constant 2005 US$

Region/Income Group	Population (millions)	Total Wealth	Intangible Capital	Produced Capital	Natural Capital	Crop Land	Pasture Land	Forest/ Timber	Forest/ Nontimber	Protected Areas	Oil	Natural Gas	Hard Coal	Soft Coal	Minerals
East Asia and the Pacific	155	8,445	4,394	2,893	1,157	243	129	152	9	104	106	187	159	1	67
Europe and Central Asia[a]	0	17,609	17,274	231	104	−1,203	−1,124	−214	−472	−896	1,800	1,914	185	28	87
Latin America and the Caribbean	72	7,658	5,412	706	1,541	12	−336	901	7	57	362	170	13	0	355
Middle East and North Africa	37	3,978	−468	1,026	3,420	15	−1	−8	8	30	1,638	1,715	0	0	25
South Asia	228	2,849	2,743	699	−592	−456	−308	86	−3	−85	33	76	39	1	24
Sub-Saharan Africa	147	593	2,378	−78	−1,707	−725	−866	−327	−58	−106	252	76	56	0	−8
Low income	124	848	965	165	−282	−130	−43	−110	−13	−52	38	39	0	0	−10
Lower middle income	436	5,573	3,422	1,756	395	−189	−83	104	−3	49	205	172	93	1	45
Upper middle income	80	7,814	6,114	612	1,087	54	−989	616	3	−187	541	636	84	0	329
High income OECD	57	109,870	95,239	14,040	591	−429	−448	−581	121	273	550	827	150	15	113
High income non-OECD	11	10,840	−4,438	302	14,977	−526	33	−9	17	−1,404	11,784	5,084	0	0	−3
World[b]	707	17,164	14,138	2,503	523	−217	−259	7	15	18	426	362	91	3	78

Source: Authors' calculations based on World Bank data.
a. Changes are from 2000 to 2005.
b. World figures are for those countries for which we have wealth data.

Notes

1 All figures are reported in constant 2005 U.S. dollars.

2 Analysis of wealth accounts in this chapter is based on data for 124 countries for which wealth accounts are available for 1995, 2000, and 2005, as described in annex 1. An additional 28 countries for which wealth accounts are available only from 2000 are not included in this analysis.

3 As discussed in chapter 1, high-value ecosystem services associated with nonagricultural land, such as aesthetic services provided by natural landscapes, are missing from the wealth accounts due to lack of data. They are likely to be of particular importance in developed countries. If they were included, they would probably increase the share of natural capital in total wealth, at least in some countries.

4 Including those that make up the vast majority of countries in the low-income region.

5 Although the high-income oil producers are excluded, there are a number of developing countries in the region that rely heavily on oil and natural gas as well as other minerals.

6 Data are not available for most of these countries in 1995, so the analysis is reported for 2000 and 2005 only.

Reference

World Bank. 2006. *Where Is the Wealth of Nations? Measuring Capital for the 21st Century.* Washington, DC: World Bank.

CHAPTER   3

Changes in Natural Capital: Decomposing Price and Quantity Effects

AS NOTED IN CHAPTER 2, WORLDWIDE GROWTH IN WEALTH between 1995 and 2005 has been driven by growth in intangible capital, which accounted for nearly 80 percent of the change. Developing countries differ sharply from developed countries with respect to the composition of new wealth. In developing countries, growth in intangible capital contributed 60 percent to growth in total wealth, compared to 86 percent in countries of the Organisation for Economic Co-operation and Development (OECD); growth in produced capital contributed 24 percent, versus 14 percent in OECD countries; and growth in natural capital contributed 13 percent, versus 1 percent in OECD countries (figure 3.1).

Developing countries, however, are not a homogeneous group. Investments in produced capital drive much of the total wealth growth in East Asia and the Pacific (33 percent), Middle East and North Africa (25 percent), and South Asia (22 percent). Growth in intangible capital is most important for changes in total wealth in Europe and Central Asia (106 percent), Sub-Saharan Africa (100 percent, dropping to 78 percent if South Africa and Nigeria are excluded), and South Asia (80 percent).[1] The contribution of growth in natural capital to growth in total wealth is very high in the Middle East and North Africa, and is relatively high in Latin America and the Caribbean and in East Asia and the Pacific; natural capital actually declined in Sub-Saharan Africa. But natural capital's contribution to changes in total wealth is often hidden by the opposite signs of changes in land and subsoil assets. Therefore, to understand the impact natural capital has on changes in total wealth, we need to decompose the effects of different natural assets such as land, forests, and nonrenewable resources.

This chapter explores what has driven the changes in natural capital over the period 1995–2005. In addition to examining different types of assets, it decomposes the effects of changes in prices, or unit rents, from the effects of changes in physical stocks.[2] Agricultural land values can change because of changes in crop prices, input costs, yields, and area under production. Forest land values can change because of a change in production forest, which can result in a higher extraction rate or a change in depletion time, or because of a change in the value of timber. Subsoil asset values can change because of new discoveries, which extend the exhaustion time of the resources, changes in the unit rents from existing assets, or changes in forecasted production patterns.[3] The first section of the chapter provides a short description of the methodology (a more detailed description can be found in annex 3.1). Subsequent sections analyze the data appearing in annex 3.2.

Decomposition: A Note on the Methodology

Annex 3.1 explains the application of the decomposition methodology, so a few brief observations will suffice here. We may think of the value of an asset as being determined by a combination of three factors: (a) the unit rent it generates over time, (b) the quantity of the resource it is possible to extract in any given period, and (c) the length of time over which the resource is expected to be available. For simplicity, let us assume the three terms are combined with each other in a multiplicative manner:[4]

$$\text{Asset value } (V) = \text{Unit rent } (R) \times \text{Production quantity } (Q) \\ \times \text{Exhaustion time } (T). \tag{3.1}$$

Assume we wish to decompose changes in the asset value (V) between period 1 and period 2. We are interested in the relative importance of each factor in the right-hand side of equation (3.1):

$$V_2 - V_1 = R \text{ effect} + Q \text{ effect} + T \text{ effect}. \tag{3.2}$$

Imagine for the moment that the only thing that changes between period 1 and period 2 is the unit rent the resource generates. In this case the decomposition is very simple, since the Q effect and the T effect are zero:

$$V_2 - V_1 = (R_2 - R_1)Q_1T_1 + 0 + 0. \tag{3.3}$$

Notice that the higher the change in unit rents and the higher the initial values of Q and T, the higher will be the R effect. The same logic can be applied to the case in which production quantity and exhaustion time change one at a time. Let us now assume both unit rents and quantity change. The decomposition will have two positive terms, the R effect and the Q effect (the T effect will be zero), and a residual term:

$$V_2 - V_1 = (R_2 - R_1)Q_1T_1 + (Q_2 - Q_1)R_1T_1 + 0$$
$$+ (Q_2 - Q_1)(R_2 - R_1)T_1. \quad (3.4)$$

The residual term in the right-hand side of equation (3.4) serves to balance the equation. Provided price and quantities do not change too much, the fourth term will be negligible compared to the other effects and can be ignored. The important issue here is that the decomposition works by looking at changes in each factor separately, holding everything else constant, and then adding up the various effects. It allows us to separate the effects of price changes from the effects of physical quantity changes. We turn now to the analysis of the numbers.

Contribution of Land and Subsoil Assets to Changes in Wealth

Changes in natural capital often account for a large part of the variation in total wealth over time (see annex 3.2 and chapter 2). For example, between 1995 and 2005, changes in natural capital accounted for 56 percent of the change in total wealth in the Middle East and North Africa and for 46 percent of the change in high-income oil exporters. Other regions have suffered declines in natural capital values, notably Sub-Saharan Africa, where the decline amounted to 15 percent of the change in total wealth. In some regions, changes in natural capital have a negligible effect, such as in the OECD countries. In others, such as South Asia and Europe and Central Asia, values for different natural assets have changed with opposite signs, offsetting each other's effects.

In developing countries, increases in subsoil asset values have driven most of the growth in natural capital. Land values, on the other hand, have had a relatively small effect (figure 3.1). This is somewhat surprising given that land accounts for a large share of total wealth in many low- and middle-income countries. We can shed light on this issue by disentangling the effects of changes in unit rent, or price, and changes in physical quantity, such as yields and production area. Figure 3.2 shows that in developing countries, production-side variables such as area and yield have increased by an amount equal to 7 percent of the change in total wealth, while price declines have amounted to 5 percent of the change. The detailed data in annex 3.2 show that yields for all crops have increased throughout the developing world. This can be observed across income groups and regions.

FIGURE 3.1
Decomposition of Changes in Natural Capital by Asset and Income Group, 1995-2005

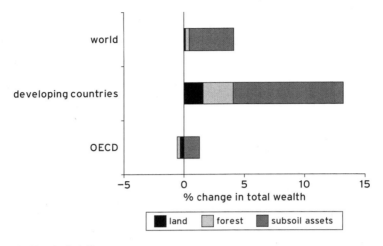

Source: Authors' calculations.
Note: Europe and Central Asia countries are excluded.

FIGURE 3.2
Decomposition of Changes in Natural Capital by Factor in Developing Countries, 1995-2005

Source: Authors' calculations.
Note: Europe and Central Asia countries are excluded.

The story of subsoil assets is qualitatively different from that of land values: price and quantity changes have both been positive. However, as can be seen in figure 3.4, changes in unit rents account for the majority of the growth in subsoil asset values in both developed and developing countries.

The different regions in the developing world have distinctive natural resource endowments. It is useful, therefore, when decomposing changes in natural capital to summarize the changes by region.

Sub-Saharan Africa and South Asia

In Sub-Saharan Africa and South Asia, declining land values are only partly offset by increases in subsoil asset values. Drops in land values amounted to 25 percent of the change in total wealth in Sub-Saharan Africa.[5] These declines diminish in absolute value but keep the same sign if we exclude Nigeria and South Africa (see annex 3.3). In South Africa, the decline in land values amounted to 29 percent of the change in total wealth. In Nigeria the effect is even greater (−170 percent).

The decomposition analysis shows that a sharp decline in unit rents drove the drop in value of land assets in Sub-Saharan Africa (figure 3.3). The fall in crop prices contributed −17 percent and was not offset by the relatively modest increases in area under cultivation (+4 percent) and yields (+5 percent). It is important to note that the effect is mostly explained by drops in real prices rather than in nominal prices. Nominal prices have not shown substantial changes between

FIGURE 3.3
Decomposition of Changes in Land Values by Region, 1995–2005

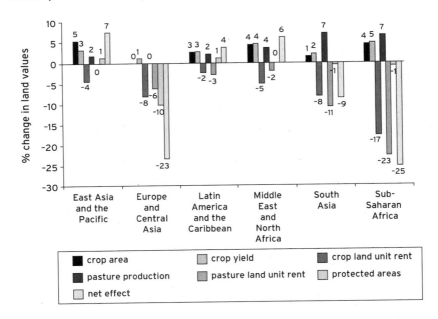

Source: Authors' calculations.
Note: Values for Europe and Central Asia refer to the change between 2000 and 2005.

1995 and 2005, but once they are adjusted for inflation, the value of most crops goes down substantially. Also in Sub-Saharan Africa, pasture price drops have contributed −23 percent to the change in total wealth. The results do not change qualitatively if one excludes Nigeria and South Africa from the sample (see annex 3.3). Most of the effect is due to changes in real prices, but prices for pasture land products have also declined substantially in nominal terms.

In South Asia, drops in crop prices have contributed −8 percent to the change in total wealth, and drops in pasture product prices have contributed −11 percent. Inflation played an important role here as well. Price drops have been just barely offset by increases in cultivated crop area (+1 percent), yields (+2 percent), and pasture production (+7 percent).

While land values declined, subsoil asset values in Sub-Saharan Africa and South Asia increased between 1995 and 2005 (figure 3.4). In Sub-Saharan Africa, subsoil assets contributed 17 percent to the growth in total wealth, and the effect remains substantial even after Nigeria is excluded from the sample. This has partially offset the slump in agricultural land values. The increase in subsoil assets has been driven partly by unit rents and partly by production increases.

FIGURE 3.4
Decomposition of Changes in Subsoil Asset Values by Region, 1995–2005

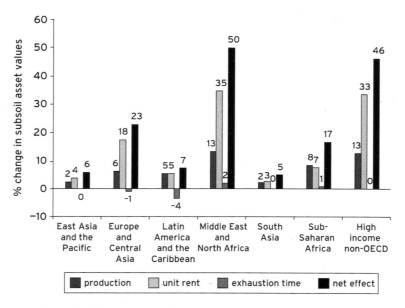

Source: Authors' calculations.
Note: Values for Europe and Central Asia refer to the change between 2000 and 2005.

Increases in oil prices have contributed 5 percent to total wealth growth in the region, while increases in oil production have contributed 6 percent. Natural gas prices have contributed 1 percent, and increases in gas production 2 percent. Across all subsoil assets, price increases accounted for 45 percent of increases in value. That figure goes up to 53 percent if one excludes Nigeria from the sample. Nigeria stands out from other major oil producers in that it increased production at a much faster pace, and prices only accounted for 34 percent of the rise in subsoil asset values.

In South Asia, increases in subsoil asset values and timber values have also helped offset part of the agricultural land declines. This has been driven mainly by unit rent increases, particularly for oil, natural gas, and timber, and to a lesser extent by increases in production of natural gas, coal, and minerals.

Europe and Central Asia

In Europe and Central Asia, changes in natural capital show features that are broadly similar to those in South Asia and Sub-Saharan Africa. But there are some differences. For this reason, and because our dataset only allows us to estimate changes for the period 2000–2005 in this region, we keep the discussion of Europe and Central Asia separate.

Natural capital's contribution to changes in wealth appears to be modest (−4 percent), but this is because land values and subsoil asset values are moving in opposite directions. In fact, the value of land assets and forest assets has declined substantially over the period between 2000 and 2005, while the value of subsoil assets has increased in the same period by a similar order of magnitude (annex 3.2).

The data on change in land value show that there has been a consistent drop in unit rents for cereals, fruits, vegetables, sugar crops, and other crops (including roots, pulses, and oil crops). At the aggregate level, unit rent declines accounted for 116 percent of the decline in crop land values. This has been partially offset by increases in yields, particularly for cereals and vegetables (+1 percent). Pasture product prices have also declined, causing a drop in pasture land values. Unit rent declines in agriculture substantially affect our estimates of protected areas, which are conservatively valued using a quasi–opportunity cost. The estimates show a negative contribution of 10 percent. Forest land values also declined, driven by a drop in both the unit rents for timber and the value of nontimber forest products.

In this region the increase in subsoil asset value completely offset the decline in agricultural land values. The change is largely driven by the increase in oil and gas unit rents, which cumulatively account for 70 percent of the change in subsoil assets. Increases in oil and gas production account for 26 percent and are only marginally offset by a decline in the exhaustion time of oil reserves.

Middle East and North Africa

Subsoil asset value increases between 1995 and 2005 have driven 50 percent of total wealth growth in the Middle East and North Africa. They explained 46 percent of wealth growth in high-income non-OECD countries. A common feature of oil exporters in the Middle East and North Africa and in the non-OECD group is that mostly unit rent increases—and not production increases — explain the growth in natural capital. Production increases accounted for only 27–28 percent of total increase in subsoil asset values. In the Middle East and North Africa, production only contributed 6 percent to the increase in oil wealth. In high-income non-OECD countries, production contributed 20 percent to the increase in oil wealth. In the case of natural gas, the relative contribution of unit rents and production increases has been more even.

As seen in annex 3.3, the values for the Middle East and North Africa are determined by a few countries, namely Algeria, the Arab Republic of Egypt, the Islamic Republic of Iran, and the Syrian Arab Republic. In the Islamic Republic of Iran, production has only contributed 10 percent to the increase in oil wealth; unit rent increases contributed the other 90 percent. In Syria, production of oil declined and the increase in exhaustion time and unit rents each contributed nearly 50 percent to the oil wealth increase. Algeria is the country in the group with the largest increases in oil production, accounting for 51 percent of growth in oil wealth.

The decomposition analysis shows that the Middle East and North Africa and the group of high-income oil exporters have been investing in produced capital and accumulating financial assets. On the other hand, the numbers show a very small growth in intangible capital, which contributed only 9 percent of total wealth growth in the Middle East and North Africa and 10 percent in high-income non-OECD countries. This fact is consistent with the idea that high resource dependence, while making it possible to boost infrastructure and financial assets, may hinder the process of institution building and human capital creation that is the basis of income growth in the long term.

Latin America and the Caribbean and East Asia and the Pacific

Between 1995 and 2005, natural capital contributed 17 percent of total wealth growth in Latin America and the Caribbean and 15 percent in East Asia and the Pacific. In both regions, agricultural land, forest land, and subsoil assets all grew in value over the period.

Agricultural land has been gaining importance, thanks in particular to production increases. It contributed 4 percent of total wealth growth in Latin America and the Caribbean and 7 percent in East Asia and the Pacific. Changes in production area and yields have been positive and have more than offset the decline in crop and pasture prices that we observed globally. In Latin America and the Caribbean, increased crop land area and yields each contributed 2 percent to growth in total wealth, and pasture production increases contributed 1 percent. In East Asia and the Pacific, increases in area under crops contributed 5 percent to growth in total wealth, yield increases contributed 3 percent, and pasture production contributed 2 percent.

In Latin America and the Caribbean, increases in the value of timber land have contributed 7 percent to the growth in total wealth. This is in large part the effect of a rise in timber prices, which contributed 6 percent to the change in total wealth. Particularly noteworthy is the case of Brazil, where the rise in forest land value contributed 14 percent of the change in total wealth. That increase has been driven mainly by a price rise (12 percent) and to a lesser extent by an increase in production (2 percent). Timber price increases have also been relatively important in East Asia and the Pacific and in South Asia, where they contributed 2 percent of the growth in total wealth.

Subsoil assets also contributed to the growth in natural capital wealth and in total wealth. In Latin America the subsoil asset contribution to total wealth growth was driven both by production increases in oil, natural gas, and minerals, and by unit rent increases, coming mostly from oil. A decrease in exhaustion time for oil in our dataset contributed a 3 percent reduction to the change in total wealth. In South Asia, an increase in unit rents for oil and natural gas contributed 2 percent to total wealth growth, and increases in production of oil, natural gas, coal, and minerals contributed 3 percent.

Summing Up: Land Values and Subsoil Assets

Prices, or unit rents, have played a major role in boosting or reducing natural capital's contribution to changes in total wealth over the period 1995–2005(see figure 3.3). Declining prices for crop and pasture products have led to low or declining natural capital values in a number of countries. Sub-Saharan Africa, South Asia, and Europe and Central Asia, where natural capital changes have resulted in a deduction to total wealth, are a case in point. Such declines have been partially offset by increases in production and yields, but in most cases the price effect has dominated. Land values have contributed positively to growth in total wealth in other regions, namely East Asia and the Pacific and Latin America and the Caribbean. All in all, increases in land asset values have contributed 8 percent to total wealth growth in low-income countries. This is much higher than the 2 percent contribution in lower-middle-income countries and the −1 percent contribution in upper-middle-income countries. This result has been driven in large part by increases in production area for crops (which contributed 4 percent of growth in total wealth), crop yields (5 percent), and pasture production (4 percent). A slump in agricultural and pasture prices has partially offset these effects, contributing −5 percent (see figure 3.4).

Over the period from 1995 to 2005, prices of subsoil assets increased sharply. This has contributed to large increases in natural capital in some regions. The effect has been greater in regions where subsoil assets are a greater share of total wealth. Consequently, in upper-middle-income countries, which are relatively well endowed with nonrenewable resources, the growth in subsoil asset values has contributed 11 percent to the growth in total wealth. In lower-middle-income countries the contribution was 8 percent, and in low-income countries 4 percent. In OECD countries, subsoil assets have contributed only 1 percent to the growth in total wealth.

Worldwide, the growth in subsoil asset values has been driven by increases in unit rents, which accounted for 71 cents of every dollar increase in total asset value. In developing countries, unit rent increases contributed 65 percent of the increase in subsoil asset values, but in OECD countries the contribution was 82 percent. The reason for the difference is that many developing countries have increased production over the period under study. Energy and mineral extraction increases have contributed as much as 13 percent to total wealth growth in the Middle East and North Africa, 8 percent in Sub-Saharan Africa, and 5 percent in Latin America and the Caribbean.

Price rises have affected some regions more than others. Price increases accounted for 70 percent of subsoil asset increases in the Middle East and North Africa, but only 45 percent in Sub-Saharan Africa. The value goes up to 53 percent if one excludes Nigeria from the sample. By contrast, prices have represented 75 percent of the subsoil asset value increase in the Islamic Republic of Iran and 62 percent in Algeria.

Annex 3.1: Decomposition Methodology

Total wealth in a given year is the sum of produced capital, natural capital, net foreign assets, and intangible capital (or residual). In our database, we estimate total wealth and the different types of capital for the period 1995–2005. Hence, we are able to estimate the change in wealth between 1995 and 2005 (for Europe and Central Asia the estimate is from 2000 to 2005). Decomposition of changes in total wealth into its four major categories (produced, natural, intangible, and net foreign assets) is straightforward since these are all additive. We are interested in going one step further by carrying out decomposition of certain categories, particularly natural capital and intangible capital, into their subcomponents. Since produced capital is estimated as the accumulated stock of investment series, its decomposition would not yield new information. Decomposition of intangible capital is undertaken in chapter 5, so natural capital is our focus here.

Since we build the estimates of natural capital using information on prices and on physical quantities such as area and yield, we are interested in decomposing the effects of different factors to show their relative importance. In this section we lay out a decomposition methodology adapted from Bacon and Bhattacharya (2007). Natural capital is composed of the present value of the returns to land from crops, pasture and protected areas, forests (timber and nontimber) and subsoil assets (oil, gas, coal, and minerals). Each component in turn is estimated using information on area and yield (or production), prices or unit rents, and exhaustion time. Equation (3A.1) shows how crop wealth (CW) is estimated as an example:

$$CW_t = area \times yield \times real\ price \times rentalrate \times \alpha(T, d). \qquad (3A.1)$$

Wealth is expressed as the product of area cultivated, yield, real price, rental rate, and a value $\alpha(T, d)$. The term $\alpha(T, d)$ captures the effect of taking the present value of current rents. Alpha depends on the resource's exhaustion time (when applicable) or the time span over which the present value is taken—expressed by T—and the value of the discount rate d.

The logarithmic mean Divisia index (LMDI) is used to decompose change in crop wealth into the additive effects of changes in area, yield, real price, and alpha (rental rates for crops are assumed constant over time and across countries). For details, see Bacon and Bhattacharya (2007). The change in crop wealth from 2000 to 2005 can then be written as follows:

$$\triangle CW \equiv CW(2005) - CW(2000) \equiv A_{eff} + Y_{eff} + P_{eff} + W_{eff}. \qquad (3A.2)$$

In equation (3A.2), A_{eff} is the effect of changes in area under crop cultivation; Y_{eff} is the effect of changes in yield of crops; P_{eff} is the effect of changes in real prices, since wealth in 1995 and 2005 is expressed in constant 2005 U.S. dollars; and W_{eff} is the effect of changes in alpha. In our estimates, the rental rate is assumed to be constant. Applying the LMDI index, each one of these effects can be calculated as shown in equation (3A.3) for the changes in price:

$$P_{eff} = \left\{ \frac{[CW(2005) - CW(1995)]}{\log\left[\frac{CW(2005)}{CW(1995)}\right]} \right\} \times \log\left[\frac{P(2005)}{P(1995)}\right] \qquad (3A.3)$$

Hence, change in crop land value can be decomposed into the sum of the effects of changes in alpha, real prices, yields, and areas from 1995 to 2005. The change in total natural capital in turn can then be summed over changes in each one of these effects, capturing changes in the value of crop land, pasture land, protected areas, forests, and subsoil resources.

Annex 3.2: Decomposition of Changes in Total Wealth by Income Group and Region, 1995-2005

TABLE 3A.1
Decomposition of Changes in Total Wealth by Income Group and Region, 1995–2005
% change in total wealth

	Low Income	Lower Middle Income	Upper Middle Income	High Income Non-OECD	OECD	East Asia and the Pacific	Europe and Central Asia[a]	Latin America and the Caribbean	Middle East and North Africa	South Asia	Sub-Saharan Africa
Change in total wealth (2005 US$ billions)	1,150	24,072	10,389	3,110	130,323	16,305	7,160	9,232	1,879	5,834	2,362
Intangible capital	75	55	74	10	86	49	106	72	9	80	100
Produced capital	15	29	13	18	14	33	1	13	25	22	10
Net foreign assets	0	3	–1	25	0	3	–3	–2	10	0	4
Natural capital	10	13	14	46	1	15	–4	17	56	–1	–15
Land	8	2	–1	0	0	7	–23	4	6	–9	–25
Cereals area	1	0	0	0	0	0	0	0	0	0	0
Cereals yield	2	1	0	0	0	0	1	0	0	1	1
Cereals price, real	–2	–2	0	0	0	–1	–2	0	–1	–2	–2
Fruits area	1	1	0	0	0	1	0	0	2	1	1
Fruits yield	1	1	0	0	0	1	0	0	1	0	0
Fruits price, real	1	–1	0	0	0	–1	–1	0	–2	–1	–2
Vegetables area	0	4	0	0	0	5	0	0	2	1	–1
Vegetables yield	1	1	0	0	0	1	0	0	2	0	1
Vegetables price, real	0	–2	0	0	0	–2	–2	0	–2	–1	–2
Sugar crops area	–1	0	1	0	0	0	0	1	0	–1	0
Sugar crops yield	0	0	1	0	0	0	–2	1	0	0	0

Sugar crops price, real	-1	-1	-1	0	0	0	-1	0	-2	-2
Other crops area	2	0	1	0	0	0	1	0	0	3
Other crops yield	2	1	1	0	1	-1	1	1	1	3
Other crops price, real	-3	-1	0	0	0	-2	0	-1	-1	-10
Pasture production	4	3	2	0	2	0	2	4	7	7
Pasture price, real	-2	-4	-6	0	0	-6	-3	-2	-11	-23
Protected areas	0	1	1	0	0	0	1	0	0	0
Protected areas value per hectare, real	1	1	-1	0	1	-10	0	0	-1	-1
Forest	-1	2	4	0	2	-4	6	0	2	-6
Timber exhaustion time	-11	0	0	0	0	0	-1	0	0	-7
Timber production	1	0	0	0	0	0	1	0	0	1
Timber price, real	7	2	4	0	2	-1	6	0	2	0
Nontimber forest exhaustion time	0	0	0	0	0	0	0	0	0	0
Nontimber forest area	1	0	0	0	0	0	0	0	0	1
Nontimber forest value per hectare, real	0	0	0	0	0	-2	0	0	0	-1
Subsoil assets	4	8	11	46	6	23	7	50	5	17
Oil exhaustion time	0	0	-2	0	0	-1	-3	2	0	1
Oil production	1	1	3	7	0	5	3	2	0	6
Oil unit rent, real	1	3	4	29	1	6	4	23	1	5

(continued)

TABLE 3A.1 *(continued)*

	Low Income	Lower Middle Income	Upper Middle Income	High Income Non-OECD	OECD	East Asia and the Pacific	Europe and Central Asia[a]	Latin America and the Caribbean	Middle East and North Africa	South Asia	Sub-Saharan Africa
Gas exhaustion time	0	0	−1	0	0	0	0	−1	0	0	0
Gas production	1	1	2	6	0	1	1	1	12	1	2
Gas unit rent, real	1	1	3	5	1	1	10	1	12	1	1
Coal exhaustion time	0	0	0	0	0	0	0	0	0	0	0
Coal production	0	1	0	0	0	1	0	0	0	1	0
Coal unit rent, real	0	1	0	0	0	1	1	0	0	0	2
Minerals exhaustion time	0	0	0	0	0	0	0	0	0	0	0
Minerals production	−1	1	2	0	0	1	0	2	0	1	0
Minerals unit rent, real	0	0	0	0	0	0	0	0	0	0	0

Source: Authors' calculations.
a. Values for Europe and Central Asia refer to the change between 2000 and 2005.

Annex 3.3: Decomposition of Changes in Total Wealth in Selected Countries in Middle East and North Africa and Sub-Saharan Africa, 1995-2005

TABLE 3A.2
Decomposition of Changes in Total Wealth in Selected Countries in the Middle East and North Africa and Sub-Saharan Africa, 1995-2005

% change in total wealth

	Algeria	Egypt, Arab Rep.	Iran, Islamic Rep.	Syrian Arab Republic	Other Middle East and North Africa[a]	Nigeria	South Africa	Other Sub-Saharan Africa
Change in total wealth (2005 US$ billions)	-25	528	734	86	555	150	1,067	1,145
Intangible capital	1,744	62	-24	0	79	94	124	78
Produced capital	-146	8	38	18	16	52	1	13
Net foreign assets	-349	3	10	37	-3	54	-1	3
Natural capital	-1,149	27	75	45	7	-100	-25	6
Land	-18	10	5	-9	6	-170	-29	-2
Cereals area	1	0	0	-1	0	-1	0	1
Cereals yield	-5	1	1	3	0	3	0	1
Cereals price, real	5	0	-1	-4	0	-23	0	-1
Fruits area	-15	1	3	1	0	5	0	1
Fruits yield	-10	1	1	1	0	-3	0	1
Fruits price, real	26	0	-3	-7	0	-38	0	0
Vegetables area	-9	3	2	-1	1	-21	0	1
Vegetables yield	-15	1	2	5	1	5	0	1
Vegetables price, real	30	0	-2	-8	-1	-10	0	-1
Sugar crops area	0	2	0	0	0	-1	2	-1

Sugar crops yield	0	0	1	0	0	−1	−1	1
Sugar crops price, real	0	0	0	0	0	−1	−1	−2
Other crops area	−3	0	0	2	0	41	0	2
Other crops yield	−10	0	1	3	0	8	0	3
Other crops price, real	11	0	−1	−5	0	−123	0	−3
Pasture production	−46	3	3	10	2	3	1	10
Pasture price, real	27	−2	−2	−7	1	−14	−28	−16
Protected areas	0	0	1	1	0	0	0	0
Protected areas value per hectare, real	−7	0	0	0	0	−2	−3	0
Forest	−4	0	0	0	0	−59	−1	−4
Timber exhaustion time	12	0	0	0	0	−24	−1	−10
Timber production	−3	0	0	0	−1	3	0	2
Timber price, real	−13	0	0	0	1	−36	0	5
Nontimber forest exhaustion time	0	0	0	0	0	0	0	0
Nontimber forest area	−1	0	0	0	0	0	0	2
Nontimber forest value per hectare, real	1	0	0	0	0	−1	0	−2
Subsoil assets	−1,128	17	70	54	1	129	6	12
Oil exhaustion time	68	2	0	21	1	0	0	2
Oil production	−197	−4	4	−4	0	61	0	4
Oil unit rent, real	−254	6	42	23	1	37	0	6
Gas exhaustion time	0	0	0	0	0	0	0	0
Gas production	−296	7	12	9	0	24	0	0

(continued)

TABLE 3A.2 (continued)

	Algeria	Egypt, Arab Rep.	Iran, Islamic Rep.	Syrian Arab Republic	Other Middle East and North Africa[a]	Nigeria	South Africa	Other Sub-Saharan Africa
Gas unit rent, real	−448	6	11	5	0	6	0	0
Coal exhaustion time	0	0	0	0	0	0	0	0
Coal production	0	0	0	0	0	0	1	0
Coal unit rent, real	0	0	0	0	0	0	3	0
Minerals exhaustion time	0	0	0	0	0	0	0	0
Minerals production	−1	0	1	0	0	0	2	−1
Minerals unit rent, real	0	0	0	0	0	0	−1	1

Source: Authors' calculations.
a. Other Middle East and North Africa consists of Jordan, Morocco, and Tunisia.

Notes

1   The value for Europe and Central Asia is limited to the 2000–05 period.

2   The analysis in this chapter concentrates on changes in real prices, that is, after accounting for inflation.

3   Unit rents increase as world prices of energy and mineral commodities increase, as unit rents are equal to price minus production costs. For low-production-cost countries, the effect of an increase in prices will be higher than for high-production-cost countries.

4   In reality, the way the three terms interact is given by the present value formula

$$V_0 = \sum_{t=0}^{T} \frac{R_t Q_t}{(1+d)^t}$$

It is easy to show that for a constant discount rate d and assuming quantity and prices increase at a constant rate, the formula for V_0 indeed becomes multiplicative.

5   Note that there can be relatively large figures for the changes in individual components of wealth, such as quantity changes, but the net effect of summing up these changes in components can be small owing to the cancellation of positive and negative factors.

Reference

Bacon, Robert W., and Soma Bhattacharya. 2007. "Growth and CO_2 Emissions: How Do Different Countries Fare?" Environment Department Paper 113, World Bank, Washington DC.

PART 2

A Deeper Look at Wealth

CHAPTER 4

Wealth Accounting in the Greenhouse

THE RELEASE OF THE STERN REVIEW ON THE ECONOMICS OF
climate change (Stern 2006), the Fourth Assessment Report of the Intergovernmental Panel on Climate Change (IPCC 2007b), and *World Development
Report 2010* on development and climate change (World Bank 2010) has given
a significant boost to the profile of climate change as a development issue. Data
on the emission of greenhouse gases have become central to the monitoring of
emission reduction commitments by individual countries, while discussions
about historical responsibility for the causes of climate change have focused on
the accumulation of greenhouse gases emitted by individual countries (see, for
example, den Elzen et al. 1999).

In this chapter we approach the greenhouse gas problem from a wealth
accounting perspective. This is important because the damages produced by
these gases will have an impact on future well-being and on the sustainability of
individual countries and the world. Greenhouse gases, and carbon dioxide (CO_2)
in particular, have distinctive economic characteristics that affect the analysis of
the wealth of nations.

Our goal is to estimate, for each country, the economic value of both the
flow of CO_2 emissions and the stock of atmospheric CO_2 that is the result of
historical emissions. The value of CO_2 emissions is directly linked to the *social
cost of carbon*, discussed below. Establishing the value of CO_2 stocks requires an

economic rationale and methodology for valuing these stocks, and this is one of the contributions of the chapter.

The chapter is best viewed as an exercise in what Paul Samuelson famously termed "positive economics." Our contribution to the climate debate is to establish values of CO_2 stocks and flows by applying economic principles of valuation, without considering normative issues. But we obviously recognize that normative and ethical issues are at the heart of the climate debate, and so we offer some reflections on application of the principles of corrective justice as well as on the range of ethical principles that can be brought to bear on the climate problem.

Climate change is driven by the emission of a range of substances with different warming potentials and atmospheric lifetimes, including methane, nitrous oxide, and black carbon, in addition to CO_2. For the purposes of this chapter we will focus only on CO_2, a choice that is driven by purely practical considerations: carbon dioxide is by far the largest contributor to climate change, and long time-series estimates of CO_2 emissions are available.

Below we outline the economics of climate change, highlighting the social cost of carbon as a key element. This is followed by an examination of how property rights to the global commons influence how we should do the wealth accounting. Finally, we present our estimates of the value of CO_2 stocks and flows for 2005. We begin by presenting the scientific consensus on climate change and drawing out the implications for developing countries.

Climate Science and the Development Consensus

The successive assessment reports of the Intergovernmental Panel on Climate Change (IPCC) reflect an evolving scientific consensus on whether the global climate is changing and whether human activity has been the main driver of change. The fourth and latest assessment (IPCC 2007b) draws the strongest conclusions to date. A summary for policy makers (IPCC 2007a) makes the following assertions, among others:

> Warming of the climate system is unequivocal, as is now evident from observations of increases in global average air and ocean temperatures, widespread melting of snow and ice and rising global average sea level.

> Most of the observed increase in global average temperatures since the mid-20th century is very likely due to the observed increase in anthropogenic GHG [greenhouse gas] concentrations. It is likely that there has been significant anthropogenic warming over the past 50 years averaged over each continent (except Antarctica).

> Continued GHG emissions at or above current rates would cause further warming and induce many changes in the global climate system during the 21st century that would very likely be larger than those observed during the 20th century.

Anthropogenic warming could lead to some impacts that are abrupt or irreversible, depending upon the rate and magnitude of the climate change.

The scientific consensus presented by the IPCC is strong and clear, therefore. Below we draw upon the scientific literature to establish baselines for how much of the anthropogenic CO_2 that was emitted historically still resides in the atmosphere, and we estimate each country's share of that stock.

Climate change as a development challenge is the central focus of *World Development Report (WDR) 2010*. A key finding of the report is that up to 80 percent of the damages from climate change will be borne by developing countries. This outcome is largely driven by the high dependence of developing countries on natural resources, particularly agricultural land, as a source of income. Other chapters of this book highlight the dependence of low-income countries, in particular, on natural resources as a share of total wealth.

One of the principal policy messages of *WDR 2010* is that the development process itself must be transformed in a greenhouse world. High-carbon growth, which has been the historical norm, is no longer an option. While low-income countries have contributed only a little over 1 percent of the anthropogenic stock of CO_2, developing countries as a whole are now the largest annual emitters of CO_2, and most of the growth in emissions during this century is likely to take place in developing countries.[1]

This establishes the setting for the analysis in this chapter. Climate change is happening now, is driven by human activities, and will likely accelerate unless action is taken to reduce greenhouse gas emissions very substantially. Its greatest impact will be on countries most dependent upon climate-sensitive sectors of the economy: developing countries characterized by high dependence on natural resources as a share of wealth. Accounting for carbon stocks and flows can contribute to the needed transformation of the development process.

Some Economics of Climate Change

In order to account for and value CO_2 stocks and flows, it is essential to understand some of the basic economics of this pollutant. Two basic physical properties of CO_2 have a profound influence on the economics of climate change: (a) it is a uniformly mixed pollutant, meaning that emissions at one point on the globe will affect the whole globe, and (b) it is a highly persistent pollutant.[2]

The high persistence of CO_2 in the atmosphere is an important element in the economic analysis of climate change. Carbon cycles naturally through the biogeosphere, with stocks held in the atmosphere, in living matter, in soils, and in the ocean. The rate of decay of CO_2 from the atmosphere after it has been emitted has been modeled by the United Nations Framework Convention on Climate Change (UNFCCC 2002), and this model has been applied in the Climate Analysis

Indicators Tool (CAIT) used in this chapter.[3] To give a feel for the extent of this persistence, the model predicts that, while 50 percent of CO_2 will have dissipated from the atmosphere 15 years after emission, 36 percent will remain in the atmosphere after 50 years, and 30 percent will remain after 100 years.

This has two basic implications. First, in accounting for the stocks of CO_2 in the atmosphere that have been emitted by any given country, long time series of country emissions will be required. This is provided by the CAIT dataset. Second, in establishing the value of damages inflicted by a ton of CO_2 that is emitted now (or has been emitted in the past), it will be necessary to model damages a century or more into the future and to take the present value of this flow of damages. This is how we measure the *social cost of carbon*. As this definition suggests, any estimate of the social cost of carbon is scenario- or model-dependent and is subject to all of the uncertainties that integrated climate-economy modeling entails.[4]

Table 4.1 summarizes the range of estimates of the social cost of marginal carbon emissions constructed by Tol (2005). Depending on model assumptions, and particularly on discounting assumptions tied to the pure rate of time preference, the range in mean values is from roughly $4 to $70 per ton of CO_2 in 2005 dollars. In this chapter we use a figure derived by Fankhauser (1995) of $20 per ton of carbon in 1995, the same figure used in estimates of adjusted net saving published by the World Bank since 1999. Translated to dollars per ton of CO_2 ($/tCO_2$) and 2005 dollars, this amounts to *$6.69 per ton of additional CO_2 emissions*. This figure lies within the range of estimates in table 4.1, roughly one-half of the mean social cost of carbon appearing in peer-reviewed papers, and nearly twice the median.

TABLE 4.1
Distribution of Published Marginal Social Costs of CO_2 Emissions
constant 2005 US$ per ton of CO_2

	Mode	Mean	5%	10%	Median	90%	95%
Base	0.40	25.40	−2.60	−0.40	3.80	45.00	95.50
Author weights	0.40	35.20	−2.90	−0.40	4.40	60.00	173.20
Peer reviewed	1.40	13.60	−2.40	−0.40	3.80	34.10	66.80
CoV = 0.5	1.40	25.10	−0.20	0.50	4.60	43.60	94.10
CoV = 1.5	0.40	25.60	−6.70	−2.10	3.80	46.40	102.30
No equity weights	0.40	24.50	−2.10	−0.40	2.70	32.50	81.80
Equity weights	0.10	27.50	−5.40	−0.40	14.70	68.20	107.70
PRTP = 3% only	0.40	4.40	−1.50	−0.40	1.90	9.50	16.90
PRTP = 1% only	1.30	13.90	−3.70	−0.40	0.80	34.10	45.00
PRTP = 0% only	1.90	71.20	−6.40	−0.40	10.60	205.90	439.10

Source: Tol 2005, with data converted to $/tCO_2$.
Note: PRTP = pure rate of time preference; CoV = coefficient of variation.

Note that the social cost of carbon is a marginal figure, that is, it represents the damage inflicted by one extra ton of CO_2 emitted. It is like a price in this regard, and is therefore useful in many aspects of the economic analysis of climate change. When we value flows of carbon emitted, in the next section of this chapter, it is the marginal value of the social cost of carbon that is applied. However, when it comes to valuing *stocks* of CO_2, it is clear that a marginal value of the social cost of carbon looking forward is not appropriate.

To value CO_2 stocks, we first turn to the question of starting points. The approach applied in this chapter is to measure a country's entire stock of CO_2 residing in the atmosphere as a result of emissions dating from the start of the Industrial Revolution.[5] To value this CO_2 stock, we evaluate the reduction in global damages that would have occurred if that country's stock had not been emitted. That is, we invoke the assumption of *ceteris paribus*—"other things being equal." Because this value assumes that all other stocks of CO_2—the result of emissions by all other countries—are still in the atmosphere, it is not possible to add up the stock values across countries to arrive at a global total because this would violate the "other things being equal" assumption. This also implies that the value of the CO_2 stock for an aggregation of countries, such as the European Union (EU), will not equal the sum of the stock values for the individual countries in the group.

Figure 4.1 presents the stylized approach to valuing an atmospheric stock of CO_2. It assumes that the social cost of carbon is a quadratic function of the atmospheric concentration of CO_2. At the 2005 CO_2 atmospheric concentration level of 379.8 parts per million by volume (ppmv), the social cost of carbon is $6.69, as indicated above.[6] Since the social cost of carbon measures damages from *anthropogenic* emissions of CO_2, it is assumed to be zero when its atmospheric concentration was at preindustrial levels: 284.0 ppmv.

Suppose now that country X has emitted a stock of atmospheric CO_2 that, if removed from the atmosphere, would bring concentrations down to 359.8 ppmv. Then the reduction in global damages that would be incurred if country X's stock had not been emitted is measured by the area under the curve between points *a* and *b*, times the conversion factor from ppmv to tons of CO_2.[7] This is the "other things being equal" value of the stock of CO_2 attributed to country X.

To make this question of average versus marginal social values of the stock of carbon more concrete, we can take the example of the EU, treated as a single emitter in this instance. CAIT estimates that the EU's share of the stock of anthropogenic CO_2 in 2006 is 23.8 percent. Applying the approach shown in figure 4.1, we calculate the average social value of the EU stock of CO_2 to be $5.72 per ton, obtained by dividing the value of damage (the area under the curve in figure 4.1) by the CO_2 stock, measured in tons, attributed to the EU. This compares with the marginal social value of $6.69 per ton.

FIGURE 4.1
The Value of a Reduction in the Stock of CO_2

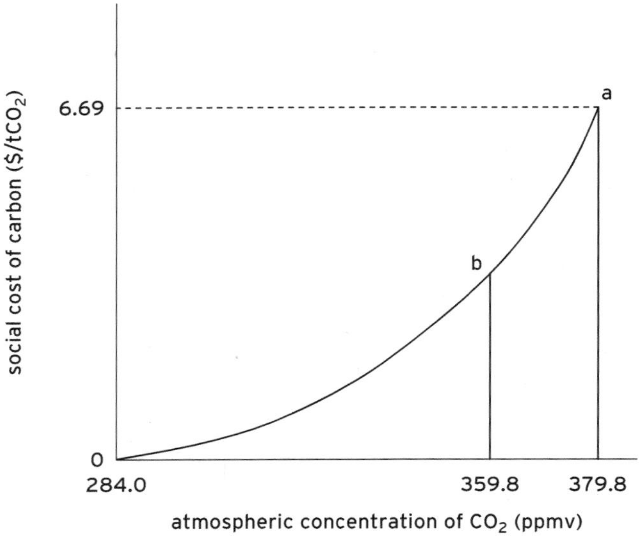

Source: Authors.

Estimated Values of Carbon Stocks and Flows in 2005

The CAIT database covers most countries in the world, providing estimates of each country's share of the stock of CO_2 remaining in the atmosphere in 2006. It includes emissions from fossil fuel combustion and cement manufacture from 1850 to 2006 and emissions from land use change since 1990. These shares of the stock in 2006 are in effect discounted emissions, since they are estimated by summing up the amount of each year's historical emission net of dissipation from the atmosphere since the time of emission. We combine the shares of the stock from CAIT with an estimate of the total stock of anthropogenic CO_2 in the atmosphere in 2005 to arrive at estimated stocks by country.[8]

Figure 4.2 shows the estimated stock of CO_2 for the top 10 emitters, where EU countries feature both as part of the EU aggregate (of 27 countries) and singly. The stocks for the United States and the EU clearly dominate, but China and India feature in the top 10, as does the Russian Federation.

The value of these stocks of CO_2 is shown in figure 4.3, normalized to gross national income (GNI) measured at nominal exchange rates. Here, we see a very different picture of the top 10 historical emitters, with Russia, China, and India exhibiting the largest value of CO_2 stocks as a share of national income. Compared with the United States and the EU, these countries have had higher ratios of CO_2 emissions to GNI.

FIGURE 4.2
Stock of CO$_2$: Top 10 Emitters

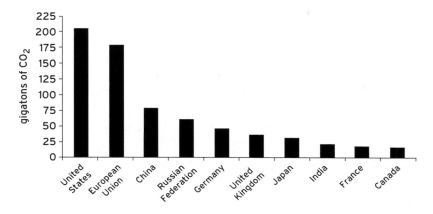

Source: Authors' calculations based on CAIT data for 2009.

FIGURE 4.3
Value of CO$_2$ Stock as a Percentage of GNI: Top 10 Emitters

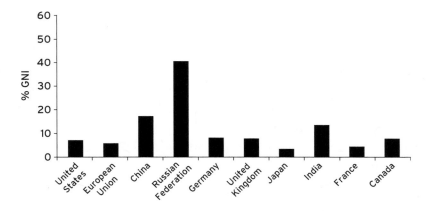

Source: Authors' calculations based on CAIT data for 2009 and World Bank (2007).

Table 4.2 summarizes both stocks and flows of anthropogenic CO$_2$ for all countries exceeding 1 percent of the total atmospheric stock in 2005. In terms of shares of the stock, high-income countries dominate with 60 percent of the total, compared with 40 percent for developing countries (comprising upper-middle-income, lower-middle-income, and low-income countries). Looking at values of CO$_2$ stocks per capita, the top countries, at over $3,000 per capita, are the United States, Germany, the United Kingdom, and Canada; China and India are notably low. For CO_2 stocks as a share of total wealth (a better comparator than GNI, since one stock is being compared to another), the big figures belong to developing and transition countries, including China, Russia, India, Ukraine, Poland, and South Africa. In aggregate, developing countries exhibit a value of CO_2 stocks exceeding 1 percent of total wealth.

Turning to current emissions, table 4.2 shows that the big emitters per capita are high-income countries—the United States, Japan, Canada, and Australia—plus the Russian Federation. However, when share of GNI is considered, the

TABLE 4.2
CO_2 Stock and Current Emissions, 2005

Emitter	CO_2 Stock					CO_2 Emissions		
	Share (%)	t/capita	$/capita	% GNI	% wealth	t/capita	$/capita	% GNI
United States	27.3	691	3,865	9.1	0.5	19.7	132	0.3
European Union	23.8	363	2,079	7.4	0.5	8.2	55	0.2
China	10.5	60	377	21.9	2.0	4.3	29	1.7
Russian Federation	8.1	422	2,684	51.5	3.7	10.6	71	1.4
Germany	6.1	549	3,535	10.3	0.7	9.7	65	0.2
United Kingdom	4.7	586	3,808	9.9	0.6	9.2	61	0.2
Japan	4.2	248	1,617	4.4	0.3	10.2	68	0.2
India	2.8	19	125	17.0	1.2	1.3	9	1.2
France	2.5	301	1,984	5.6	0.3	6.5	43	0.1
Canada	2.2	507	3,347	9.7	0.6	17.3	116	0.3
Ukraine	2.1	337	2,223	123.0	7.6	6.9	46	2.6
Poland	1.8	353	2,335	30.0	1.7	7.9	53	0.7
Italy	1.7	218	1,358	4.5	0.3	8.0	54	0.2
Australia	1.2	433	2,875	9.0	0.6	17.9	120	0.4
Mexico	1.2	84	559	6.9	0.4	4.2	28	0.3
South Africa	1.2	185	1,229	24.2	1.4	8.7	58	1.2
Korea, Rep.	1.1	166	1,105	6.3	0.5	9.8	66	0.4
Spain	1.0	172	1,146	4.5	0.3	8.2	55	0.2
Upper middle income	18.6	150	891	17.2	1.1	5.0	34	0.6
Lower middle income	19.8	41	244	19.1	1.4	2.6	18	1.4
Low income	1.5	12	80	23.8	1.2	0.5	3	1.0

Source: Authors' calculations based on CAIT data for 2009 and World Bank (2007).

largest emitters are developing countries—China, India, and South Africa—plus Russia and Ukraine.[9]

The large number of transition economies seen in table 4.2 reflects an important legacy of the years of central planning. Table 4.3 takes a closer look at the countries of Eastern Europe and Central Asia. The values of CO_2 stocks per capita exceed \$2,000 in Kazakhstan, Poland, Russia, and Ukraine. As a share of total wealth, CO_2 stocks exceed 5 percent in Azerbaijan, Kazakhstan, Moldova, Turkmenistan, Ukraine, and Uzbekistan. The value of current CO_2

TABLE 4.3
Eastern Europe and Central Asia: CO$_2$ Stock and Current Emissions, 2005

Emitter	Share (%)	CO$_2$ Stock				CO$_2$ Emissions		
		t/capita	\$/capita	% GNI	% wealth	t/capita	\$/capita	% GNI
Albania	0.02	48	322	11.7	0.6	1.5	10	0.4
Armenia	0.04	98	653	39.8	2.2	1.4	9	0.6
Azerbaijan	0.19	169	1,133	82.0	7.4	4.2	28	2.0
Belarus	0.36	275	1,844	59.6	3.9	6.6	44	1.4
Bosnia and Herzegovina	0.06	119	794	26.8	1.2	6.8	45	1.5
Bulgaria	0.27	261	1,746	49.6	2.7	6.1	41	1.2
Georgia	0.06	101	673	46.4	2.5	1.1	7	0.5
Kazakhstan	0.89	439	2,942	86.6	7.8	11.7	78	2.3
Kyrgyz Republic	0.05	73	487	105.5	4.6	1.1	7	1.6
Latvia	0.05	163	1,088	15.8	0.9	3.1	21	0.3
Lithuania	0.09	197	1,320	17.8	1.0	4.1	27	0.4
Macedonia, FYR	0.04	147	984	34.8	1.7	5.5	37	1.3
Moldova	0.07	139	932	104.7	5.4	2.2	14	1.6
Poland	1.80	353	2,335	30.0	1.7	7.9	53	0.7
Romania	0.59	204	1,365	30.1	1.7	4.2	28	0.6
Russian Federation	8.08	422	2,684	51.5	3.7	10.6	71	1.4
Serbia	0.20	201	1,346	39.4	1.9	–	–	–
Tajikistan	0.03	34	230	67.2	3.4	0.9	6	1.7
Turkey	0.56	59	394	5.9	0.3	3.5	23	0.3
Turkmenistan	0.16	247	1,654	48.2	8.0	8.6	58	1.7
Ukraine	2.12	337	2,223	123.0	7.6	6.9	46	2.6
Uzbekistan	0.52	149	995	182.3	18.7	4.3	29	5.3

Source: Authors' calculations based on CAIT data for 2009 and World Bank (2007).
Note: – = not available.

emissions as a share of GNI exceeds 1 percent in the majority of countries in the region.

Discussion: Issues of Law and Equity

While it is tempting to consider the value of these stocks of CO_2 as a type of "environmental debt," and thus as figures that would appear as liabilities in the national balance sheet accounts, doing so would require a legal framework that first establishes responsibility for all the past emissions included in our calculations and then creates an obligation for emitters to pay the countries harmed by their emissions. Similar difficulties accompany any attempt to establish liability for current CO_2 emissions. An insightful article by Weisbach (2009) describes the major obstacles these endeavors would face.

Taking the common law of tort as the model of corrective justice, Weisbach identifies the central issue as finding fault. To take just a few examples, are high CO_2 emitters like Canadians at fault for living in a cold climate? Is consumption of meat unethical in the climate context, given that meat production is a major source of CO_2 emissions? Do countries that industrialized earlier, before widespread awareness of the connection between emissions and the greenhouse effect, necessarily bear full historical responsibility? Weisbach notes, "To determine fault on a global scale for pervasive activities that span more than a century is simply impossible."

The alternative to finding fault is to impose strict liability. In the climate context this would imply that all emitters of CO_2 would be liable for damages, without the need for a finding of fault as in tort law. But as Weisbach notes, applying strict liability retroactively—which would be required if historical emissions were to be subject to corrective justice—is almost unprecedented. As a general principle of due process, agents who would be subject to strict liability should be entitled to advance notice prior to any assumption of liability.

In addition, corrective justice requires that there be some demonstrable connection between the agent causing harm and the party being harmed. When we consider the problem of damages from CO_2 emitted over time, it is difficult at this time to see how this evidentiary requirement would be met.

Finally, as already noted, imposing some form of sanction on developing-country emitters, whether the emissions of CO_2 are current or historical, raises serious questions of equity. As a general principle it seems inequitable to require developing countries to finance a global public good, particularly when the largest portion of historical emissions creating the need for that public good has come from high-income countries.

If we wish the solution to the climate problem to be equitable, the inevitable next question concerns the equity criteria to be applied. A variety can be identified, including egalitarianism (implying equal per capita emission rights, for example), ability to pay, sovereignty (implying status quo rights), "maxi-min" (maximize net benefits to the poorest nations), horizontal equity (similar economic circumstances receive similar emission rights), vertical equity (higher compliance burdens should fall on those with higher ability to pay), Pareto compensation, and market justice (seek efficient solutions to the climate problem) (Rose et al. 1998; Rose and Kverndokk 2008).

Applying any of these equity criteria would result in different outcomes concerning who pays for dealing with climate change, and making a choice among them is ultimately the responsibility of the nations of the world as they progress toward a comprehensive solution to the climate problem.

Summing Up

Our purpose in this chapter has not been to join the rancorous debate about historical responsibility for climate change. The CAIT figures are, on their own, sufficient to fuel that debate.

Our contribution has been to devise an approach to economic valuation of the stocks of CO_2 that can be attributed to each country and to present the resulting figures both in per capita terms and as a share of total wealth. In per capita terms the stock values are particularly large in high-income countries, while they are large in proportion to total wealth in the large middle-income countries, particularly in the transition economies of Eastern Europe and Central Asia. We also value current emissions, using the social cost of carbon. These figures are also large in per capita terms in high-income countries and large as a share of GNI in the large middle-income countries.

It is clear that assigning property rights would be a necessary step in bringing these CO_2 values into the national income, savings, and wealth accounts that are the focus of this book. If we assume that countries have the right not to be polluted by their neighbors—a fundamental principle of international environmental law—then each country's value of CO_2 emissions could be accounted as a *notional* deduction from savings, while the value of the stock of CO_2 attributed to the country could be a *notional* liability in the asset accounts. But any attempt to move from notional values to damages owed would raise the issues discussed earlier about the applicability of the model of corrective justice and the associated ethical questions.

The social cost of carbon employed in this chapter falls within the range of peer-reviewed estimates, $6.69 per ton of CO_2. By way of comparison, the U.K. Department of Energy and Climate Change has published guidelines suggesting a central estimate of the value of carbon lying between £21 and £50 per ton of CO_2 in 2008 (DECC 2009). The lower of these figures amounts to about $40 per ton of CO_2 in 2005 dollars, and at this social cost of carbon the average value of the U.S. stock of CO_2 per citizen would amount to over $23,000, representing nearly 55 percent of GNI per capita or 3 percent of total wealth per capita. In addition, if the world were to agree on an emissions cap that would lead to stabilization of the global stock of CO_2, the social cost of carbon would rise at the rate of interest, say 5 percent per year.[10] But the rate of decay of CO_2 stocks is much lower, averaging about 1.2 percent a year over 100 years. It is therefore likely that the value of these CO_2 stocks will increase over time.

The rate of depreciation of these stocks of CO_2 is driven by physical processes. Unlike financial obligations, therefore, these stocks cannot be reduced by saving more today. But the rate of accumulation of *new* stocks of atmospheric CO_2 is very much driven by the combination of economic and climate policy.

This brings us back to one of the main messages of *WDR 2010*: the development process itself must be transformed because high-carbon growth is no longer sustainable. Achieving this transformation across a broad range of countries is part of what the United Nations Framework Convention on Climate Change terms the "common but differentiated responsibilities" of all countries.

Annex: Sources and Technical Details

This annex provides the sources of the data used in this chapter, as well some key technical details concerning the empirical estimates used.

Stock of CO_2 in 2005

A standard source for historical CO_2 concentration data is the Carbon Dioxide Information Analysis Center (CDIAC) of the U.S. Department of Energy, which has published data on recent greenhouse gas concentrations (Blasing 2010).

For this chapter we assume a preindustrial atmospheric CO_2 concentration of 284 parts per million by volume (ppmv), based on work by Etheridge et al. (1998). We use a current concentration figure of 379.76 ppmv in 2005 based upon the Mauna Loa time series from Pieter Tans (2010) of the Earth System Research Laboratory, National Oceanic and Atmospheric Administration, U.S. Department of Commerce.

The difference between these two figures gives a concentration of anthropogenic atmospheric CO_2 equal to 95.76 ppmv. Concentrations are then converted to mass, based upon information from CDIAC (2010):

$$1 \text{ ppmv } CO_2 = 2.13 \text{ Gt C} = 7.81 \text{ Gt } CO_2.$$

Our estimated mass of anthropogenic atmospheric CO_2 for 2005 is therefore 747.9 Gt CO_2.

As noted in the text, CAIT assumes a rate of dissipation of CO_2 from the atmosphere based upon UNFCCC (2002). The formula assumes different rates of decay for distinct fractions of the gas in the atmosphere. If we denote the fraction of emitted CO_2 still in the atmosphere t years after emission as $f(t)$, and emissions in year s as $e(s)$, then the year 2005 stock S is calculated as

$$S(2005) = \sum_{t=1,850}^{2005} e(t) \cdot f(2005 - t)$$

As reported in the CAIT indicator framework paper (WRI 2009), CAIT calculates an anthropogenic CO_2 concentration in year 2000 of 83 ppmv compared with the observed figure of 90 ppmv. The difference is ascribed to the simple model of the carbon cycle used in the calculation and the omission of land-use change and forestry emissions prior to 1990.

CAIT reports only the country shares of the anthropogenic stock of CO_2, which are shown in tables 4.2 and 4.3. We multiply these shares by the total stock estimate of 747.9 Gt CO_2 to arrive at country stocks, but the omission of emissions from land-use change in the nineteenth century probably biases developed-country stocks downward.

Average Versus Marginal Social Cost of Carbon

Figure 4.1 presents the logic for how nonmarginal changes in the stock of atmospheric CO_2 should be valued. We use a quadratic form of the relationship between the marginal social cost of carbon and the atmospheric concentration of CO_2, based upon an approximation of the damage function in the DICE (Dynamic Integrated Model of Climate and the Economy) 2007 model documented by Nordhaus (2008).

The DICE 2007 integrated assessment model employs a piece-wise polynomial damage function to relate global damages (measured in percentage of gross domestic product lost) to the mean global temperature rise, with damage assumed to be zero for a zero rise in temperature. Since the temperature rise is an increasing function of the atmospheric concentration of CO_2, and the social cost of carbon (SCC) is an increasing function of damages, we approximate these relationships as:

$$SCC = 0.00018407 \cdot x(x - 284)$$

Here x is the atmospheric concentration of CO_2, and the leading numerical constant ensures that the social cost of carbon is equal to \$6.69 when concentrations are at the 2005 level, 379.76 ppmv. The $(x - 284)$ term ensures that the social cost of carbon is zero when CO_2 concentrations are at the preindustrial level of 284 ppmv.

A superior solution to dealing with nonmarginal values of the social cost of carbon would be to run the DICE 2007 model (or another integrated assessment model) with alternative initial conditions for the current atmospheric concentration of CO_2, and then measure the associated social cost of carbon. Repeating this step would permit the tracing out of a more precise curve for figure 4.1, and numerical integration of the curve would yield the nonmarginal values of the social cost of carbon desired. This is a subject for future research.

Notes

1 As the analysis will show, however, per capita emissions of CO_2 in low- and middle-income countries are still much lower than in developed countries.

2 This list of characteristics is obviously not exhaustive. A key point, though not directly germane to the analysis in this chapter, is that climate mitigation is a global public good, creating strong incentives for countries to free ride on the efforts of their neighbors. Free riders increase their own profits by not applying costly CO_2 abatement technologies while at the same time benefiting from abatement efforts by others. In the absence of an effective global regulatory regime, reducing climate change is a classic coordination problem. Barrett (2003) explores this problem at length.

3 CAIT Version 7.0 was developed by the World Resources Institute in Washington, DC (http://cait.wri.org/).

4 For an example of an integrated assessment model, see the DICE (Dynamic Integrated Model of Climate and the Economy) model of Nordhaus (2008). Integrated assessment models are linked economy-climate system models.

5 This seems a reasonable starting point, but it is not uncontroversial, as our discussion of finding fault will make clear.

6 The data underlying figure 4.1 and its functional form are referenced in the annex to this chapter.

7 Obviously, if country X's stock of CO_2 is small, then points a and b nearly coincide, and marginal valuation of the stock is a reasonable approximation.

8 For sources and caveats on the data presented, see the annex to this chapter. Note that shares of anthropogenic CO_2 in 2006 would not be significantly different from those for 2005, and so we apply the 2006 shares to the 2005 total stock in order to arrive at 2005 stocks of CO_2 by country.

9 Note that the figures for the value of emissions are equal to the level of an efficient tax on carbon emissions in these countries. Some countries have suggested that taxing carbon at the point of emission is unfair, because much of the carbon is emitted in the production of export goods consumed in other countries; these producer countries therefore suggest taxing on the basis of carbon consumed. However, the logic of taxing consumption requires that there be border taxes on imports (see, for instance, Whalley 1979), so the suggested tax on carbon consumption would not necessarily reduce the tax burden on emitting nations. Atkinson et al. (2010) show that U.S. border taxes on the carbon content of imports from China, India, Russia, and South Africa could be very large, up to 10 percent of the total value of imports for a tax rate of $50 per ton of CO_2.

10 The intuition here is that implementing a stabilization target is roughly equivalent to having a finite stock of emission rights that will be depleted over time. The Hotelling rule therefore applies to the price of these emission rights—that is, the social cost of carbon.

References

Atkinson, Giles, Kirk Hamilton, Giovanni Ruta, and Dominique van der Mensbrugghe. 2010. "Trade in 'Virtual Carbon': Empirical Results and Implications for Policy." Policy Research Working Paper 5194, World Bank, Washington, DC.

Barrett, Scott. 2003. *Environment and Statecraft: The Strategy of Environmental Treaty-Making.* New York: Oxford University Press.

Blasing, T. J. 2010. "Recent Greenhouse Gas Concentrations." Carbon Dioxide Information Analysis Center, Oak Ridge National Laboratory, U.S. Department of Energy, Oak Ridge, TN. http://cdiac.ornl.gov/pns/current_ghg.html.

CDIAC (Carbon Dioxide Information Analysis Center). 2010. "Frequently Asked Global Change Questions." CDIAC, Oak Ridge National Laboratory, U.S. Department of Energy, Oak Ridge, TN. http://cdiac.ornl.gov/pns/faq.html.

DECC (Department of Energy and Climate Change). 2009. "Carbon Valuation in UK Policy Appraisal: A Revised Approach." U.K. Department of Energy and Climate Change, London.

den Elzen, M., M. Berk, M. Schaeffer, J. Olivier, C. Hendriks, and B. Metz. 1999. "The Brazilian Proposal and Other Options for International Burden Sharing: An Evaluation of Methodological and Policy Aspects Using the FAIR Model." National Institute of Public Health and the Environment, Bilthoven, Netherlands.

Etheridge, D. M., L. P. Steele, R. L. Langenfelds, R. J. Francey, J.-M. Barnola, and V. I. Morgan. 1998. "Historical CO_2 Records from the Law Dome DE08, DE08-2, and DSS Ice Cores." In *Trends: A Compendium of Data on Global Change.* Oak Ridge, TN: Carbon Dioxide Information Analysis Center, Oak Ridge National Laboratory, U.S. Department of Energy.

Fankhauser, Samuel. 1995. *Valuing Climate Change: The Economics of the Greenhouse.* London: Earthscan.

IPCC (Intergovernmental Panel on Climate Change). 2007a. *Climate Change 2007: Synthesis Report—Summary for Policymakers.* Contribution of Working Groups I, II, and III to the Fourth Assessment Report of the Intergovernmental Panel on Climate Change. Geneva: IPCC.

———. 2007b. *IPCC Fourth Assessment Report: Climate Change 2007.* Geneva: IPCC.

Nordhaus, William. 2008. *A Question of Balance: Weighing the Options on Global Warming Policies.* New Haven, CT: Yale University Press.

Rose, A., and S. Kverndokk. 2008. "Equity and Justice in Global Warming Policy." Nota di Lavoro 80.2008, Fondazione Eni Enrico Mattei, Milan.

Rose, A., B. Stevens, J. Edmonds, and M. Wise. 1998. "International Equity and Differentiation in Global Warming Policy." *Environmental and Resource Economics* 12 (1): 25–51.

Stern, Nicholas. 2006. *The Economics of Climate Change: The Stern Review.* Prepared for the U.K. Government. New York: Cambridge University Press.

Tans, Pieter. 2010. "Trends in Atmospheric Carbon Dioxide." Earth System Research Laboratory, National Oceanic and Atmospheric Administration, U.S. Department of Commerce, Boulder, CO. http://www.esrl.noaa.gov/gmd/ccgg/trends.

Tol, Richard. 2005. "The Marginal Damage Costs of Carbon Dioxide Emissions: An Assessment of the Uncertainties." *Energy Policy* 33: 2064–74.

UNFCCC (United Nations Framework Convention on Climate Change). 2002. *Scientific and Methodological Assessment of Contributions to Climate Change: Report of the Expert Meeting.* Document FCCC/SBSTA/2002/INF.14. Bonn: UNFCCC.

Weisbach, David. 2009. "Responsibility for Climate Change, by the Numbers." Law and Economics Working Paper 448, University of Chicago Law School, Chicago.

Whalley, John. 1979. "A Simple Neutrality Result for Movements between Income and Consumption Taxes." *American Economic Review* 69 (5): 974–76.

World Bank. 2007. *World Development Indicators 2007*. Washington, DC: World Bank.

————. 2010. *World Development Report 2010: Development and Climate Change*. Washington, DC: World Bank.

WRI (World Resources Institute). 2009. "CAIT: Indicator Framework Paper." World Resources Institute, Washington, DC.

C H A P T E R   5

Intangible Capital and Development

IT HAS BEEN UNDERSTOOD SINCE AT LEAST THE TIME OF
Irving Fisher (1906) that income is the return on wealth. But if we scale up this
idea to the level of the national economy, we arrive at a puzzle: if we measure
wealth only as produced capital, we see from the national balance sheet accounts
of countries such as Canada that wealth is only a small multiple of gross national
income (GNI). This implies unrealistically high implicit rates of return on wealth.
Table 5.1 shows Canadian figures for 2009.

The value of produced capital is less than three times GNI, while net worth
(which includes commercial land and net financial assets) is a bit less than four
times GNI. The implicit rates of return on wealth are correspondingly high, 35.9
percent and 25.4 percent respectively. Canadians appear to be a very productive
bunch.[1]

The "solution" to this puzzle, of course, is that the national balance sheet
accounts of the System of National Accounts (SNA) exclude values for many
intangible assets, such as human capital and social/institutional capital.[2]
Moreover, the Canadian balance sheets highlighted in table 5.1 exclude the value
of commercial natural resources.[3] Since a "normal" rate of return on assets should
be on the order of 5 percent, a comprehensive measure of national wealth should
be approximately 20 times national income. The gap between such a measure

TABLE 5.1
National Wealth and Income in Canada, 2009
Can$ millions

Net financial assets	−109,452	
Land assets	1,846,753	
Produced capital (K)	4,191,919	
Net worth	5,929,220	
GNI	1,505,817	
K/GNI	2.78	Implicit rate of return 35.9%
Net worth/GNI	3.94	Implicit rate of return 25.4%

Source: Statistics Canada 2010a, 2010b.

of comprehensive national wealth and the SNA balance sheet value is what we have termed intangible capital.

However, there is a risk that the intangible capital estimates derived in this book are simply a black box. We therefore revisit the analysis of the composition of intangible capital presented in chapter 7 of *Where Is the Wealth of Nations?* (World Bank 2006), bringing to bear our new wealth accounts for 1995, 2000, and 2005. We extend this analysis by exploring the role of intangible capital in production. But we begin by presenting the theoretical underpinnings of the measure of total wealth and intangible capital.

Theoretical Considerations

As documented in appendix A, total or comprehensive wealth is measured as the present value of future consumption, and intangible wealth is the residual derived by subtracting physical, natural, and net financial assets from total wealth. It is therefore important to understand in some detail how the total wealth estimates are derived.

Hamilton and Hartwick (2005) show how to estimate a comprehensive measure of national wealth for a competitive economy with constant returns to scale. For production function $F = F(K, L, R)$ with factors K (produced capital), labor L, natural resource flow R, and interest rate r, comprehensive wealth is given by

$$W = K + H + S = \int_t^\infty C(s) \cdot e^{-\int_t^s r(z)dz} \, ds. \tag{5.1}$$

That is, comprehensive wealth can be measured either by adding up asset values K, H (human capital), and S (the value of the natural resource stock), or by measuring the present value of consumption C along the competitive development path. The intuition behind this result is clear: future consumption must be bounded by current wealth.

To apply expression (5.1) we have to make assumptions about future consumption growth and the discount rate. To choose the discount rate we apply the Ramsey formula, which tells us how much a consumer would need to be compensated for deferring a unit of consumption from the current period to the next period. This is given by

$$r = \rho + \eta g, \qquad (5.2)$$

where ρ is the pure rate of time preference, η is the elasticity of the marginal utility of consumption, and g is the growth rate of per capita consumption. The discount rate is therefore the sum of the rate of impatience plus the rate of change of the marginal utility of consumption. If ρ, η, and g are constant, then expression (5.1) reduces to

$$W(t) = \frac{C(t)}{\rho - (1 - \eta)g}. \qquad (5.3)$$

Empirical estimates of ρ are typically small (Pearce and Ulph 1999), on the order of 1–2 percent, while for η they typically range from 1 to 2. However expression (5.3) implies that for $\eta > 1$, total wealth is a decreasing function of the growth rate of future consumption, a counterintuitive result. Based on this analysis, we therefore choose ρ equal to 1.5 percent and η equal to 1 in order to calculate total wealth.

As seen in expression (5.1), the underlying growth theory assumes an infinite lifetime for the analysis. As a practical matter, we have chosen to carry out the wealth accounting on a generational basis, assuming a maximum lifetime for all assets of 25 years. Our total wealth estimates are therefore calculated as the present value of the current level of consumption (held constant), taken over 25 years and discounted at the pure rate of time preference, 1.5 percent. We assume an optimistic future rate of per capita consumption growth of 2.5 percent (historical values are typically less than 1.5 percent), so that our calculated interest rate using the Ramsey formula is 4 percent.

Given these parameter choices, the logical next question is whether the resulting total wealth estimates are "reasonable." We define reasonability in terms of the implicit rate of return on wealth, as we did in the discussion of table 5.1. To test this we derive the following additional result from Hamilton and Hartwick (2005): if interest rate r is constant, δ is the depreciation rate for produced capital, and $F_R R$ is the value of resource depletion, then net income is just equal to the return on total wealth. That is:

$$C + \dot{K} - \delta K - F_R R = rW = r \int_t^\infty C(s) \cdot e^{-r(s-t)} \, ds. \qquad (5.4)$$

FIGURE 5.1
Distribution of Implicit Rates of Return on Comprehensive Wealth, 2005

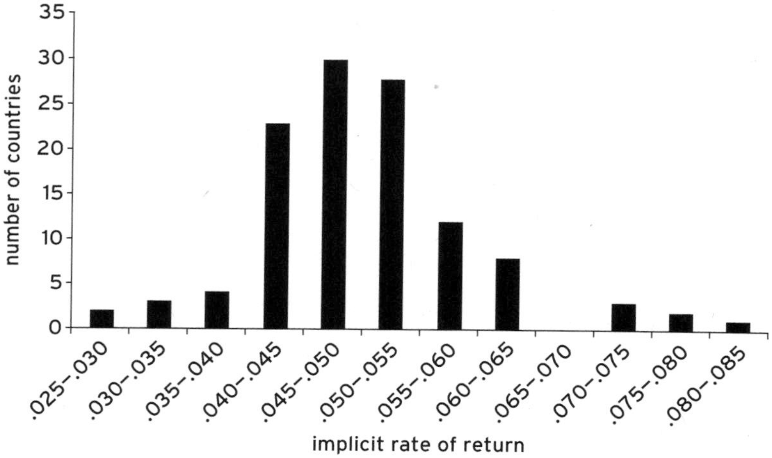

Source: Authors' calculations.

We use data from the World Bank's *World Development Indicators* (2010) to calculate net income and then apply expression (5.4) in order to derive the implicit rate of return on comprehensive wealth in each country. The distribution of rates of return across countries is plotted in figure 5.1, which shows that 80 percent of the rates lie between 4 percent and 6 percent.

As this discussion makes clear, calculating a value for total wealth involves questions of judgment, including the choice of the pure rate of time preference, the elasticity of the marginal utility of consumption, and the lifetime over which present values are calculated. Alternatives to the choices we have made are clearly possible, but the calculation of the implicit rate of return on wealth provides an essential reality check for any total wealth estimates that result.

Finally, another caveat. Since intangible capital is measured residually, it implicitly includes all "missing" asset values. For example, since data on the value of diamond and fishery resources are not widely available, these natural assets are implicitly (and erroneously) included as part of the intangible capital for countries where these resources are important.

Explaining Intangible Capital

Chapter 7 of *Where Is the Wealth of Nations?* (World Bank 2006) attempted to open the black box of intangible capital by analyzing the extent to which other factors could explain the total variation in intangible capital across countries.

The factors chosen—measures of human capital and institutional/social capital—were selected on the basis of their plausibility as constituents of intangible wealth.

Where Is the Wealth of Nations? estimated the composition of intangible wealth based upon a cross-sectional dataset of wealth estimates for the year 2000. This analysis had a number of limitations imposed by the cross-sectional nature of the data: in particular, there could be omitted variables relating to fixed country characteristics or to common shocks at a point in time that affect all countries. In addition, the analysis used a particular functional form (Cobb-Douglas) to carry out the decomposition, without sufficient discussion of the underlying theory of wealth accounting. Finally, the measure of human capital used in the analysis, average years of schooling per capita, did not account for declining marginal returns to education or for the quality of human capital. In this chapter we address all of these shortcomings.

Marking an advance since the 2006 work, we now have a panel dataset with observations for 115 countries for the years 1995, 2000, and 2005. This permits the use of country and time fixed effects, which in turn helps mitigate omitted variable bias as long as the unobserved variables are constant over time and/or across countries.

With regard to measuring human capital, the current consensus approach in the literature uses a log-linear relationship between earnings and years of schooling, first formulated by Mincer (1974). It expresses the human capital per worker h as an exponential function of years of schooling, $h = e^{\theta(s)}$, where the function $\theta(s)$ represents the efficiency of a unit of labor with s years of schooling relative to one with no schooling. We follow common practice and use $\theta(s) = \varepsilon s$, where ε is the rate of return to education. Our benchmark is $\varepsilon = 8.5$ percent return on years of schooling, as in Klenow and Rodríguez-Clare (1997, 2005). This is the average of returns to education in Psacharopoulos and Patrinos (2004). Our estimates of years of schooling per worker are from Barro and Lee (2001).

Next, we augment our indicator of human capital to account for the health of the population and of the workforce, based on the analysis by Caselli (2005), who introduces adult survival rates (equal to 1 minus the mortality rate for individuals between the ages of 15 and 60) as a proxy for health status. Shastry and Weil (2003) argue that differences in health status proxied by adult mortality rates map into substantial differences in energy and capacity for effort. For adult survival rate a we therefore calculate quality-adjusted human capital as

$$h = e^{\sigma a} \cdot e^{\theta s}. \tag{5.5}$$

Adult survival rates are available in consistent form for a large cross-section of countries from *World Development Indicators* (World Bank 2010), while Weil (2007) estimates a value of $\sigma = 0.653$.

Turning to institutional quality, we follow *Where Is the Wealth of Nations?* in using a rule of law index from Kaufmann, Kraay, and Mastruzzi (2009) as the proxy measure. This index measures the extent to which agents have confidence in and abide by the rules of society. In particular, it measures the quality of contract enforcement, property rights, the police, and the courts, as well as the likelihood of crime and violence.[4]

The next issue is the functional form for estimating the constituents of intangible capital. The most parsimonious model is provided by expression (5.1). The underlying growth theory shows that total wealth (the present value of future consumption) is simply the sum of the different assets owned by a country. This suggests a linear model specification for decomposing intangible capital:

$$ic_{it} = \alpha_i + \beta_t + \gamma_h h_{it} + \gamma_w w_{it} + \varepsilon_{it}. \tag{5.6}$$

Here *ic* is intangible capital, α_i is the country fixed effect, β_t is the time dummy, *h* is human capital, and *w* is the rule of law.

In estimating expression (5.6) we use three different models: (a) pooled data (no fixed effects or time dummies) with income dummies[5] and human capital measured by years of schooling; (b) pooled data with income dummies and human capital measured as in expression (5.5); and (c) panel data with fixed effects, time dummies, and human capital measured as in expression (5.5). The results of the estimation (the values of coefficients γ_h and γ_w) are shown in table 5.2.[6]

The first column in table 5.2 bears a strong resemblance to the results in *Where Is the Wealth of Nations* (World Bank 2006 chapter 7, table 7.4). A one-unit increase in the rule of law index (out of a possible 100 units) yields $3,000 of intangible wealth, while one additional year of schooling per capita yields $11,025. The second model uses the human capital index rather than years of

TABLE 5.2
Estimated Constituents of Intangible Wealth
2005 US$

	Pooled Data, Years of Schooling	Pooled Data, Human Capital	Country Fixed Effects, Human Capital
Rule of law	3,000	2,819	..
Years of schooling	11,025		
Human capital		46,178	92,899
Time			10,013

Source: Authors' estimates. Detailed estimation results are reported by Ferreira and Hamilton (2010).
Note: .. = statistically insignificant coefficient. All other coefficients are significant at the 1% or 5% level. The time dummy is for 2005 relative to 1995.

schooling. This index compresses the human capital scale, as shown in expression (5.5). In both models the rule of law index coefficient is statistically significant and close to $3,000. In the fixed effects model the rule of law index becomes insignificant, while the coefficient on human capital doubles and the time dummy (for 2005 relative to 1995) is positive and significant.

The results shown in table 5.2 require careful interpretation. With the theoretically preferred specification of human capital based on expression (5.5), the pooled data model shows that both human capital and institutional quality (proxied by the rule of law index) are statistically significant components of intangible wealth. However, the fixed effects model is preferred because it controls for unobserved variable bias.[7] With this specification, rule of law ceases to be a significant determinant of intangible capital. This suggests that the country fixed effects in expression (5.6) are picking up the effects of institutional quality, which makes sense given the short time span involved; institutional quality likely did not vary that much from 1995 to 2005. But the country fixed effects are also picking up other important endowment effects, potentially including geography and history. The data do not permit us to dig deeper into these other constituents.

The other point to note in table 5.2 is the large coefficient on the passage of time from 1995 to 2005, over $10,000. This coefficient of time is typically considered to be a proxy measure of technical progress. The table can therefore be interpreted as saying that there is evidence for a considerable increase in intangible wealth per capita associated with technological change.

Table 5.3 presents the value of the human capital index, the estimated value of human capital (based on the price of $92,899 shown in table 5.2), and the country fixed effects for selected countries. It is clear that human capital is the dominant form of intangible wealth in rich countries, but a sizable "residual of the residual" (that is, intangible wealth excluding human capital) remains in most cases.[8] Other factors, such as total factor productivity, may be part of the intangible wealth story in high-income countries.

As table 5.3 also shows, the fixed effects for developing countries are large, negative, and significant, often more than $-$200,000 per capita. This could be viewed as an artifact of using a single average global price for human capital. But an alternative interpretation is that this average global price represents the *potential* value of a unit of human capital, potential that is not realized in developing countries owing to negative endowments, including institutional quality, geography, and history.

The Role of Intangible Capital in Development

In growth accounting (see, for instance, Mankiw, Romer, and Weil 1992) there is a long tradition of using data on factor accumulation to explain the growth

TABLE 5.3
**Human Capital and Country Fixed Effects in Selected Countries,
Average 1995-2005**
2005 US$

Country	Intangible Capital ($/capita)	Human Capital Index	Human Capital ($/capita)	Fixed Effects ($/capita)	Residual ($/capita)
G7 countries					
Canada	385,939	4.9	455,093	..	−69,154
France	441,169	3.5	324,988	..	116,181
Germany	413,737	4.3	399,283	..	14,454
Italy	377,822	3.4	312,546	..	65,276
Japan	364,893	4.1	380,438	..	−15,545
United Kingdom	499,841	4.0	375,106	..	124,735
United States	562,835	5.0	464,335	..	98,500
BRICS					
Brazil	52,822	2.6	237,230	−198,561	
China	6,662	3.0	281,606	−288,846	
India	4,441	2.5	236,169	−248,193	
Russian Federation	14,407	3.7	343,350	−347,306	
South Africa	58,802	2.4	226,898	−184,072	
Low-income countries (selected)					
Bangladesh	4,341	2.0	189,857	−197,557	
Ghana	4,660	2.2	207,742	−217,626	
Haiti	7,456	2.0	186,968	−188,202	
Kenya	5,219	2.1	194,752	−200,795	
Nepal	1,872	2.0	186,030	−197,573	
Senegal	9,571	2.2	199,972	−204,724	
Tajikistan	2,633	4.1	380,434	−395,415	
Uganda	1,253	1.9	172,075	−182,969	
Vietnam	4,196	2.6	245,243	−271,825	
Zambia	6,292	2.0	187,064	−193,728	

Source: Authors' calculations.
Note: .. = statistically insignificant coefficient.

in economic output. The basic approach is to estimate a production function, using panel or cross-sectional data for countries, to relate output to factor inputs.

We follow this tradition using our panel data set on produced, natural, and intangible wealth. First we regress the logarithm of output against the logarithms of the production factors. As a variant, we also use our calculated human capital index as a production factor in place of intangible capital. The log-log specification means that we can interpret the resulting regression coefficients as elasticities of output with respect to the different production factors, since the underlying functional form for the production function is Cobb-Douglas.

Table 5.4 reports the results of our estimation of output elasticities across different production factors and different subsets of countries. In all cases we use country fixed effects and time dummies. The first column reports the results of estimating the production function for all countries using our human capital index rather than intangible capital as a factor of production. In this formulation, only produced capital has a significant coefficient; the elasticities for natural and human capital are not significantly different from zero.

In the second column we report the estimated coefficients for a production function where we use intangible capital rather than human capital as a production factor. The largest elasticity is for produced capital, but now both natural and intangible capital are significant factors of production. The final two columns in table 5.4 report the estimated elasticities when we split the sample into developed and developing subsets of countries. In each case we treat intangible wealth as a factor of production. For developing countries the results are very similar to those obtained when the sample consists of all countries—produced, natural, and intangible capital have significant output elasticities, and the magnitude is similar in both samples. When the sample is limited to countries of the Organisation for Economic Co-operation and Development (OECD), however, only intangible capital is significant and the elasticity is very large, roughly 0.5.

Summing up, we would intuitively expect that produced, natural, and human capital would all be statistically significant factors of production, but we obtain this result only when we treat intangible capital, rather than the human capital index, as a factor of production. This is consistent with the preceding subsection on explaining intangible capital, which shows that intangible capital

TABLE 5.4
Elasticities of Output with Respect to Production Factors

	All Countries	All Countries	Developing Countries	OECD Countries
Produced capital	0.398	0.320	0.313	..
Natural capital	..	0.068	0.072	..
Human capital index	..			
Intangible capital		0.176	0.169	0.502

Source: Authors' calculations. Detailed estimation results are reported by Ferreira and Hamilton (2010).
Note: .. = statistically insignificant coefficient.

certainly includes the value of human capital but clearly measures more than that, including elements of institutional quality and technical progress as well. The results for the OECD country subsample suggest a different, and perhaps more substantial, role for intangible capital in high-income countries.

Summing Up

The finding that intangible capital makes up 60–80 percent of total wealth in most countries raises important questions for policy. As long as intangible capital is a black box, governments may be tempted to conclude that all public expenditures (excluding physical infrastructure) are in some sense investments in intangible wealth. Considerable unproductive expenditures could ensue, wasting precious fiscal resources. The analysis in this chapter helps clarify the composition and contribution of intangible capital to development.

On composition, the key finding is the dominance of human capital as a constituent of intangible wealth. An expected result, this turns out to be unequivocally true for high-income countries. For developing countries the potential value of human capital is extremely high when a single average global price is used for human capital, but this is offset by the negative endowment measured by the country fixed effects. It is certainly conceivable that the quality of institutions and the legacy of geography and history for developing countries can explain these large, negative fixed effects.

Our analysis also shows that intangible capital is a significant factor of production across all countries. It would be surprising if this were not the case; the striking finding is that intangible capital is the *only* significant factor of production in OECD countries. This suggests that the accumulation of tangible factors—produced and natural capital—is not a significant contributor to growth in high-income economies. In these advanced economies all of the potential constituents of intangible capital—the quantity and quality of human capital, the constituents of total factor productivity, and institutional quality beyond the rule of law—may be the key drivers of production and growth.

The policy conclusion for developing country governments from this analysis is that investments in human capital are an important part of the development process. This is no surprise. But the analysis also suggests that strengthening institutions and developing the capacity to generate and use knowledge—the precursors to total factor productivity growth—will also be wealth-enhancing. Finally, our growth accounting analysis leads us to a model where an increase in the quantity of one factor will increase the marginal product of all other factors. So governments also need to ensure that complementary investments in infrastructure and natural resource management will support these investments in intangible capital, and vice versa.

Notes

1 As will be seen in the next section, it is *net* income, rather than GNI, that equals the return on total capital. The implicit rates of return reported in table 5.1 should therefore be multiplied by a factor of about 0.85.

2 The SNA has precise definitions for intangible fixed and intangible nonproduced assets, which include items such as mineral exploration expenditures and the value of patents. In this chapter we use the term "intangible" to include all nonphysical, nonfinancial assets.

3 While SNA 1993 requires inclusion of the value of commercial natural resources in the balance sheet accounts, to date only Australia has published such accounts.

4 In our analysis we transform the Kaufmann-Kraay-Mastruzzi rule of law figures into an index ranging from 0 to 100.

5 We include dummies for upper-middle-income, lower-middle-income, and low-income countries.

6 Chapter 7 of *Where Is the Wealth of Nations?* (World Bank 2006) also included remittances as a type of return to human capital in its model specification. Remittances were not significant in any of the specifications of the model of intangible wealth presented here.

7 We also performed F-tests for the joint significance of country and time fixed effects. In both cases we rejected the hypothesis that the fixed effects are equal to zero.

8 The exceptions are Canada and Japan.

References

Barro, Robert J., and Jong-Wha Lee. 2001. "International Data on Educational Attainment: Updates and Implications." *Oxford Economic Papers* 53 (3): 541–63.

Caselli, Francesco. 2005. "Accounting for Cross-Country Income Differences." In *Handbook of Economic Growth*, vol. 1A, ed. Philippe Aghion and Steven N. Durlauf, chap. 9. Amsterdam: North-Holland.

Ferreira, S., and K. Hamilton. 2010. "Comprehensive Wealth, Intangible Capital, and Development." Development Economics Research Group, World Bank, Washington, DC.

Fisher, Irving. 1906. *The Nature of Capital and Income*. London: Macmillan.

Hamilton, Kirk, and John M. Hartwick. 2005. "Investing Exhaustible Resource Rents and the Path of Consumption." *Canadian Journal of Economics* 38 (2): 615–21.

Kaufmann, Daniel, Aart Kraay, and Massimo Mastruzzi. 2009. "Governance Matters VIII: Aggregate and Individual Governance Indicators 1996–2008." Policy Research Working Paper 4978, World Bank, Washington, DC.

Klenow, Peter J., and Andrés Rodríguez-Clare. 1997. "The Neoclassical Revival in Growth Economics: Has It Gone Too Far?" In *NBER Macroeconomics Annual 1997*, ed. Ben S. Bernanke and Julio Rotemberg, 73–103. Cambridge, MA: MIT Press.

———. 2005. "Externalities and Growth." In *Handbook of Economic Growth*, vol. 1A, ed. Philippe Aghion and Steven N. Durlauf, chap. 11. Amsterdam: North-Holland.

Mankiw, N. Gregory, David Romer, and David N. Weil. 1992. "A Contribution to the Empirics of Economic Growth." *Quarterly Journal of Economics* 107 (2): 407–37.

Mincer, Jacob. 1974. *Schooling, Experience, and Earnings*. New York: Columbia University Press.

Pearce, David, and David Ulph. 1999. "A Social Discount Rate for the United Kingdom." In *Economics and Environment: Essays on Ecological Economics and Sustainable Development*, ed. David Pearce, 268–85. Cheltenham, UK: Edward Elgar.

Psacharopoulos, G., and H. Patrinos. 2004. "Returns to Investment in Education: A Further Update." *Education Economics* 12 (2): 111–34.

Shastry, Gauri K., and David N. Weil. 2003. "How Much of Cross-Country Income Variation Is Explained by Health?" *Journal of the European Economic Association* 1 (2–3): 387–96.

Statistics Canada. 2010a. "National Income and Expenditure Accounts: Data Tables." Publication 13-019-XWE, Ottawa.

———. 2010b. "National Balance Sheet Accounts: Data Tables." Publication 13-022-XWE, Ottawa.

Weil, D.N. 2007. "Accounting for the Effect of Health on Economic Growth." *Quarterly Journal of Economics* 122 (3): 1265–306.

World Bank. 2006. *Where Is the Wealth of Nations? Measuring Capital for the 21st Century.* Washington, DC: World Bank.

———. 2010. *World Development Indicators 2010.* Washington, DC: World Bank.

CHAPTER 6

Human Capital and Economic Growth in China

WEALTH ACCOUNTS SHOW THAT INTANGIBLE CAPITAL IS THE
largest component of wealth in virtually all countries and that human capital accounts for the majority of intangible capital. Many analysts believe that human capital is an important source of economic growth and innovation, an important factor in sustainable development, and a means of reducing poverty and inequality (see, among others, Stroombergen, Rose, and Nana 2002; Keeley 2007). For example, a detailed analysis of human capital accounts for Canada, New Zealand, Norway, Sweden, and the United States unambiguously shows that human capital is a leading source of economic growth.

Developed countries have recognized the importance of monitoring human capital accumulation. Toward this end, they have established national and international efforts to measure human capital stock and develop national human capital accounts. Seventeen countries have joined a consortium under the auspices of the Organisation for Economic Co-operation and Development to develop human capital accounts: Australia, Canada, Denmark, France, Italy, Japan, the Republic of Korea, Mexico, the Netherlands, Norway, New Zealand, Poland, Romania, the Russian Federation, Spain, the United Kingdom, and the United States. Two international organizations, Eurostat and the International

---

This chapter is based on a more detailed report by Li et al. (2009).

Labour Organization, are also participating. But most developing countries have yet to start programs to measure human capital. Recent work to estimate human capital stocks in China represents an important step toward filling that gap.

The Chinese economy has grown at a dramatic rate since the start of economic reforms in the 1980s. There is evidence that human capital has played a significant role in the Chinese economic miracle (see, for example, Fleisher and Jian 1997; Démurger 2001). Studies also show that human capital has an important effect on productivity growth and on reducing regional inequality in China (Fleisher, Li, and Zhao 2010). Despite the important role of human capital in the Chinese economy, however, there has been until now almost no comprehensive measurement of the total stock of human capital, and none that quantifies the changes in human capital in rural and urban areas and among males and females.

Human capital measures for China can contribute greatly to an understanding of the global importance of human capital, for a number of reasons. First, China is the most populous country in the world. It is important to understand how the dynamics of human capital in China are affected by demographic changes (driven, for example, by the one-child policy, migration, and urbanization) and by the rapid expansion of education during the course of economic development. Second, such measures would allow for better assessment of the contribution of human capital to growth, development, and social well-being in empirical and theoretical research. Construction of human capital measures is an important step in assessing the contribution of human capital to economic growth. To date, such studies have used only partial measurement of human capital, having to do with education characteristics, for example.[1]

Additional benefits from human capital measures include the provision of useful information for policy makers, such as data that can be used to assess how the education policies of central and local governments affect the accumulation of human capital. This is especially important given the long-term nature of human capital investment. For example, since the early 1980s there has been a remarkable increase in the educational attainment of the Chinese population. In 1982 the largest population group was concentrated in the "no schooling" category. By 2007 the largest category was "junior middle school," equivalent to seven to nine years of schooling.

This chapter summarizes an estimate of China's human capital stock from 1985 to 2007 by Li et al. (2009). Their work contributes to the objectives of this book in two ways: it provides an in-depth case study of an important asset, human capital, and how it has changed over time, and it provides an example of asset valuation derived entirely from country-specific data.

Li and colleagues use the Jorgenson-Fraumeni (J-F) lifetime income method to estimate human capital in China. While there are several alternative approaches to estimating human capital,[2] the J-F method is the most widely used, particularly in the growth literature. It has an advantage because of its sound theoretical foundation, and the data needed for estimation are relatively easy to obtain (Jorgenson and Fraumeni 1989, 1992a, 1992b).

Under the J-F approach, an individual's human capital stock is equal to the discounted present value of all future incomes he or she is expected to generate. Human capital accumulates through formal education as well as on-the-job training. Using data for wage rates and labor market participation cross-classified by gender, age, rural-urban location, and educational attainment, the expected lifetime earnings for each individual can be estimated. Annex 6.1 provides a brief summary of the methodology as applied to China. Annex 6.2 explains how the original figures from Li et al. (2009) were recast to be consistent with the methodology of the World Bank wealth accounts reported in this book.

Stocks of Human Capital in China

China's total real human capital increased rapidly between 1985 and 2007, from $11,709 billion to $21,960 billion (in 2005 prices; see table 6.1). Average annual growth in this period was 2.9 percent. Growth actually declined between 1985 and 1994, but it accelerated to 9.6 percent in the period that followed. Growth in human capital overall was slower than economic growth; over the same period, gross domestic product (GDP) grew at an average annual rate of 9.3 percent. As a result, the ratio of human capital to GDP fell from 11 in 1985 to 7 in 2007. However, human capital has grown much faster in China than in other countries. For example, in 1970–2000 the annual average growth of human capital in Canada was 1.7 percent per year (Gu and Wong 2009).

Like other countries, China has much more human capital than physical capital, but physical capital has been growing much faster than human capital since 1985. Important unanswered questions for China are whether investment has been overly weighted toward physical capital relative to human capital and how to determine optimal relative values of human and physical capital for sustainable economic growth.

Growth of human capital is attributable to several factors. Part of the growth is due to the increase in China's population, from 1.02 billion in 1982 to 1.32 billion in 2007 (figure 6.1). There has also been a rapid increase in the urban share of total population, from 21 percent in 1982 to 45 percent in 2007; this is important because urban dwellers have higher per capita human capital than rural dwellers. A large part of the increase in human capital, however, is due to an increase in

TABLE 6.1
Total Human Capital in China, 1985-2007
US$ billons

Year	Nominal Human Capital	Real Human Capital (2005 US$)	Nominal GDP	Ratio of Human Capital to GDP (nominal prices)
1985	3,295	11,709	306	10.8
1986	3,100	10,362	298	10.4
1987	3,247	10,126	325	10.0
1988	4,034	10,591	403	10.0
1989	4,905	10,926	452	10.9
1990	4,161	8,998	391	10.6
1991	4,084	8,533	410	10.0
1992	4,450	8,730	488	9.1
1993	5,336	9,116	613	8.7
1994	4,827	6,639	559	8.6
1995	6,127	7,193	728	8.4
1996	7,424	8,041	856	8.7
1997	8,627	9,084	953	9.1
1998	9,330	9,897	1,019	9.2
1999	10,139	10,902	1,084	9.4
2000	11,170	11,954	1,198	9.3
2001	12,082	12,831	1,325	9.1
2002	12,877	13,777	1,453	8.9
2003	14,034	14,840	1,641	8.6
2004	15,571	15,854	1,932	8.1
2005	17,251	17,251	2,236	7.7
2006	19,482	19,196	2,658	7.3
2007	23,364	21,960	3,280	7.1

Source: Adapted from Li et al. 2009, with adjustments described in annex 6.2.

educational attainment and the resulting increases in labor productivity and earnings. Five categories of educational attainment are identified:

- No schooling
- Primary school (grades 1–6)
- Junior middle school (grades 7–9)
- Senior middle school (grades 10–12)
- College and above

FIGURE 6.1
Population of China, 1982-2007

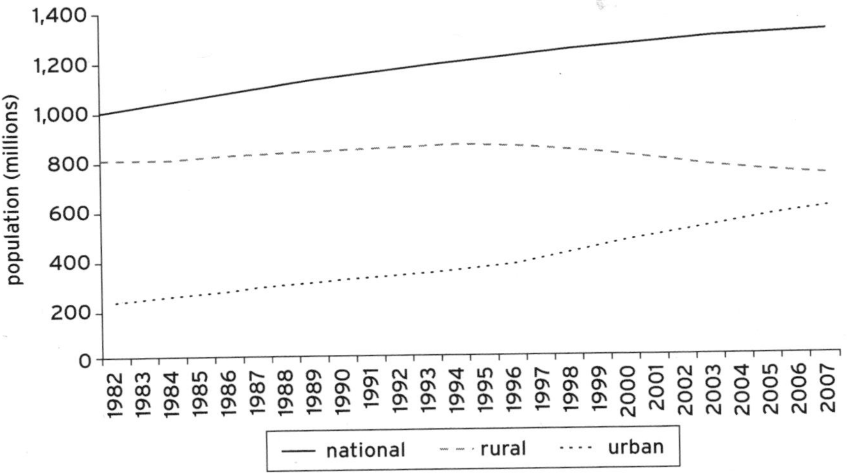

Source: Based on Li et al. 2009.

The two categories with the least schooling saw their combined share of population fall dramatically, from roughly 75 percent in 1982 to 45 percent in 2007, while the three categories with more schooling increased from 25 percent to 55 percent over the same period (figure 6.2). The population with no schooling at all was cut by half, from 402 million in 1982 to 201 million in 2000, where it remained to 2007; this represents a decline from nearly 40 percent of the population to just 15 percent. The population with only a primary school education increased in absolute numbers, but its share of the population fell from 35 percent to 30 percent. Junior middle school registered the largest growth among all education levels: the number of junior middle school graduates increased from 181 million in 1982 to 471 million in 2007, roughly doubling their share of total population. But the most rapid growth was seen among college graduates: starting from a very low base of around 6 million in 1982, the number increased more than twelvefold by 2007 to more than 76 million.

Human Capital by Rural-Urban Location and by Gender

Table 6.2 shows total real human capital separately for the urban and rural populations. In 1985, rural China held more human capital ($6,935 billion) than urban China ($4,774 billion). This continued until 1993, when accumulation of human capital in urban areas overtook rural human capital. While human capital

FIGURE 6.2
Population of China by Educational Attainment, 1982-2007

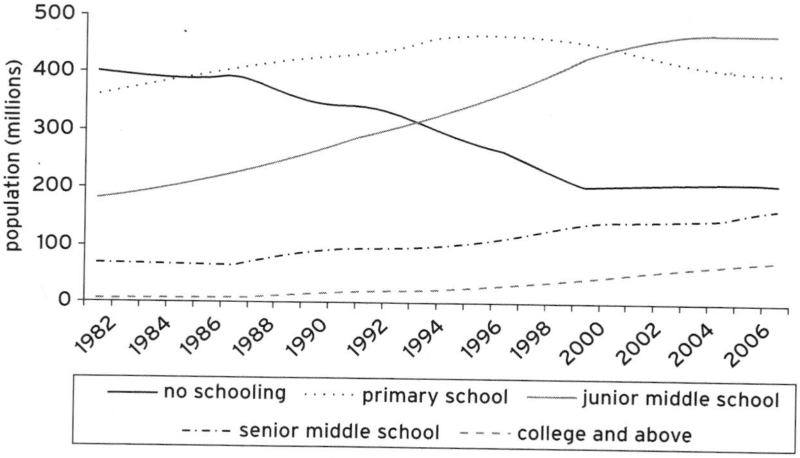

Source: Based on Li et al. 2009.

increased in both urban and rural China, urban human capital grew very fast and by 2007 the situation was reversed: human capital in urban areas is now 73 percent higher than in rural areas.

A major factor in the rising urban-rural human capital gap is simply the growth in the urban population due to migration. The share of the urban population more than doubled, from 21 percent in 1982 to 45 percent in 2007. Rapid economic growth and the transition toward a market-oriented economy have provided opportunities for human capital to realize much higher returns throughout the Chinese economy, but especially in urban areas. The other major reason for the shift in human capital from rural to urban areas is the education gap. In urban areas, the population with education at college level or above accounted for 2.5 percent of the population in 1985 and increased to 13 percent by 2007. But in rural areas, the corresponding figures remained well below 1 percent even by 2007.

Human capital increased for both males and females, but more slowly for females than for males. As a result, the gender disparity in human capital, already established in 1985, increased slightly by 2007. While females accounted for 44 percent of total human capital in 1985, their share decreased to 41 percent in 2007. Gaps can be the result of differential population growth, demographic changes, rural-urban migration, trends in educational attainment, differential rates of return to education and on-the-job training, and so on.

In comparison to other countries, China's total human capital is quite large, more than that of any country except the United States. But this is due to its very

TABLE 6.2
Total Real Human Capital in China by Rural-Urban Location and Gender
2005 US$ billions

Population	1985	2007	Growth 1985-2007 (%)
National	11,709	21,960	88
By location			
Urban	4,774	13,922	192
Rural	6,935	8,038	16
By gender			
Male	6,529	12,852	97
Female	5,180	9,108	76

Source: Adapted from Li et al. 2009, with adjustments described in annex 6.2.

TABLE 6.3
Per Capita Real Human Capital in China by Rural-Urban Location and Gender
2005 US$

Population	1985	2007	Growth 1985-2007 (%)
National	12,171	19,687	62
By location			
Urban	20,865	27,452	32
Rural	9,458	13,214	40
By gender			
Male	12,938	21,952	70
Female	11,325	17,185	52

Source: Adapted from Li et al. 2009, with adjustments described in annex 6.2.

large population. China's per capita human capital is still relatively low. Per capita real human capital increased 62 percent, from $12,171 in 1985 to $19,687 in 2007 (table 6.3). All of the growth occurred in the period after 1994, when human capital increased at an annual rate of 9.2 percent. Therefore, although population growth contributed significantly to the total human capital accumulation before 1994, per capita human capital growth was the primary driving force after 1995. The substantial increase in educational attainment during 1985–2007 contributed significantly to the growth in both total and per capita real human capital.

Changes in per capita human capital are much more uniform for each population group compared to the changes in total human capital reported in table 6.2. In 2007, total male human capital was about 41 percent higher than total female human capital, but on a per capita basis they are similar: female per capita human capital is nearly 78 percent of male per capita human capital. The gender gap appears to have widened over time, as per capita female human capital was 87 percent of male human capital in 1985. Most of the gender gap in total human capital can be attributed to differences in the size of the working population, returns to schooling and work experience, and gender differences in mandatory retirement age. (Retirement age is 55 for females but 60 for males under Chinese labor law; thus, men have an extra five years in which to generate income, increasing their human capital.)

Although total urban human capital was lower than rural human capital in 1985, this gap reflects the very small urban population at that time. On a per capita basis, urban human capital was greater than rural, a gap that has decreased only slightly since then. The advantage of urban per capita human capital combined with the large migration from rural to urban areas shifted total human capital to urban areas by 2007.

Comparison with World Bank Estimates of Human Capital

In constructing global wealth accounts, the World Bank must use data readily available for all countries; often the same or slightly modified parameters are applied to many countries because of a lack of country-specific information. Naturally, when a country applies wealth accounting, using country-specific data instead of global parameters, the results may differ from the World Bank estimates.

The estimated value of human capital in China reported in table 6.1, $17,251 billion in 2005, is 44 percent higher than the World Bank estimate of $12,007 billion.[3] There is a fundamental difference between the two approaches to measuring human capital: the World Bank uses the residual approach, while Li and colleagues use the J-F lifetime earning approach. But these different approaches need not produce significantly different results if consistent assumptions are made in both cases. Norway constructed human capital accounts using both approaches and found them to be very similar (Graeker 2008).

Why does the estimated value of human capital from the China case study differ from the World Bank estimate? The difference is explained by assumptions about a key parameter, the growth of future earnings—that is, the return to human capital.[4] The case study authors based their assumptions on an analysis of growth in earnings over the past 30 years. Li et al. (2009) found that the average annual growth rate of real earnings was 4.1 percent in rural areas and 6.0 percent in urban areas and predicted that these growth rates for human capital will continue in the future. In the World Bank wealth accounts, the growth rate is 4 percent in all countries. Since most of China's human capital is in urban areas, the higher growth rate assumed in the Li case study will result in much higher human capital than the estimate in the World Bank wealth accounts. The human capital accounts for China demonstrate the importance of implementing wealth accounting at the national level, using country-specific information.

Summing Up

Both total and per capita human capital have grown rapidly in China since 1995, especially in urban areas. The main driver of this growth has been increases in educational attainment and in opportunities provided by a market-driven economy, rather than population growth. A gender gap exists for total human capital, and on a per capita basis the difference between male and female human capital has increased somewhat since 1985. A large urban-rural gap has developed as well, mainly because of urbanization and large-scale migration from the rural areas to the cities. Reducing the urban-rural disparity will require more investment in rural human capital.

Global evidence presented in this book indicates that the share of human capital in total wealth increases as national income increases. Assessing the optimal investment in different capital assets is essential to ensuring China's long-term sustainable development. The human capital accounts provide critical information that can inform growth analysis and investment strategy in China.

Annex 6.1: Methodology–Jorgenson-Fraumeni Lifetime Income Approach

Jorgenson and Fraumeni estimate human capital using a lifetime income approach (1989, 1992a, 1992b). In principle, human capital includes both market and nonmarket components, but for China only market human capital was estimated because of data limitations. Lifetime income is estimated for the population based upon current education levels and income and expected future survival, education, income, and real wage growth rates. All estimated future income is discounted to the present to create estimates of human capital for a particular year.

Jorgenson and Fraumeni separated an individual's lifetime into five stages.

Stage 1. No school and no work:

$$mi_{y, s, a, e} = sr_{y+1, s, a+1} \times mi_{y, s, a+1, e} \times \frac{1 + G}{1 + R}$$

where the subscripts y, s, a, and e denote, respectively, year, sex, age, and educational attainment, respectively; mi stands for lifetime market labor income per capita; and sr is the survival rate, defined as the probability of becoming one year older, G is the real income growth rate, and R is the discount rate.

Stage 2. Schooling but no work:

$$mi_{y, s, a, e} = [senr_{y+1, s, a+1, e+1} \times sr_{y+1, s, a+1} \times mi_{y, s, a+1, e+1} + (1 - senr_{y+1, s, a+1, e+1})$$
$$\times sr_{y+1, s, a+1} \times mi_{y, s, a+1, e}] \times \frac{1 + G}{1 + R}$$

where $senr$ is school enrollment rate and subscript $e+1$ refers to the grade level of enrollment, the probability that an individual with educational attainment e is enrolled in education level $e+1$.

Stage 3. Both schooling and work:

$$mi_{y, s, a, e} = ymi_{y, s, a, e} + [senr_{y+1, s, a+1, e+1} \times sr_{y+1, s, a+1} \times mi_{y, s, a+1, e+1}$$
$$+ (1 - senr_{y+1, s, a+1, e+1}) \times sr_{y+1, s, a+1} \times mi_{y, s, a+1, e}] \times \frac{1 + G}{1 + R}$$

where ymi denotes annual market income per capita.

Stage 4. Work but no further schooling:

$$mi_{y, s, a, e} = ymi_{y, s, a, e} + sr_{y+1, s, a+1} \times mi_{y, s, a+1, e} \times \frac{1 + G}{1 + R}$$

Stage 5. Retirement—no school or work:

$$mi_{y, s, a, e} = 0$$

Estimation is conducted in a backward recursive fashion, from those age 75, 74, 73, and so forth to those age 0. Expectations about future relative wage rates, enrollment, annual market income, and survival come from data on cohorts of older individuals alive in the year the estimates are constructed. Per capita estimates are multiplied by population estimates to derive total market human capital for each year. Divisia indexes are constructed using nominal human capital as weights and population growth rates to create estimates of real human capital.

Expected Lifetime Earnings of Individuals

To measure lifetime earnings of all individuals in the population, future incomes are projected, discounted back to the present,[5] and weighted for each individual by the age- and gender-specific probability of survival. This is done in two steps. First, imputed earnings equation parameters are used to estimate earnings for all individuals in a given year by applying the Mincer (1974) equation to micro-survey data.[6] Mincer's approach has been widely adopted in empirical research on earnings determination for numerous countries and time periods:

$$in(inc) = \alpha + \beta \cdot e + \gamma \cdot exp + \delta \cdot exp^2 + u$$

where $in(inc)$ is the logarithm of earnings; e is years of schooling; exp and exp^2 are, respectively, years of work experience and experience squared; and u is a random error.

The coefficient β is an estimate of the return to an extra year of schooling, and γ and δ measure the return to investment in on-the-job training. To ensure that income estimates are as accurate as possible, the parameters are estimated separately for the rural and urban populations by gender and year, using survey data in selected years. These are used to impute values for missing years over the period 1985–2007.

Second, earnings are derived for future years until retirement by assuming that real earnings grow at the same average annual rates of growth as labor productivity. Growth in labor productivity for the period 1978 to 2007 was 4.1 percent and 6.0 percent per year in the rural and urban sectors, respectively. It is assumed that labor productivities (and, hence, the real income) will continue to grow annually at these average rates in the future.

Annex 6.2: Recasting the Data to be Consistent with World Bank Methodology

The work by Li et al. (2009) was recalculated to make it more consistent with the World Bank database in two ways. First, results are reported here in constant 2005 U.S. dollars, while Li et al. carried out their analysis in 1985 yuan. Some of the trends over time may differ depending on the currency used for analysis. For example, Li et al.'s analysis in constant yuan found much higher growth in human capital than did the same analysis carried out in 2005 U.S. dollars.

More important, a social discount rate was derived using the same methodology used for the World Bank wealth accounts; this rate is considerably higher than the one used in the original report by Li et al. (2009). That study used a very low discount rate of 3.14 percent, based on the average real return on long-term government bonds from 1996 to 2007. However, there is little reason to think that the return on bonds reflects the real social discount rate, because financial markets are subject to control. A low discount rate leads to very high human capital estimates.

The discount rate used in World Bank calculations was derived from the Ramsey formula (see appendix A). Under the Ramsey formula, r, the discount rate, equals the pure rate of time preference, ρ, plus the elasticity of utility with respect to consumption. The pure rate of time preference is assumed to be 1.5 percent, while the elasticity of utility with respect to consumption is assumed to be 1. The annual growth of real per capita consumption in China from 1970 to 2008 has been 6.76 percent. This results in a social discount rate for China of 8.26 percent. A high discount rate substantially lowers the present value of future earnings, resulting in much lower estimates of human capital.

Notes

1 See, for example, Cai and Wang (1999), Hu Angang (2002), Zhou Ya (2004), Hou and Cao (2000), and Hu Yongyuan (2005). Zhang (2000) and Qian and Liu (2007) calculated China's human capital stock based on total investment (cost side); Zhu and Xu (2007) and Wang and Xiang (2006) estimated human capital from the income side. Zhou Delu (2005) and Yu (2008) used a weighted average of human capital attributes to construct a measurement.

2 See Stroombergen, Rose, and Nana (2002) for a comprehensive survey of methodologies.

3 This is the estimate for intangible capital.

4 There may also be differences in the working lifespan over which human capital is generated, but this effect is likely to be small relative to the expected rate of growth in earnings.

5 A discount rate of 3.14 percent was used, equivalent to the average real return on 10-year government bonds from 1996 to 2007.

6 Data used to estimate the Mincer equations come from two well-known household surveys in China: the annual Urban Household Survey and the China Health and Nutrition Survey (the latter covers both rural and urban households).

References

Cai Fang and Wang Dewen. 1999. "The Sustainability of China's Economic Growth and Labor Contributions." *Economic Research* (in Chinese) 10: 62–68.

Démurger, Sylvie. 2001. "Infrastructure Development and Economic Growth: An Explanation for Regional Disparities in China?" *Journal of Comparative Economics* 29 (1): 95–117.

Fleisher, Belton, and Jian Chen. 1997. "The Coast-Noncoast Income Gap, Productivity, and Regional Economic Policy in China." *Journal of Comparative Economics* 25 (2): 220–36.

Fleisher, Belton, Haizheng Li, and Min Qiang Zhao. 2010. "Human Capital, Economic Growth, and Regional Inequality in China." *Journal of Development Economics* 92 (2): 215–31.

Graeker, Mads. 2008. "Sustainable Development and Changes in National Wealth for Norway in the Period from 1985 to 2007." Statistics Norway, Oslo.

Gu, Wulong, and Ambrose Wong. 2009. "Human Development and Its Contribution to the Wealth Accounts in Canada." Paper presented at the Canadian Economics Association Annual Conference, Toronto, May 29.

Hou Yafei and Cao Yin. 2000. "Analysis of the Quality of Human Capital Stock." *Chinese Journal of Population Science* (in Chinese) 6: 43–48.

Hu Angang. 2002. "From the Most Populous Country to a Country with Great Power of Human Capital: 1980–2000." *Chinese Journal of Population Science* (in Chinese) 5: 1–10.

Hu Yongyuan. 2005. "Human Capital and Economic Growth: A Co-integration Analysis." *Science and Technology Management Research* (in Chinese) 4: 88–90.

Jorgenson, Dale W., and Barbara M. Fraumeni. 1989. "The Accumulation of Human and Nonhuman Capital, 1948–84." In *The Measurement of Saving, Investment and Wealth*, ed. R. Lipsey and H. Tice, 227–82. NBER Studies in Income and Wealth, vol. 52. Chicago: University of Chicago Press.

————. 1992a. "Investment in Education and U.S. Economic Growth." *Scandinavian Journal of Economics* 94, supplement: S51–70.

————. 1992b. "The Output of the Education Sector." In *Output Measurement in the Service Sectors*, ed. Z. Griliches, 303–41. NBER Studies in Income and Wealth, vol. 56. Chicago: University of Chicago Press.

Keeley, Brian. 2007. *Human Capital: How What You Know Shapes Your Life*. Paris: Organisation for Economic Co-operation and Development.

Li, Haizheng, Barbara M. Fraumeni, Zhiqiang Liu, and Xiaojun Wang. 2009. "Human Capital in China." NBER Working Paper 15500, National Bureau of Economic Research, Cambridge, MA.

Mincer, Jacob. 1974. *Schooling, Experience, and Earnings*. New York: Columbia University Press.

Qian Xuya and Liu Jie. 2007. "Empirical Study of Human Capital in China." *Statistic Research* (in Chinese) 3: 39–45.

Stroombergen, Adolph, Dennis Rose, and Ganesh Nana. 2002. "Review of the Statistical Measurement of Human Capital." Statistics New Zealand, Wellington.

Wang Dejin and Xiang Rongmei. 2006. "Estimates of Human Capital Stock in China." *Statistics and Decision* (in Chinese) 5: 100–102.

Yu Shujing. 2008. "Comprehensive Evaluation and Dynamic Analysis on China's Provincial-Level Regional Human Capital." *Modern Management Science* (in Chinese) 4: 36–37.

Zhang Fan. 2000. "Estimates of Physical Capital and Human Capital in China." *Economic Research* (in Chinese) 8: 66–71.

Zhou Delu. 2005. "Population-Based Indicators of Human Capital Accounting Theory and Empirical Study." *Chinese Journal of Population Science* (in Chinese) 3: 56–62.

Zhou Ya. 2004. "Study on the Distribution Differences of China's Human Capital." *Education & Economics* (in Chinese) 2: 17–20.

Zhu Pingfang and Xu Dafeng. 2007. "Estimation of Human Capital in Chinese Cities." *Economic Research* (in Chinese) 8: 84–95.

C H A P T E R   7

Linking Governance to Economic Consequences in Resource-Rich Economies: EITI and Wealth Accounting

NATURAL CAPITAL CONSTITUTES A MAJOR COMPONENT OF wealth and is a principal source of income for many developing countries. At first glance, resource-rich economies appear to have an economic advantage over less-well-endowed countries because natural resources, especially oil, gas, and minerals (referred to hereafter as extractives), can provide funds to finance rapid development and poverty reduction. But the large incomes and foreign exchange generated by these exports must be carefully managed in order to avoid the "resource curse"—the paradox that such riches do not always lead to long-term, inclusive, and equitable prosperity and can even undermine development outcomes.

It has been argued that the resource curse is caused by several factors, some related to macroeconomic management, and others to political economy and governance.[1] The major problems include (a) currency appreciation that can reduce the competitiveness of nonextractive exports, (b) more difficult macroeconomic management due to volatile commodity prices, (c) inefficient management of the extractive sector, (d) corruption and serious political conflicts over rent capture and management of revenues generated by the extractive sector, and (e) dissipation of rents on current consumption rather than investment. Evidence has shown that the economic performance of less-developed countries is often inversely related to their natural resource wealth.

However, this relationship is not deterministic: some countries such as Chile and Botswana have done well with their natural capital. Having the right policy matters, and wealth accounting can enrich our understanding of the context and thereby improve policy making.

The overarching development challenge for resource-rich economies is to transform nonrenewable natural capital into other forms of productive wealth, so that once the extractive wealth is exhausted there are other income-generating assets to take its place. Mining is not sustainable, but the revenue from extractive sectors can be invested in other forms of wealth, such as infrastructure, human capital, renewable natural capital, and institutions (social capital), to build economies that are sustainable.

To achieve this transformation requires effective policy in three areas:

- Policies to promote efficient resource extraction in order to maximize resource rent generated by the extractive sector
- A system of taxes and royalties that allows government to recover equitable and proportionate shares of rent
- A clear policy for investment of resource rent in productive assets

This last point is especially important: the analysis of wealth accounts in earlier chapters shows that to achieve sustainable economic development, income from nonrenewable resources must be invested, not used to fund consumption.

Getting policy right in all three areas presents a considerable challenge, cutting across a broad swath of the economic and political landscape. There are areas where the best policy is relatively well understood but implementation is difficult. Regarding recovery of resource rent, for example, Hilson and Maconachie (2009) and Campbell (2003) show that African governments receive negligible shares of mining revenues compared to the shares of the (usually foreign) mining companies. For example, just 1.7 percent of the value of gold that companies mined in Ghana from 1990 to 2002 went to the Ghanaian treasury via royalties and corporate income taxes (Campbell 2003). This implies that policy makers should be just as concerned with ensuring that states receive a fair share of revenues as they are with setting macroeconomic policy.[2]

Regarding policies on investment of rents, the best path may depend on a variety of factors, and more analytical work is needed. For example, in a very poor country, should all rent be invested, or should some of it be used for current consumption to alleviate extreme poverty? Should the rent be managed entirely by a dedicated government investment fund, as in Norway, or should part of the rent be redistributed directly to citizens in order to promote private investment, as is done with oil revenues in the U.S. state of Alaska? If the revenues are managed by government, how should government balance investment in public infrastructure, support for domestic private sector development, and investment for the highest return even if that means investing abroad?

The political economy in each country plays an important role, and the best action in one country may not be appropriate in another (see Brahmbhatt, Canuto, and Vostroknutova 2010).

Governance, Accountability, and Transparency along the Extractives Value Chain

Governance and accountability are central elements in achieving these policies and overcoming the resource curse (Eifert, Gelb, and Tallroth 2002; Bannon and Collier 2003). However, ways of building accountability and good governance in resource-rich countries are not well understood. Transparency is widely recognized as an important element in this effort (see, for example, Le Billon 2001; Collier and Venables 2009; Collier 2008). Transparency alone does not guarantee accountability and good governance, but it is the first step, reflecting the adage, "What you do not measure, you cannot manage."[3]

Information and evidence have been referred to as the "currency of accountability" (Dye and Stapenhurst 1998), implying that transparency is the minting process in this analogy.[4] Transparency allows the generation of information, which can then be communicated and used to place pressure on decision makers or hold them to account. However, the process by which information goes from minting into circulation is not straightforward. Strong institutions are of fundamental importance: on the whole, countries with strong institutions and good policies do better than those with weak institutions and weak policies. And those that start off with weak institutions may find that the process of resource exploitation weakens them further. Parliaments, political parties, civil society organizations, think tanks, universities, and the media—which collectively we can term the "public sphere"—can use information to build accountability, while institutional context, such as free speech laws and courts, provides the framework in which this takes place.[5] In simple terms, accountability can be built through transparency and equitable participation in the governance process.

By quantifying natural resources as a dwindling and depreciable source of income, wealth accounting provides the basis for an important conceptual shift in how people think of natural resources. In this way, wealth accounting can help people hold policy makers to account, leading to better policy making. This in turn can improve governance and help build stronger institutions.

Accountability and transparency are needed along the entire extractives "value chain," that is, the full range of extractives-related activities and processes.[6] Figure 7.1 depicts the extractive industries value chain, encompassing the key decision points from the award of licenses and contracts through regulation and monitoring of operations, collection of taxes and royalties, distribution of revenues, and use of those revenues to support sustainable development policies and projects.

FIGURE 7.1
The Extractive Industries Value Chain

Source: Adapted from Alba 2009.

Given the complexity of the extractive industries sector, it is helpful to consider any one intervention in the context of the whole system. Wealth accounting provides critical information at different points along the value chain and links management of extractives to the macro economy. This provides an added dimension of transparency to the management of extractives, revealing the extent to which nonrenewable resources are being used to build wealth and sustainable development.

The concept of a value chain for the sector promotes understanding of the individual links in the extractive industries development and management process and the need for a systemwide approach. Hence, a well-functioning revenue distribution system is of limited value if the contract is not balanced and does not allow the government to capture sufficient taxes and royalties, or if the revenue collection system is weak. Alternatively, a country might skillfully negotiate a petroleum or mining deal but then lack capacity at other points along the chain to turn that deal into concrete investments for current and future prosperity.

A number of local and international initiatives to improve accountability have been introduced. Prominent among them is an international multi-stakeholder initiative known as the Extractive Industries Transparency Initiative (EITI), launched in 2002 at the World Summit on Sustainable Development in Johannesburg. This international exercise promotes accountability by requiring transparency of revenue flows and validation of both data and process by civil society organizations. The EITI represents a novel use of multi-stakeholder partnerships between governments, the private sector, and civil society organizations. But ensuring the transparency and validation of these revenues is just the first step in making sure that wealth is harnessed for sustainable development. The World Bank Group has developed an approach called the EITI++, which is an internal guiding framework for improved, structured engagement with client countries receiving significant resource revenues.[7]

EITI and EITI++ emphasize monitoring processes in the value chain that are expected to promote sustainable development in resource-rich economies. The EITI++ approach describes the processes along the value chain needed to generate, capture, and invest rents, going as far as "implementation of projects and policies." But EITI++ is not designed to monitor long-term wealth creation and the transformation of extractive wealth into other forms of wealth, a condition necessary for sustainable development.

Long-term accountability can only be monitored using the comprehensive wealth approach that reveals whether a government is using nonrenewable natural capital to build long-term, sustainable development. Comprehensive wealth accounts extend the principle of transparency and accountability beyond EITI++ to monitor whether the loss of natural capital through depletion is being offset by investments in manufactured capital and human capital. Together, EITI++ and wealth accounting provide a way to monitor whether the extractive sector does, in fact, contribute to long-term development. EITI and EITI++ introduce transparency and foster accountability for extractives-related processes, and wealth accounts provide a tool to monitor the economic consequences, that is, wealth creation and the transformation of natural capital into other forms of wealth.

The rest of this chapter describes the EITI and EITI++ approaches and suggests ways in which wealth accounting can be linked to them to strengthen monitoring and accountability in resource-rich economies.

EITI and Transparency

As already noted, for many countries natural resources offer the most immediate path to development, but for countries that rely on exports of nonrenewables, the revenue stream represents a one-time opportunity. The challenge is to develop effective, contextualized governance processes and increase informed decision making along the value chain.

The EITI process is built around a multi-stakeholder model that brings together governments, extractive companies, and civil society in each country. It is voluntary: countries must apply for candidate status and meet certain preconditions. To retain membership there is a process of validation, which reviews EITI implementation with domestic stakeholders to ensure that EITI standards are upheld. Three countries have been formally validated as EITI-compliant: Azerbaijan, Liberia, and Timor-Leste. Another 29 have candidacy status and are working toward validation.[8]

EITI++: Extending Good Governance along the Value Chain

Disclosure of revenues does not in itself reveal whether a country is receiving a fair share of rents, nor does it indicate whether government is investing the revenues for development outcomes. Every step in managing extractive industry resources is important. Committed governments should receive support to help them implement good policy and practice along the entire value chain through greater transparency and accountability.

EITI++ extends the EITI principle of transparency along the length of the chain. These emphasize the need for appropriate policy frameworks, institutional capacity to implement policies effectively, and accountability mechanisms. The EITI++ initiative focuses on resource-rich countries in Sub-Saharan Africa that account for about 70 percent of Africa's gross domestic product (GDP). It seeks to develop national capability to handle natural resource management and channel the growing revenue streams into fighting poverty, hunger, malnutrition, illiteracy, and disease.

Wealth Accounts: Extending Transparency to Macroeconomic Performance

Accountability depends in part on the availability of transparent, easy-to-understand information. Wealth accounts were developed to address the three policy issues raised at the beginning of this chapter: maximizing resource rents, recovering a fair share of rents, and investing rents in productive assets. The accounts provide indicators that can be used to monitor the economic performance of resource-rich economies. In particular, wealth accounting implemented at the country level provides indicators for tracking recovery of resource rent through taxes and royalties, as well as management of those revenues, and extends the monitoring of the value chain to include the impact on national wealth. Wealth accounts show whether natural capital is being used to build and transform the wealth of a nation, and they provide information about various steps in the process where management success or failure may be occurring. The use of wealth accounting in Botswana is a case in point.

Botswana is well known for sound management of its mineral wealth, as well as for transparency and good governance. Botswana does not participate in EITI, as it already has appropriate institutions in place and carries out the recommended processes. The government reports mineral revenues annually in publicly available documents, and there is open discussion of how to make best use of these revenues. In the 1990s the Ministry of Finance and Development Planning introduced the Sustainable Budget Index to monitor the extent to which mineral revenues were used for investment in the government budget.

The Department of Environmental Affairs piloted wealth accounting, extending the principle of wealth building for sustainable development to the macroeconomy (Botswana 2007). Wealth accounts were constructed for produced capital, natural capital, and net foreign financial assets; data were insufficient to construct human capital accounts. The wealth accounts were used to monitor recovery of resource rent and investment of rents, the second and third areas of policy necessary for transforming mineral wealth into other forms of capital. The wealth accounts show that the government of Botswana

FIGURE 7.2
Recovery of Resource Rent from Mining in Botswana, 1980–2005

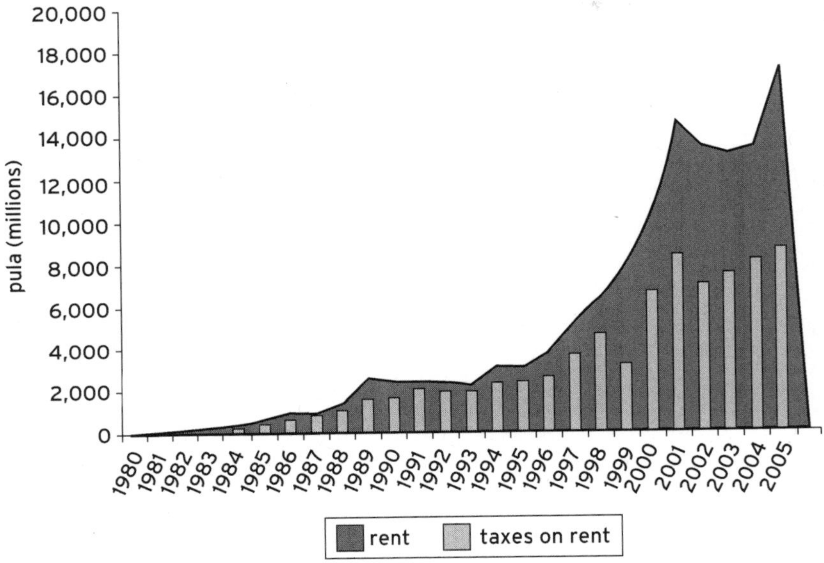

Source: Botswana 2007; Lange 2004. Estimates for 1998 to 2005 are from unpublished updates of the Botswana wealth accounts by Lange.

has consistently recovered a large share of the rents generated by mining (figure 7.2). Analysis of government's capital and development budget in the 1980s and 1990s showed that all mining revenues were invested until the late 1990s; since then, some of the revenues have been used for government consumption, but most is still invested (Lange and Wright 2004).

As a result of its sound management of mineral revenues, Botswana has seen rapid growth in its real wealth and GDP per capita (figure 7.3; wealth does not include human capital). By contrast, the results of a similar analysis for neighboring Namibia show less success in using mineral assets to build national wealth.

Summing Up

Many countries have made a commitment to sustainable development but lag behind in implementing the necessary policies to achieve this goal. The key long-term development challenge for resource-rich economies is to transform natural capital, particularly nonrenewable capital, into other forms of wealth. For these countries, avoiding pitfalls associated with extractive wealth is a pressing challenge that should be at the forefront of country development planning and

FIGURE 7.3
**Growth of Real Per Capita Wealth and GDP in Botswana and Namibia,
1980-2005**

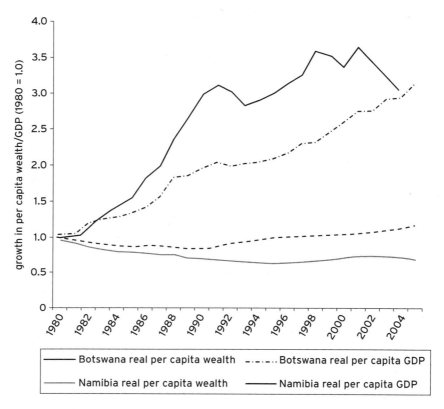

Source: Botswana 2007; Lange 2004. Estimates for 1998 to 2005 are from unpublished updates
of the Botswana wealth accounts by Lange.
Note: Wealth does not include human capital.

poverty reduction strategies. There are now a number of initiatives that have been
launched to improve accountability and governance in resource-rich countries,
including local efforts in specific countries, initiatives by bilateral and multilateral
agencies, and international efforts such as EITI.

EITI++ is a more comprehensive initiative to promote accountability and
good governance through transparency in national processes to generate, capture,
and invest rents. But it does not show whether investment of rents is sufficient to
compensate for depletion of natural capital. Comprehensive wealth accounting
adds a new and conceptually important dimension to the accountability fostered
by EITI and EITI++. It provides a simple tool to monitor wealth creation and,

specifically, to reveal whether natural capital is being transformed into other forms of wealth. This constitutes a fundamental shift in how natural resources are conceived of and thus how public and private actors might be held to account. Without transparency in wealth transformation and creation—the conditions for long-term sustainable development—accountability in resource-rich countries may not be considered complete.

Notes

1 For reviews of the resource curse literature, see, for example, Auty (1993), Barma, Kaiser, and Le (2010); Frankel (2010); and Humphreys, Sachs, and Stiglitz (2007).

2 A "fair" share of rents is not always easy to establish. The rent generated by a commodity, such as gold, can vary enormously across countries because of the nature of the reserves, local conditions that affect the cost of mining (including perceived risk due to domestic conditions), and volatility in world market commodity prices. In some countries a high-risk premium is legitimately included in the cost of mining. Rents from oil and gas are almost always positive and large.

3 Transparency leads to good governance through active participation of a well-informed society using transparency of information to hold decision makers to account. This process from transparency to good governance requires a well-functioning civil society.

4 Although Dye and Stapenhurst (1998) focused their attention on supply-side accountability—for example, through audit offices and structures of accountability—this chapter stresses the importance of both supply-side and demand-side (or bottom-up) accountability processes.

5 The role of the public sphere in ensuring accountability is complex. The public sphere is not a single, unified area in which information is disseminated and discussed; multiple, fractured public spheres often exist. Furthermore, in many countries participation is limited by restrictions on free speech or by lack of knowledge and engagement.

6 For a comprehensive introduction to the value chain approach, see Alba (2009).

7 The EITI++ is not a formalized independent initiative in the mold of EITI; rather, it complements EITI's focus on transparency in reporting revenues by offering a slate of coordinated options for improved management of resource wealth.

8 For a full list of member countries and their status, see the EITI website at http://www.eiti.org.

References

Alba, Eleodoro Mayorga. 2009. "Extractive Industries Value Chain: A Comprehensive Integrated Approach to Developing Extractive Industries." Extractive Industries for Development Series 3/Africa Region Working Paper 125, World Bank, Washington, DC.

Auty, Richard M. 1993. *Sustaining Development in Mineral Economies: The Resource Curse Thesis.* New York: Routledge.

Bannon, Ian, and Paul Collier, eds. 2003. *Natural Resources and Violent Conflict: Options and Actions.* Washington, DC: World Bank.

Barma, N., K. Kaiser, and T. M. Le. 2010. "Rents to Riches? The Political Economy of Natural Resources Led Development." World Bank, Washington, DC.

Botswana. 2007. "Towards Mineral Accounts for Botswana." Department of Environmental Affairs and Centre for Applied Research, Gaborone.

Brahmbhatt, M., O. Canuto, and E. Vostroknutova. 2010. "Natural Resources and Development Strategy after the Crisis." In *The Day After Tomorrow: The Future of Economic Policy in the Developing World*, ed. Otaviano Canuto and Marcelo Giugale, 101–18. Washington, DC: World Bank.

Campbell, Bonnie. 2003. "Factoring in Governance Is Not Enough: Mining Codes in Africa, Policy Reform and Corporate Responsibility." *Minerals and Energy* 18 (3): 2–13.

Collier, Paul. 2008. *The Bottom Billion: Why the Poorest Countries Are Failing and What Can Be Done about It*. New York: Oxford University Press.

Collier, Paul, and Anthony J. Venables. 2009. "Natural Resources and State Fragility." OxCarre Research Paper 31, Department of Economics, University of Oxford, U.K.

Dye, Kenneth, and R. Stapenhurst. 1998. *Pillars of Integrity: Importance of Supreme Audit Institutions in Curbing Corruption*. Washington, DC: World Bank Institute.

Eifert, Ben, Alan Gelb, and Nils Borje Tallroth. 2002. "The Political Economy of Fiscal Policy and Economic Management in Oil Exporting Countries." Policy Research Working Paper 2899, World Bank, Washington, DC.

Frankel, Jeffrey A. 2010. "The Natural Resource Curse: A Survey." NBER Working Paper 15836, National Bureau of Economic Research, Cambridge, MA. http://www.nber.org/papers/w15836.

Hilson, G., and R. Maconachie. 2009. "'Good Governance' and the Extractive Industries in Sub-Saharan Africa." *Mineral Processing and Extractive Metallurgy Review* 30 (1): 52–100.

Humphreys, Macartan, Jeffrey Sachs, and Joseph Stiglitz, eds. 2007. *Escaping the Resource Curse*. New York: Columbia University Press.

Lange, G. 2004. "Wealth, Natural Capital, and Sustainable Development: Contrasting Examples from Botswana and Namibia." *Environmental and Resource Economics* 29 (3): 257–83.

Lange, G., and M. Wright. 2004. "Sustainable Development in Mineral Economies: The Example of Botswana." *Environment and Development Economics* 9 (4): 485–505.

Le Billon, Philippe. 2001. "The Political Ecology of War: Natural Resources and Armed Conflicts." *Political Geography* 20 (5): 561–84.

C H A P T E R   8

Country Experiences with Wealth Accounting

IN ADDITION TO ANALYTIC WORK CARRIED OUT BY THE WORLD
Bank, other agencies and individual scholars have done a considerable amount
of work on wealth accounting over the past two decades. Taken together, these
studies have deepened our knowledge of wealth accounting and have clarified
issues related to it. Along with the study by Hamilton and Clemens (1999),
economists Kenneth Arrow, Partha Dasgupta, and Karl-Göran Mäler have
achieved substantial theoretical advances in comprehensive wealth accounting
for sustainable development, reporting their findings in a series of publications.
The academic community and nongovernmental organizations (NGOs) have
produced a large body of empirical work on natural capital accounting at the
national, regional, and local levels.

Wealth accounting has also been taken up by national government agencies, by international organizations such as the Organisation for Economic
Co-operation and Development (OECD) and Eurostat, and by the United
Nations Statistical Commission as part of a comprehensive framework for environmental accounting. The recent report by Stiglitz, Sen, and Fitoussi (2009)
proposed ways to modify and extend conventional national accounts in order
to provide a more accurate and useful guide for policy. These authors endorsed
the comprehensive wealth approach to development and the compilation of
accounts for certain categories of capital.

This chapter reports the progress on wealth accounting by national government agencies, focusing particularly on natural capital. While the contribution of academics, NGOs, and other researchers is important, the implementation of wealth accounting by national governments is necessary for long-term institutionalization of the accounts. Although the World Bank will continue to compile and improve global wealth accounts, the eventual goal is for countries to implement wealth accounting themselves under standard guidelines. Compared to intergovernmental organizations, countries have much greater resources and access to information that enables them to compile more accurate and comprehensive wealth accounts. Once they are engaged in this task, the role of the World Bank would be to collect this information, as it does data on gross domestic product (GDP) and other national economic indicators, for publication in reports such as *World Development Indicators.*

The country experience with wealth accounting is quite varied. The most comprehensive wealth accounting is done by Norway, which was also the first country to introduce environmental accounting on a regular basis as part of official statistics in the late 1970s. For the most part, however, countries have introduced limited asset accounts for select natural resources, most often only for subsoil assets and, among the subsoil assets, most often for oil and natural gas. An important parallel development has been the compilation of a system for environmental accounting, including wealth accounts, under the aegis of the United Nations Statistical Commission; it is known as the System of Integrated Environmental and Economic Accounting, or SEEA (United Nations et al. 2003). The compilation of guidelines for wealth accounting is critical for international acceptance; it establishes consensus on methodology and international comparability for work carried out by national statistical agencies and the policy agencies that use the accounts.

The concept of national balance sheets and wealth accounting has been part of national accounts for some time and was explicitly identified in the 1993 System of National Accounts. However, as we will see, wealth accounting has not yet been widely implemented.

Current Country Practices

Table 8.1 provides an overview of current country practices in national wealth accounting. It focuses on the real economy, breaking down data by the types of nonfinancial assets covered. This assessment of country practices provides a conservative picture of the state of wealth accounting because the set of countries included has been restricted in several ways.

First, countries are included only when wealth accounting is carried out as part of, or in relation to, an official statistics program under the auspices of a

TABLE 8.1
Overview of Country Practices in Wealth Accounting for Nonfinancial Assets

Country	Minerals and Energy	Timber	Fish	Land	Human Capital	Other Assets[a]	Balance Sheet for Produced Assets	Natural Capital Included in Balance Sheet
Australia	Reg	Reg		Reg	P		yes	yes
Austria	P	P					yes	no
Belgium							yes	n.a.
Botswana	S						no	no
Brazil		I					no	no
Canada	Reg	Reg		Reg	P		yes	yes
Chile							yes	n.a.
Czech Republic	Reg			Reg			yes	yes
Denmark	Reg	P		P			yes	no
Estonia		P					no	no
Finland		Reg			P		no	no
France	Reg	P		R			yes	yes
Germany		Reg		P			yes	no
Guatemala		I					no	no
Hungary							yes	n.a.
Iceland			P				yes	no
India	P	P					no	no
Indonesia	Reg	P					no	no
Israel							yes	n.a.
Italy							yes	n.a.
Japan	Reg	Reg	Reg	Reg			yes	yes
Korea, Rep.	Reg	Reg		Reg			yes	yes
Mexico	Reg	Reg	I			yes	no	no
Namibia	S			S			no	no
Netherlands	Reg			P	I	yes	yes	no
New Zealand		P	Reg		P	yes	no	no
Norway	Reg	Reg	Reg		P	yes	other[b]	no
Philippines	S	S	S				no	no
Portugal							no	no
Slovak Republic				Reg			no	no
South Africa	S						no	no
Sweden		S	S				no	no

(continued)

TABLE 8.1
Overview of Country Practices in Wealth Accounting for Nonfinancial Assets
(*continued*)

Country	Minerals and Energy	Timber	Fish	Land	Human Capital	Other Assets[a]	Balance Sheet for Produced Assets	Natural Capital Included in Balance Sheet
United Kingdom	Reg		P				yes	no
United States	S			S	P		yes	no
Total	18	19	7	11	7	3	19	6
Of which regular	12	7	2	7	0	0		

Source: OECD statistics database (accessed February 23, 2010); United Nations Statistics Division, Searchable Archive of Publications on Environmental-Economic Accounting (http://unstats.un.org/unsd/envaccounting/ceea/archive); results from the Global Assessment of Environment Statistics, Environmental-Economic Accounting and related statistics (http://unstats.un.org/unsd/envaccounting/ceea/assessment.asp); websites of national statistical offices; personal interviews.
Note: Reg = accounts published on a regular basis (e.g., annually); I = accounts recently initiated but without results yet; P = accounts compiled as a pilot project that has not yet been taken into regular production; S = accounts compiled regularly in the past but currently suspended; Blank cell = no accounts initiated; n.a. = not applicable.
a. For example, other forest asset values, water, and hydroelectric power.
b. Norway publishes annual, comprehensive wealth accounts but not as part of official balance sheets.

government agency such as a national statistical office, central bank, or relevant ministry. Academic institutions, research organizations, and NGOs have done a large number of pilot studies on wealth and environmental accounting,[1] but we consider such studies only when they have involved government agencies as well.

Second, countries are included only when they compile complete asset accounts in monetary units, that is, accounts that record opening and closing stocks and changes therein (such as depletion, discoveries, or growth) during the accounting period. This excludes countries that, for example, compile the value of extracted timber but do not estimate the total stock of timber.

The table was compiled in three stages. First, we reviewed existing surveys in different wealth accounting areas (subsoil, land, etc.) to draw up a first rough draft. These included surveys by the United Nations Statistics Division (UNSD 2009) and Pasquier, Quirino, and Kesey (2007). Second, we consulted existing country publications as well as the OECD statistics database to get a more precise picture. Third, we visited the websites of national statistical offices and conducted follow-up interviews with country experts and other environmental accounting experts.

As of 2010, more than 30 countries have compiled wealth estimates; 16 of them compile at least one type of natual capital stock regularly.[2] The great majority of countries use the SEEA as a reference. Country wealth accounting practices are classified as follows:

Reg: accounts published on a regular basis (e.g., annually)
I: accounts recently initiated but without results yet
P: accounts compiled as a pilot project that has not yet been taken into regular production
S: accounts compiled regularly in the past but currently suspended

The table clearly demonstrates that wealth accounting is being practiced in both developed and developing countries. Several developing countries have strong environmental accounting programs, although some of these programs have been suspended due to lack of resources and/or capacity. Sweden and the United States have had strong wealth accounting programs in the past, but have now stopped. In Sweden, measurement issues and waning policy interest caused the focus of the environmental accounting program to shift from stock accounts to flow accounts (e.g., air emissions) and economic accounts (environmental taxes and subsidies, etc.). Recently, new initiatives by Brazil, China, and India have given impetus to environmental accounting.[3]

In terms of types of assets covered, timber and subsoil accounts have been tried most often, followed by land accounts. Produced assets are compiled most regularly by countries, followed by subsoil assets. We will now discuss compilation practices in more detail by type of resource.

Mineral and Energy Accounts

Among the natural capital accounts, stock accounts for mineral and energy resources are compiled most regularly. Table 8.2 identifies some characteristics of mineral and energy asset accounts for those countries identified as regular compilers in table 8.1.

The net present value (NPV) method is the one used by the World Bank in its wealth accounts and recommended in the SEEA. It is the most widely used, although two developing countries, Mexico and Indonesia, use the net price method or the El-Serafy method, considered easier to implement. Japan uses the Hoskold or sinking-fund method, while the Czech Republic estimates stock values as the residual value of the stock of tangible, nonproduced assets minus the stock of land, both of which are available from statistical surveys (OECD 2008).

Country practices differ regarding the assumptions used in application of the NPV method: the chosen discount rates are often around 4 percent, but rates of return vary between 4 and 8 percent. Canada calculates several variants of the NPV method, resulting in upper and lower boundary values. The available time series vary across countries, and some countries do not compile physical

TABLE 8.2
Country Practices in Mineral and Energy Asset Accounting

Country	All Subsoil	Energy	Minerals	Valuation Method	Constant Prices	Time Series
Australia	yes	yes	yes	NPV	yes	>15
Canada	yes	yes	yes	NPV (variants)	·no	>40
Czech Republic	yes	–	–	other	no	>5
Denmark	yes	yes	no	NPV	no	>15
France	yes	–	–	NPV	no	>20
Indonesia	yes	yes	–	net price	no	>10
Japan	yes	–	–	Hoskold	no	>40
Korea, Rep.	yes	yes	yes	NPV	no	>5
Mexico	yes	yes	–	net price, El Serafy	no	>10
Netherlands	yes	yes	yes	NPV	no	>15
Norway	yes	yes	no	NPV	yes	>25
United Kingdom	yes	yes	no	NPV	no	>30

Note: − = unknown; > x = a time series of at least x years was found.

stock accounts (volume measures). Australia and Norway appear to be the only countries that also publish stock values in constant prices.

One of the main findings of the Global Assessment of Energy Accounts (UNSD 2009) was that in all responding countries, the total stock of reserves that is valued is broader than mere proven reserves, which are considered in the 2008 System of National Accounts (European Commission et al. 2009). Some part of probable and possible reserves may be included. Another finding was that the main difficulty in applying the NPV method is fluctuating resource rents. Some countries therefore use a weighted moving average to smooth the effect of price changes, while others use specific price forecasts.

Other Natural Capital Accounts

Timber Accounts

Although around 20 countries have compiled timber stock accounts, only seven of them have done so regularly. A possible explanation is that forests often provide, in addition to timber production, a broad range of services that are difficult to value because of their nonmarket nature. Many timber-rich countries, rather than pursuing stock accounts, have chosen to compile economic accounts for forestry that provide information about the overall importance of the forestry sector for the economy.

Land Accounts

There has been increasing interest lately in estimating stock values of land (Australian Bureau of Statistics 2010; Statistics Netherlands 2010). At least 11 countries currently compile estimates for land, but not all of them cover all types of land, and only six of them currently include these estimates in the national balance sheet. Several methods are used, ranging from business surveys and registers to household budget surveys (Kim 2008).

Fish Accounts

New Zealand, Norway, and Japan appear to be the only countries that regularly compile stock values for various species of fish. The Japanese estimate is based upon the capitalization method. Norway uses the NPV applied to estimated resource rent. New Zealand introduced a system of individually tradable quotas to manage its fisheries, resulting in a large competitive market for fish quota sales and rentals. This system has established a direct market price for the asset value of fisheries, which is used in the New Zealand fisheries accounts.

Several countries, such as Namibia and Iceland, have experimented with fish accounts. When no quota valuation is available the NPV method can be difficult to apply in practice. In a number of pilot studies, the resource rent from fisheries is negative. In most instances this is the result of heavy subsidies (World Bank and FAO 2009), but in some cases it may result from strong vertical integration of the fisheries industry (Harkness and Aki 2008).

Other Stock Accounts

Norway records a stock account for hydropower. New Zealand has experimented in the past with a stock account for water. The Netherlands is currently working on estimating stock values for renewable energy (wind and solar). Mexico has calculated the depletion of groundwater resources based on a calculation of the shadow price of groundwater according to the residual value method in combination with an annual water balance.

Human Capital

There is an increasing interest in the compilation of human capital accounts, and at least seven countries so far have conducted pilot studies or initiated work in this field. Most countries estimate human capital as the present value of future labor income, using the Jorgenson-Fraumeni method described in chapter 6, although differences exist regarding its precise application and scope (e.g., ages covered, treatment of nonmarket activities). Only three countries have compiled complete stock accounts, and none compile these accounts regularly. The OECD recently established a consortium to develop human capital accounts, and 17 countries have joined. Only Norway has incorporated human capital into its wealth accounts.

Balance Sheets

Although many countries estimate their financial assets and liabilities, only about 20 publish balance sheets for nonfinancial assets (covering at least produced assets).[4] Only six countries include estimates for nonproduced assets in their national accounts balance sheets.

Norway compiles stocks of produced capital, but these are not included in the balance sheets of the national accounts. Norway has a long tradition of research on wealth accounting and publishes an indicator of national wealth that is disseminated as part of the country's annual report on sustainable development indicators.

Wealth Accounting in Recent Initiatives

In response to increasing policy demands, the statistical community agreed in 2006 that it was time to mainstream environmental-economic accounting and related statistics within the national statistical system. To this end, the United Nations Statistical Commission decided to revise the SEEA and elevate it to an international statistical standard. This will put environmental accounting on the same footing as the System of National Accounts. A statistical standard requires a high degree of international agreement on methodology; while such agreement exists for certain aspects of the environmental accounts, there are other aspects on which consensus has not yet been reached. Guidelines for the former will be published in volume 1, the statistical standard, while volume 2 will address issues that are highly relevant to policy but on which no consensus exists at this time (UNSD 2008).The statistical standard will include subsoil assets, timber assets, fisheries, and land.

The Joint UNECE/OECD/Eurostat Working Group on Statistics for Sustainable Development was mandated to "articulate a broad conceptual framework for sustainable development measurement with the concept of capital at its centre" in order to propose a set of indicators to enhance international comparability (UNECE 2009). At the same time, the working group reviewed existing practices in countries that have adopted policy-based approaches to the measurement of sustainable development in order to look for commonalities between indicator sets.

Although members of the working group held diverging opinions regarding the precise interpretation of sustainable development,[5] the group's report resulted in a set of 28 indicators that are consistent with both the comprehensive wealth approach and the most commonly used physical indicators (UNECE 2009). The list includes indicators for the value of stocks of financial, produced, human, and natural capital, as well as for flow measures (net investment/depletion) for these assets. These correspond conceptually to the World Bank's wealth accounts and to adjusted net saving. The report notes the difficulty in measuring social capital and underlines the need for additional indicators in order to capture "the well-being effects of capital that cannot or should not be captured in a market-based monetary measure" and the existence of critical capital (UNECE 2009). The Joint UNECE/OECD/Eurostat Task Force on Measuring Sustainable Development, established in 2008 as a successor group, has established a research program to address some of these issues.

The *Report by the Commission on the Measurement of Economic Performance and Social Progress*, also known as the Stiglitz-Sen-Fitoussi report (2009), clearly distinguishes between assessments of current well-being and assessments of sustainability. The report concurs with several of the recommendations in the report by the Joint UNECE/OECD/Eurostat Working Group (UNECE 2009). In principle, Stiglitz, Sen, and Fitoussi endorse the comprehensive wealth approach to measuring sustainability (recommendation 3) while noting that the correct valuation of certain stocks is highly problematic.[6] They recommend accounts for stocks of resources that have market prices, such as minerals or timber, but question whether reliable values can be obtained for other natural capital.

Summing Up

Since our benchmark year of 1979, wealth accounting has become increasingly widespread in the statistical community. The strongest advances have been made in the areas of mineral and energy accounting, while recent years have seen increasing interest in assessing stock values of land and human capital. The valuation of renewable assets (like fish) lags, largely because of measurement difficulties.

At the same time, both the Stiglitz-Sen-Fitoussi (2009) report and the Joint UNECE/OECD/Eurostat Working Group report (UNECE 2009) have come out strongly in support of wealth accounting, although they recommend that physical indicators be included with the monetary indicators. The great majority of countries with environmental accounting programs use SEEA guidelines. Wealth accounting is likely to get a further stimulus from the forthcoming elevation of the revised SEEA to a statistical standard, on par with the System of National Accounts. This should provide clear guidelines and recommendations that country statistical offices can use to construct natural capital accounts.

Notes

1 For example, Mungatana, Hassan, and Lange (forthcoming) report a number of case studies for African countries.

2 That is, they compile at least one of the asset accounts and/or balance sheets regularly.

3 The focus in China has been less on stocks and more on flows (green GDP).

4 There may be additional non-OECD countries that compile balance sheets for produced assets whose practices were outside the scope of this assessment.

5 "One view within the group, referred to as the integrated view, held that the goal of sustainable development is to ensure both the well-being of those currently living and the potential for the well-being of future generations. The second, labelled the future-oriented view, held that the concern of sustainable development is properly limited to just the latter; that is, sustainable development is about ensuring the potential for the well-being of future generations" (UNECE 2009, 3).

6 The explanatory text to recommendation 3 states, "Measures of wealth are central to measuring sustainability. What is carried over into the future necessarily has to be expressed as stocks. . . " (Stiglitz, Sen, and Fitoussi 2009).

References

Australian Bureau of Statistics. 2010. "Accounting for Natural Resources—Land and Subsoil Assets—in the Australian Bureau of Statistics." Paper prepared for the Conference of European Statisticians/Group of Experts on National Accounts, Tenth Session, Geneva, April 26–29.

European Commission, International Monetary Fund, Organisation for Economic Co-operation and Development, United Nations, and World Bank. 2009. *System of National Accounts 2008*. New York: United Nations.

Hamilton, K., and M. Clemens. 1999. "Genuine Savings Rates in Developing Countries." *World Bank Economic Review* 13 (2): 333–56.

Harkness, Jane, and Luke Aki. 2008. "A Numerical Comparison of Fish Quota Values and Standard Resource Rent Calculations Using New Zealand's Commercial Fish Resource." Paper LG/13/6 presented at the 13th Meeting of the London Group on Environmental Accounting, Brussels, September 29–October 3.

Kim, Y. 2008. "Estimation of the Stock of Land in OECD Countries." Paper presented at the meeting of the OECD Working Party on National Accounts, Paris, October 14–16.

Mungatana, E., R. Hassan, and G. Lange, eds. Forthcoming. *Implementing Environmental Accounts: Case Studies from Eastern and Southern Africa*. Dordrecht, Netherlands: Springer.

OECD (Organisation for Economic Co-operation and Development). 2008. "Results of the Survey on Sub-soil Assets in OECD Countries." STD/CSTAT/WPNA(2008)7. Paper presented at the meeting of the OECD Working Party on National Accounts, Paris, October 14–16.

Pasquier, J., G. Quirino, and C. Kesy. 2007. "Environmental Accounts: State of Play of Recent Work." Final report to Eurostat, Luxembourg.

Statistics Netherlands. 2010. "Measuring Natural Assets in the Netherlands." Paper prepared for the Conference of European Statisticians/Group of Experts on National Accounts, Tenth Session, Geneva, April 26–29.

Stiglitz, Joseph E., Amartya Sen, and Jean-Paul Fitoussi. 2009. *Report by the Commission on the Measurement of Economic Performance and Social Progress.* Paris: Commission on the Measurement of Economic Performance and Social Progress.

UNECE (United Nations Economic Commission for Europe). 2009. *Measuring Sustainable Development: Report of the Joint UNECE/OECD/Eurostat Working Group on Statistics for Sustainable Development.* Prepared in cooperation with OECD and Eurostat. New York: United Nations.

United Nations, European Commission, International Monetary Fund, Organisation for Economic Co-operation and Development, and World Bank. 2003. *Handbook of National Accounting: Integrated Environmental and Economic Accounting 2003.* To be issued as Series F, No. 61, Rev. 1 (ST/ESA/STAT/SER.F/61/Rev.1). New York: United Nations.

UNSD (United Nations Statistics Division). 2008. *Environmental-Economic Accounting.* Brochure. http://unstats.un.org/unsd/envaccounting/EnvAcc_Brochure_FINAL1.pdf.

———. 2009. "Report on the Global Assessment of Energy Accounts." Background document for the 40th session of the United Nations Statistical Commission, New York, February 24–27. http://unstats.un.org/unsd/envaccounting/ceea/surveyEEA.asp.

World Bank and FAO (Food and Agriculture Organization). 2009. *The Sunken Billions: The Economic Justification for Fisheries Reform.* Washington, DC: World Bank.

APPENDIX A

Building the Wealth Estimates: Methodology

This appendix details the construction of wealth, genuine savings, and savings gap estimates.

The wealth estimates are composed of the following:

- Total wealth
- Produced capital
  - Machinery, equipment, and structures
  - Urban land
- Natural capital
  - Energy resources (oil, natural gas, hard coal, lignite)
  - Mineral resources (bauxite, copper, gold, iron, lead, nickel, phosphate, silver, tin, zinc)
  - Timber resources
  - Nontimber forest resources
  - Crop land
  - Pasture land
  - Protected areas
- Net foreign assets

Intangible capital is calculated as a residual, that is, as the difference between total wealth and the sum of produced and natural capital and net foreign assets.

141

Total Wealth

Total wealth can be calculated as

$$W_t = \int_t^\infty C(s) \cdot e^{-r(s-t)} ds$$

where W_t is the total value of wealth, or capital, in year t; $C(s)$ is consumption in year s; and r is the social rate of return to investment.[1] The social rate of return to investment is expressed as

$$r = \rho + \eta \frac{\dot{C}}{C}$$

where ρ is the pure rate of time preference and η is the elasticity of utility with respect to consumption. Under the assumption that $\eta = 1$ and that consumption grows at a constant rate, the total wealth can be expressed as

$$W_t = \int_t^\infty C(t) \cdot e^{-\rho(s-t)} ds. \tag{A.1}$$

The current value of total wealth at time t is a function of the consumption at time t and the pure rate of time preference.

Expression (A.1) implicitly assumes that consumption is on a sustainable path, that is, the level of saving is enough to offset the depletion of natural resources. The calculation of total wealth requires that two issues be considered in computing the initial level of consumption:

- *The volatility of consumption.* To solve this problem we used the five-year centered average of consumption for each one of the three years: 1995, 2000, and 2005.
- *Negative rates of saving adjusted for depletion of produced and natural capital.* When depletion-adjusted saving is negative, countries are consuming natural resources, jeopardizing the prospects for future consumption. A measure of sustainable consumption needs to be derived in this instance.

Hence, the following adjustments were made:

- Wealth calculation for 2005, for example, considered consumption series for 2003–07.
- For the years in which saving adjusted for depletion of produced and natural capital was negative, this measure of depletion-adjusted saving was subtracted from consumption to obtain *sustainable* consumption, that is, the consumption level that would have left the capital stock intact.
- The corrected consumption series were then expressed in constant 2005 U.S. dollars. Deflators are country-specific: they are obtained by dividing gross domestic product (GDP) in current dollars by GDP in constant dollars. This rule was also applied to natural capital and net foreign assets.
- The average of constant-dollars consumption between 2003 and 2007, for example, was used as the initial level of consumption for wealth calculation of 2005.

For computation purposes, we assumed the pure rate of time preference to be 1.5 percent (Pearce and Ulph 1999), and we limited the time horizon to 25 years. This time horizon roughly corresponds to a generation. We adopted the 25-year truncation throughout the calculation of wealth, in particular, of natural capital.

Machinery, Equipment, and Structures

For the calculation of physical capital stocks, several estimation procedures can be considered. Some of them, such as the derivation of capital stocks from insurance values or accounting values or from direct surveys, entail enormous expenditures and face problems of limited availability and adequacy of data. Other estimation procedures, such as the accumulation methods and, in particular, the Perpetual Inventory Method (PIM), are cheaper and more easily implemented since they require only investment data and information on the assets' service life and depreciation patterns. These methods derive capital series from the accumulation of investment series and are the most popular. The PIM is, indeed, the method adopted by most OECD (Organisation for Economic Co-operation and Development) countries that estimate capital stocks (Bohm et al. 2002; Mas, Perez, and Uriel 2000; Ward 1976).

We also use the PIM in our estimations of capital stocks. The relevant expression for computing K_t, the aggregate capital stock value in period t, is then given by

$$K_t = \sum_{i=0}^{19} I_{t-i} (1 - \alpha) \qquad (A.2)$$

where I is the value of investment in constant prices and α is the depreciation rate. In equation (A.2) we implicitly assume that the accumulation period (or service life) is 20 years.[2] The depreciation pattern is geometric, with $\alpha = 5$ percent assumed to be constant across countries and over time.[3] Finally, note that equation (A.2) implies a "one-hoss-shay" retirement pattern, that is, the value of an asset falls to zero after 20 years.

To estimate equation (A.2) we need long investment series or, alternatively, initial capital stock.[4] Unfortunately, initial capital stocks are not available for all the countries considered in our estimation, and even in the cases in which published data exist (as for some OECD countries), their use would introduce comparability problems with other countries for which data do not exist.

For the countries with incomplete series of gross capital formation data, investment series were estimated if we had data on output, final consumption expenditure (private and public), exports, and imports for the missing years. With this information we can derive investment series from the national accounting identity Y=C+I+G+(X−M) by subtracting net exports from gross domestic savings. In all cases, the ratios of the investment computed this way and the original investment in the years in which both series are available are very close to one. Still, to ensure comparability between both investment series, the investment estimates derived from the accounting identity were used only if the country-specific median of these ratios, for the period 1960–2006, was close to one. For the rest of the countries for which complete investment series are still not available, data on gross fixed capital formation are used for the missing years. Complete investment series for the 19 years preceding 1995, calculated using the three methods listed above, were available for 107 countries, while complete data series for 125 countries were used to calculate produced capital for the years 2000 and 2005.

For 20 countries for the year 1995 and two countries for 2000, all still missing complete investment series, produced capital is estimated after adjusting the values obtained using a lifetime assumption of 14–19 years (as the case may be). The adjustment made is that values obtained using less than 20 years are multiplied with the median of the ratio of capital obtained from 20 years to that obtained from less than 20 years (over 1960–2006). For the remaining countries, we tried to overcome the data limitations by using a quite conservative approach. We extended the investment series by regressing the logarithm of the investment output ratio on time, as did Larson et al. (2000). However, we did not extrapolate output, limiting the extension of the investment series to cases in which a corresponding output observation was available. In particular, the 20-year service lifetime assumption was used to estimate capital stocks from investment series predicted from a regression of the ratio of the log of investment to GDP on time. Produced capital estimates for 6, 27, and 34 additional countries were obtained using this method for the years 1995, 2000, and 2005, respectively.

Urban Land

In the calculation of the value of a country's physical capital stock, the final physical capital estimates include the value of structures, machinery, and equipment, since the value of the stocks is derived (using the Perpetual Inventory Method) from gross capital formation data that account for these elements. In the investment figures, however, only land improvements are captured. Thus, our final capital estimates do not entirely reflect the value of urban land.

Drawing on Kunte et al. (1998), we valued urban land as a fixed proportion of the value of physical capital. Ideally, this proportion would be country-specific. In practice, detailed national balance sheet information with which to compute these ratios was not available. Thus, like Kunte et al. (1998), we used a constant proportion equal to 24 percent:[5]

$$U_t = 0.24 K_t. \qquad (A.3)$$

Energy and Mineral Resources

This section describes the methodology used to estimate the value of nonrenewable resources. There are at least three reasons that such calculations may be difficult. First, it is only in the past few decades that the importance of including natural resources in national accounting systems has been widely recognized. Although efforts to broaden the national accounts are underway, they are mostly limited to international organizations such as the United Nations or the World Bank. Second, there are no private markets for subsoil resource deposits to convey information on the value of these stocks. Third, the stock size is defined in economic terms: reserves are "that part of the reserve base which could be economically extracted or produced at the time of determination."[6] Stock therefore depends on the prevailing economic conditions, namely technology and prices.

Despite these difficulties, we assigned dollar values to the stocks of the main energy resources (oil, gas, and coal[7]) and to the stocks of 10 metals and minerals (bauxite, copper, gold, iron ore, lead, nickel, phosphate rock, silver, tin, and zinc) for all the countries that have production figures.

The approach used in our estimation is based on the well-established economic principle that asset values should be measured as the present discounted value of economic profits over the life of the resource. This value, for a particular country and resource, is given by the following expression:

$$V_t = \sum_{i=t}^{t+T-1} \frac{\pi_i q_i}{(1 + r)^{(i-t)}}, \tag{A.4}$$

where $\pi_i q_i$ is the economic profit or total rent at time i, (π_i denoting unit rent and q_i denoting production), r is the social discount rate, and T is the lifetime of the resource.

Estimating Future Rents

Though well understood and seldom questioned, this approach is rarely used for the practical estimation of natural asset values, since it requires knowledge of actual future rents. Instead, future rents are implicitly predicted using the more restrictive assumptions of constant total rents and optimality in the extraction path. This corresponds to assuming a zero growth rate of rents.

The value of the resource stock can then be expressed as

$$V_t = \pi_i q_i \left(1 + \frac{1}{r}\right)\left(1 - \frac{1}{(1 + r)^T}\right). \tag{A.5}$$

Choice of T

To guide the choice of an exhaustion time value, we computed the reserves-to-production ratios for all the countries, years, and resources.[8] Where country reserves data are missing, world and regional data are substituted. Table A.1 provides the median of these ratios for the different resources, showing the abundance of energy and mineral resources relative to each other.

With the exception of the very abundant coal, bauxite, and iron, the reserves-to-production ratios tend to be around 20–30 years. We chose to cap exhaustion time at 25 years for all the resources and countries.[9] From a purely pragmatic point of view, the choice of a longer exhaustion time would require an increase in the time horizon for the predictions of total rents, to feed equation (A.4). On the other hand, rents obtained farther in the future have less weight since they are more heavily discounted. Finally, the level of uncertainty increases as we look toward a more remote future. Under uncertainty, it is unlikely that companies or governments will develop reserves to cover more than 25 years of production.

Timber Resources

The predominant economic use of forests has been as a source of timber. Timber wealth is calculated as the present discounted value of rents from roundwood

TABLE A.1
Median Lifetime in 2005 for Proven Reserves

Reserve	Median Lifetime (years)
Energy	
Oil	16
Gas	38
Hard coal	63
Soft coal	456
Metals and minerals	
Bauxite	97
Copper	33
Gold	17
Iron ore	88
Lead	16
Nickel	25
Phosphate	37
Tin	45
Silver	14
Zinc	21

Source: British Petroleum; USGS 2006a, 2006b; USEIA 2006.

production. The estimation then requires data on roundwood production, unit rents, and the time to exhaustion of the forest (if unsustainably managed) in the beginning year.

The annual flow of roundwood production is obtained from the FAOSTAT database maintained by the Food and Agriculture Organization of the United Nations (FAO).[10] Calculating the rent is more complex. Theoretically, the value of standing timber is equal to the discounted future stumpage price received by the forest owner after taking out the costs of bringing the timber to maturity. In practice, stumpage prices are usually not readily available, and we calculated unit rents as the product of a composite weighted price and a rental rate.

The composite weighted price of standing timber is estimated as the average of three different prices, weighted by production: (a) the export unit value of coniferous industrial roundwood, (b) the export unit value of nonconiferous industrial roundwood, and (c) an estimated world average price of fuelwood. Where country-level prices are not available, the regional weighted average is used.

Forestry production cost data are not available for all countries. Consequently, regional rental rates ([price − cost]/price) were estimated using available studies and consultations with World Bank forestry experts.

Since we applied a market value to standing timber, it was necessary to distinguish between forests available and forests not available for wood supply because some standing timber is simply not accessible or economically viable. The area of forest *available for wood supply* was estimated as forests within 50 kilometers of infrastructure. Data on productive areas were obtained from the FAO's *Global Forest Resources Assessments* (Global FRA) for 2005 and 2000 (UNFAO 2006, 2001).[11] Data for 1995 were imputed from Global FRA 2000 data by using the ratio of productive area to total forest area, which is then multiplied by total forest area in 1995 obtained from *State of the World's Forests 1997* (UNFAO 1997).

Rents were capitalized assuming a growth rate of zero and using a 4 percent discount rate to arrive at a stock of timber resources. The concept of sustainable use of forest resources is introduced through the choice of the time horizon over which the stream is capitalized. If roundwood harvest is smaller than net annual increments, that is, if the forest is sustainably harvested, the time horizon is 25 years. If roundwood harvest is greater than the net annual increments, then the time to exhaustion is calculated. The time to exhaustion is based on estimates of forest volume divided by the difference between production and increment. The smaller of 25 years and the time to exhaustion is then used as the resource lifetime.

Five-year-average values of production and unit export values are used to calculate the revenue from timber production. Data on coniferous and nonconiferous, industrial roundwood, and fuelwood production are obtained for the years 1991–2005 from FAOSTAT forestry data online. Fuelwood price data are also from FAOSTAT forestry data online. Roundwood export unit values are calculated from FAO online data. Studies used as a basis for estimating rental rates include those by Fortech (1997); Whiteman (1996); Tay, Healey, and Price (2001); Lopina, Ptichnikov, and Voropayev (2003); Haripriya (1998); Global Witness (2001); and Eurostat (2002).

Nontimber Forest Resources

Timber revenues are not the only economic contribution of forests. Nontimber forest benefits such as minor forest products, hunting, recreation, and watershed protection are significant but are not usually accounted. This leads to forest resources being undervalued. A review of nontimber forest benefits in developed and developing countries reveals that annual returns from hunting, recreation, and watershed benefits vary from $129 per hectare in developed countries to $27 per hectare in developing countries (based on Lampietti and Dixon [1995] and Merlo and Croitoru [2005], and adjusted to 2005 prices). We assume that only one-tenth of the forest area in each country is accessible for recreation. Thus, the per-hectare value for recreation is multiplied by one-tenth of the forest area in each country to arrive at annual recreation benefits. Estimation of watershed protection values considers deforestation; deforestation rates are from Global FRA 2005 (UNFAO 2006). The annual rate of forest area changes over 1990–2000 is used as the deforestation rate for 1995, while the annual rate of forest area changes over 2000–2005 is used for 2000 and 2005. Nontimber (minor) forest product values for 2005 are also from Global FRA 2005; these values are assumed to be constant over years. Nontimber forest resources under each type of benefit are valued as the net present value of benefits over a time horizon of 25 years. [12]

Crop Land

Country-level data on agricultural land prices are not widely published. Even if local prices were available, it could be argued that land markets are so distorted that a meaningful comparison across countries would be difficult. We have therefore chosen to estimate land values based on the net present value of land rents, assuming that the products of the land are sold at world prices.

The return to land is computed as the product of rental rate and revenues from crop production. A constant rental rate of 30 percent is assumed across all crops considered. Production is yield multiplied by harvested area. Cereals, fruits, nuts, oil crops, pulses, starchy roots, stimulants, sugar crops, and vegetables are the crop categories considered with data from the FAO. Yields and areas are from the FAO's prodSTAT database. Production is calculated based on yield and harvested area for each single crop; these data are then aggregated into the Global Trade Analysis Project (GTAP) 6 Data Base sectors to obtain output for each GTAP sector (Dimaranan 2006). Values of production are then multiplied by world prices. The World Bank's Development Economics Prospects Group is the primary data source for prices in major crop categories such as rice and wheat. For the remaining crops, world median export unit values from the FAO are used. Five-year-average values of yield and unit export values are used to do the estimates (2001–05 for 2005, 1996–2000 for 2000, and 1991–95 for 1995). Harvest areas are the current year value.

Annual land return is the summation of returns from all agricultural sectors considered. In order to reflect the sustainability of current cultivation practices, the annual return in year t is projected to the year $(t + 24)$ based on growth in production (land areas are assumed to stay constant). The growth rates are 0.97 percent and 1.94 percent in developed and developing countries, respectively (Rosengrant, Agcaoili-Sombilla, and Perez 1995). The net present value of this flow was then calculated using a discount rate of 4 percent over a 25-year time horizon.

Pasture Land

Pasture land is valued using methods similar to those for crop land. The returns to pasture land are assumed to be a fixed proportion of the value of output. On average, costs of production are 55 percent of revenues, and therefore, returns to pasture land are assumed to be 45 percent of output value. Value of output is based on the production of meat, milk, and wool valued at international prices. Annual pasture land return is calculated as the product of the total revenue from all the commodities and the rental rate for pasture land, which is assumed to be 45 percent.

In order to reflect the sustainability of current grazing practices, the annual return in year t is projected to the year $(t + 24)$ based on growth in production. The growth rates are 0.89 percent and 2.95 percent in developed and developing countries, respectively (Rosengrant, Agcaoili-Sombilla, and Perez 1995). The net present value of this flow is then calculated using a 4 percent discount rate over a 25-year time horizon.

Production and unit export values are from the FAO databases prodSTAT and tradeSTAT, respectively. Five-year-average values of production and unit export values are used to calculate revenues. Missing values for price are filled with the regional average or the world average if the regional average is missing.

Protected Areas

Protected areas provide a number of benefits that range from existence values to recreational values. They can be a significant source of tourism income.

These values are revealed by a high willingness to pay for such benefits. The establishment and good maintenance of protected areas preserves an asset for the future, and therefore protected areas form an important part of the natural capital estimates. The willingness to pay to preserve natural regions varies considerably, however, and there is no comprehensive data set on this.

Protected areas (International Union for Conservation of Nature categories I–VI) are valued at the lower of per hectare returns to pasture land and crop land—a quasi–opportunity cost. These returns are then capitalized over a 25-year time horizon, using a 4 percent discount rate. Limiting the value of protected areas to the opportunity cost of preservation probably captures the minimum value, but not the complete value, of protected areas.

Data on protected areas are taken from the World Database on Protected Areas, which is compiled by United Nations Environment Programme's World Conservation Monitoring Centre. Where the value of a protected area is missing, it was assumed to be zero.

Net Foreign Assets

Finally, net foreign assets of an economy are subtracted from total wealth net of produced and natural capital to estimate the residual or intangible capital. Net foreign assets are calculated as total assets minus total liabilities. The database used was an updated and extended version of the External Wealth of Nations Mark II database developed by Lane and Milesi-Ferretti (2007). This database contains data on total assets and liabilities in (millions of) current U.S. dollars for the period 1970–2007 and for 178 economies. Total assets are the sum of foreign direct investment (FDI) assets, portfolio equity assets, debt assets, derivatives assets, and foreign exchange reserves. Total liabilities are the sum of FDI liabilities, portfolio equity liabilities, debt liabilities, and derivatives liabilities.

Calculating Adjusted Net Saving

Adjusted net saving measures the change in value of a specified set of assets, that is, the investment/disinvestment in different types of capital (produced, human, natural). The calculations are not comprehensive, as they do not include some important sources of environmental degradation such as underground water depletion, unsustainable fisheries, and soil degradation. This results from the lack of internationally comparable data rather than from intended omissions. A detailed description of the methodology used to obtain adjusted net saving can be found on the World Bank's Environmental Economics Web site.[13] Table A.2 summarizes the definitions, data sources, and formulas used in the calculations.

Calculating Adjusted Net Saving

Component of Savings	Definition	Formula	Sources	Technical Notes	Observations
Gross national savings (GNS)	Difference between GNI and public and private consumption plus net current transfers.	GNS = GNI − private consumption − public consumption + net current transfers	WDI, OECD, UN, IMF International Financial Statistics		
Depreciation (Depr)	Replacement value of capital used up in the process of production.	(data taken directly from source or estimated)	UN	Where country data were unavailable, they were estimated as follows. Available data on depreciation as a percentage of GNI was regressed against the log of GNI per capita. This regression was then used to estimate missing depreciation data. Regression: Depr/GNI = a + (b × Ln(GNI/ cap)). The regression was estimated on a five-year basis (that is, regression in 1970 was used to estimate depreciation as a percentage of GNI in years 1970–74). Where data were missing for only a couple of years in a country, the same rate of depreciation as a percentage of GNI was applied.	UN data are not available after 1999 for most countries. Missing data are estimated.

(continued)

Component of Savings	Definition	Formula	Sources	Technical Notes	Observations
Net national savings (NNS)	Difference between gross national savings and the consumption of fixed capital.	NNS = GNS − Depr			
Education expenditure (EE)	Public current operating expenditures in education, including wages and salaries and excluding capital investments in buildings and equipment.	(data taken directly from source or estimated)	Current education expenditure (public): UNESCO	When data are missing, estimation is done as follows: (a) for gaps between two data points, missing information is filled in by calculating the average of the two data points; and (b) for gaps after the last data point available, missing information is filled in on the assumption that education expenditure is a constant share of GNI.	The variable does not include private investment in education. It only includes public expenditures, for which internationally comparable data are available. Current expenditure of $1 on education does not necessarily yield exactly $1 worth of human capital (see, for example, Jorgenson and Fraumeni 1992). However, an adjustment from standard national accounts is needed. In national accounts, non-fixed-capital expenditures on education are treated strictly as consumption. If a country's human capital is to be regarded as a valuable asset, expenditures on its formation must be seen as an investment.

Energy depletion (ED)	Ratio of present value (PV) of rents, discounted at 4%, to exhaustion time of the resource. Rent is calculated as the product of unit resource rents and the physical quantities of energy resources extracted. It covers coal, crude oil, and natural gas.	ED = PV(rent, 4% discount rate, exhaustion time)/exhaustion time rent = production volume × unit resource rent unit rent = [unit price – unit cost]/unit price exhaustion time = min(25 years, reserves/ production)	Quantities: OECD, British Petroleum, IEA, *International Petroleum Encyclopedia*, UN, World Bank, national sources. Prices: OECD, British Petroleum, national sources Costs: IEA, World Bank, national sources.	Energy depletion covers crude oil, natural gas, and coal (hard and lignite). Unit resource rent is calculated as (unit world price – average cost)/unit world price. Marginal cost should be used instead of average cost in order to calculate the true opportunity cost of extraction. Marginal cost is, however, difficult to compute.	Prices refer to international rather than local prices to reflect the social cost of energy depletion. This differs from national accounts methodologies, which may use local prices to measure energy GDP. This difference explains eventual discrepancies in the values for energy depletion and energy GDP.
Mineral depletion (MD)	Ratio of present value of rents, discounted at 4%, to exhaustion time of the resource. Rent is calculated as the product of unit resource rents and the physical quantities of mineral extracted. It covers tin, gold, lead, zinc, iron, copper, nickel, silver, bauxite, and phosphate.	MD = PV(rent, 4% discount rate, exhaustion time)/ exhaustion time rent = production volume × unit resource rent unit rent = [unit price – unit cost]/unit price exhaustion time = min(25 years, reserves/ production)	Quantities: USGS Minerals Yearbook. Prices: UNCTAD monthly Commodity Price Bulletin. Costs: World Bank, national sources.	Mineral depletion covers tin, gold, lead, zinc, iron, copper, nickel, silver, bauxite, and phosphate. Unit resource rent is calculated as (unit price – average cost)/unit price. Marginal cost should be used instead of average cost in order to calculate the true opportunity cost of extraction. Marginal cost is, however, difficult to compute.	Prices refer to international rather than local prices to reflect the social cost of mineral depletion. This differs from national accounts methodologies, which may use local prices to measure mineral GDP. This difference explains eventual discrepancies in the values for mineral depletion and mineral GDP.

(continued)

TABLE A.2 (continued)

Component of Savings	Definition	Formula	Sources	Technical Notes	Observations
Net forest depletion (NFD)	Product of unit resource rents and the excess of roundwood harvest over natural growth.	NFD = (roundwood production − increment) × average price × rental rate	Roundwood production: FAOSTAT forestry database. Increments: World Bank, FAO, UNECE, WRI, national sources. Rental rates: various sources.	In a country where increment exceeded wood extraction, no adjustment to net adjusted savings was made, no matter the absolute volume or value of wood extracted. Increment per hectare on productive forest land is adjusted to allow for country-specific characteristics of the timber industry.	Net forest depletion is not the monetary value of deforestation. Roundwood and fuelwood production are different from deforestation, which represents a permanent change in land use and, thus, is not comparable. Areas logged out but intended for regeneration are not included in deforestation figures (see WDI definition of deforestation); rather, they are counted as producing timber depletion. Net forest depletion includes only timber values and does not include the loss of nontimber forest benefits and nonuse benefits.

CO_2 damages (CO_2D)	A conservative figure of \$20 marginal global damages per ton of carbon emitted was taken from Fankhauser (1994).	CO_2D = emissions (tons) × \$20	Data on carbon emissions can be obtained from WDI.	Data lag by 2–3 years, so the data for missing years are estimated. This is done by taking the ratio of average emissions from the last three years of available data to the average of the last three years' GDP in constant local currency unit. This ratio is then applied to the missing years' GDP to estimate carbon dioxide emissions. The atomic weight of carbon is 12 and of carbon dioxide 44, and carbon is only (12/44) of the emissions. Damages are estimated per ton but the emissions data are per kilo ton. The CO_2 emissions data have therefore been multiplied with 20 × (12/44) × 1,000.	CO_2 damages include the social cost of permanent damages caused by CO_2 emissions. This may differ (sometimes in large measure) from the *market* value of CO_2 emissions reductions traded in emissions markets.
PM damages (PMD)	Willingness to pay (WTP) to avoid mortality and morbidity attributable to particulate emissions.	PMD = disability adjusted life years (DALYs) lost due to PM emissions × WTP		

(continued)

TABLE A.2 (continued)

Component of Savings	Definition	Formula	Sources	Technical Notes	Observations
Adjusted net saving (ANS)	Net national savings plus education expenditure and minus energy depletion, mineral depletion, net forest depletion, carbon dioxide damage, and particulate emissions damage.	$ANS = NNS + EE - ED - MD - NFD - CO_2D - PMD$			

Source: Authors.

Note: ANS = adjusted net saving; CO_2 = carbon dioxide; CO_2D = CO_2 damages; Depr = depreciation; ED = energy depletion; EE = education expenditure; FAO = Food and Agriculture Organization; FAOSTAT = Food and Agriculture Organization of the United Nations database; GDP = gross domestic product; GNI = gross national income; GNS = gross national savings; IEA = International Energy Agency; IMF = International Monetary Fund; MD = mineral depletion; NFD = net forest depletion; NNS = net national savings; OECD = Organisation for Economic Co-operation and Development; PM = particulate matter; PMD = particulate matter damages; PV = present value; UN = United Nations; UNCTAD = United Nations Conference on Trade and Development; UNECE = United Nations Economic Commission for Europe; UNESCO = United Nations Educational, Scientific, and Cultural Organization; USGS = U.S. Geological Survey; WDI = World Development Indicators Database; WRI = World Resources Institute; WTP = willingness to pay.

Calculating the Adjusted Net Saving Gap

Population growth is a problem in most developing nations, since it exerts pressure on the physical and natural resources of an economy. Hence, we look at two country-specific measures: change in wealth per capita and the adjusted net saving gap. Change in wealth per capita is genuine savings per capita net of the impact of population growth on per capita wealth. The adjusted net saving gap as a share of gross national income (GNI) is a measure of how much extra saving effort would be required in order for a country to break even with zero change in wealth per capita.

Under the assumption of an exogenous growth rate of population g, change in wealth per capita is expressed as

$$\Delta\left(\frac{W}{P}\right) = \frac{\Delta W}{P} - g \cdot \frac{W}{P} = \frac{W}{P}\left(\frac{\Delta W}{W} - g\right), \tag{A.6}$$

where total wealth is denoted by W and population by P, and ΔW can be interpreted as genuine savings. Hence, "total wealth per capita will rise or fall depending on whether the growth rate of total wealth ($\Delta W/W$) is higher or lower than the population growth rate" (World Bank 2006, 62).

Adjustments are made to the adjusted net saving and per capita wealth measures in order to focus on stocks and flows that are mostly *rival* in nature. The measure of *tangible* wealth excludes intangible capital. Adjusted net saving is calculated by adding education expenditures to gross national savings and subtracting depletion of physical and natural resources (energy, minerals, and forests).

Finally, the adjusted net saving gap is calculated by identifying those countries with negative changes in wealth per capita and then dividing this by GNI per capita.

Notes

1 A proof that the current value of wealth is equal to the net present value of consumption can be found in Hamilton and Hartwick (2005).

2 The choice of a service life of 20 years is intended to reflect the mix of relatively long-lived structures and short-lived machinery and equipment in the aggregate capital stock and investment series. In a study that derives cross-country capital estimates for 62 countries, Larson et al. (2000) also use a mean service life of 20 years for aggregate investment.

3 Again, by choosing a 5 percent depreciation rate we try to capture the diversity of assets included in the aggregate investment series.

4 That is, $K_t = \sum_{i=0}^{t} I_{t-i}(1 - \alpha)^i + k_0$ for $t < 20$.

5 Kunte et al. (1998) based their estimation of urban land value on Canada's detailed national balance sheet information. Urban land is estimated to be 33 percent of the value of structures, which in turn is estimated to be 72 percent of the total value of physical capital.

6 The U.S. Geological Survey definition. It is clear that an increase in, say, the price of oil, or a reduction in its extraction costs, would increase the amount of "economically extractable"

oil and thereby increase the reserves. Indeed, U.S. oil production has surpassed several times the proven reserves in 1950.

7   Coal is subdivided into two groups: hard coal (anthracite and bituminous) and soft coal (lignite and subbituminous).

8   British Petroleum maintains data on proven reserves of oil and gas for 48 and 50 countries, respectively, and production data for 48 and 47 countries, respectively. *International Energy Annual 2006* provided data on hard and soft coal reserves in 60 and 51 countries/regions and production data for 66 and 41 countries/regions, respectively (USEIA 2006, tables 8.2 and 5.1). Far fewer countries had data on reserves for the 10 metals and minerals considered; limited information came from the U.S. Geological Survey's 2006 Minerals Yearbook and Mineral Commodity Summaries (USGS 2006a, 2006b). Reserves data on bauxite, copper, lead, nickel, phosphate, tin, zinc, gold, silver, and iron ore were available for 12, 12, 10, 16, 15, 10, 7, 8, 7, and 15 countries, respectively.

9   The World Bank (1997) chose $T = 20$ in its study on indicators of environmentally sustainable development.

10   When data are missing, and if a country's forest area is less than 50 square kilometers, the value of production is assumed to be zero.

11   In Global FRA 2005, see the table titled "Designated Functions of Forest—Primary Function 2005," http://www.fao.org/forestry/32035/en/. In Global FRA 2000, see table 15, "Forest in Protected Areas/Available for Wood Supply."

12   When data are missing, and if country's forest area is less than 50 square kilometers, the value of nontimber forest benefits is assumed to be zero.

13   http://www.worldbank.org/environmentaleconomics.

References

Bohm, B., A. Gleiss, M. Wagner, and D. Ziegler. 2002. "Disaggregated Capital Stock Estimation for Austria—Methods, Concepts and Results." *Applied Economics* 34 (1): 23–37.

Dimaranan, Betina V., ed. 2006. *Global Trade, Assistance, and Production: The GTAP 6 Data Base.* West Lafayette, IN: Center for Global Trade Analysis, Purdue University.

Eurostat. 2002. *Natural Resource Accounts for Forests.* Luxembourg: Office of the European Communities.

Fankhauser, S. 1994. "The Social Costs of Greenhouse Gas Emissions: An Expected Value Approach." *Energy Journal* 15 (2): 157–84.

Fortech (Forestry Technical Services). 1997. "Marketing of PNG Forest Products: Milestone 2 Report: Logging and Processing Costs in Papua New Guinea." Fortech, Canberra.

Global Witness. 2001. *Taylor-Made: The Pivotal Role of Liberia's Forests and Flag of Convenience in Regional Conflict.* London: Global Witness.

Hamilton, K., and J. M. Hartwick. 2005. "Investing Exhaustible Resource Rents and the Path of Consumption." *Canadian Journal of Economics* 38 (2): 615–21.

Haripriya, G. S. 1998. "Forest Resource Accounting: Preliminary Estimates for the State of Maharashtra." *Development Policy Review* 16: 131–51.

Jorgenson, Dale W., and Barbara M. Fraumeni. 1992. "The Output of the Education Sector." In *Output Measurement in the Service Sectors*, ed. Z. Griliches, 303–41. NBER Studies in Income and Wealth, vol. 56. Chicago: University of Chicago Press.

Kunte, A., K. Hamilton, J. Dixon, and M. Clemens. 1998. "Estimating National Wealth: Methodology and Results." Environment Department Paper 57, World Bank, Washington, DC.

Lampietti, J., and J. Dixon. 1995. "To See the Forest for the Trees: A Guide to Non-Timber Forest Benefits." Environment Department Paper 13, World Bank, Washington, DC.

Lane, Philip R., and Gian Maria Milesi-Ferretti. 2007. "The External Wealth of Nations Mark II: Revised and Extended Estimates of Foreign Assets and Liabilities, 1970–2004." *Journal of International Economics* 73 (2): 223–50.

Larson, Donald F., Rita Butzer, Yair Mundlak, and Al Crego. 2000. "A Cross-Country Database for Sector Investment and Capital." *World Bank Economic Review* 14 (2): 371–91.

Lopina, Olga, Andrei Ptichnikov, and Alexander Voropayev. 2003. *Illegal Logging in Northwestern Russia and Exports of Russian Forest Products to Sweden.* Moscow: World Wildlife Fund Russia.

Mas, Matilde, Francisco Perez, and Ezequiel Uriel. 2000. "Estimation of the Stock of Capital in Spain." *Review of Income and Wealth* 46 (1): 103–16.

Merlo, M., and L. Croitoru, eds. 2005. *Valuing Mediterranean Forests: Towards Total Economic Value.* Wallingford, UK: CABI Publishing.

Pearce, D. W., and D. Ulph. 1999. "A Social Discount Rate for the United Kingdom." In *Environmental Economics: Essays in Ecological Economics and Sustainable Development*, ed. D. W. Pearce, 268–85. Cheltenham, UK: Edward Elgar.

Rosengrant, M. W., M. Agcaoili-Sombilla, and N. D. Perez. 1995. "Global Food Projections to 2020: Implications for Investment." Food, Agriculture, and the Environment Discussion Paper 5, International Food Policy Research Institute, Washington, DC.

Tay, John, John Healey, and Colin Price. 2001. "Financial Assessment of Reduced Impact Logging Techniques in Sabah, Malaysia." In *Applying Reduced Impact Logging to Advance Sustainable Forest Management.* Bangkok: Food and Agriculture Organization of the United Nations.

UNFAO (Food and Agriculture Organization of the United Nations). 1997. *State of the World's Forests 1997.* Rome: UNFAO.

———. 2001. *Global Forest Resources Assessment 2000: Main Report.* FAO Forestry Paper 140. Rome: UNFAO.

———. 2006. *Global Forest Resources Assessment 2005.* FAO Forestry Paper 147. Rome: UNFAO.

USEIA (U.S. Energy Information Administration). 2006. *International Energy Annual 2006.* Washington, DC: U.S. Department of Energy.

USGS (U.S. Geological Survey). 2006a. *2006 Minerals Yearbook.* Washington, DC: U.S. Department of the Interior.

———. 2006b. *Mineral Commodity Summaries.* Washington, DC: U.S. Department of the Interior.

Ward, M. 1976. *The Measurement of Capital: The Methodology of Capital Stock Estimates in OECD Countries.* Paris: OECD.

Whiteman, Adrian. 1996. "Economic Rent and the Appropriate Level of Forest Products Royalties in 1996." Jakarta: Indonesia-UK Tropical Forest Management Programme.

World Bank. 1997. *Expanding the Measure of Wealth: Indicators of Environmentally Sustainable Development.* Environmentally Sustainable Development Studies and Monographs Series No. 17. Washington, DC: World Bank.

———. 2006. *Where Is the Wealth of Nations? Measuring Capital for the 21st Century.* Washington, DC: World Bank.

Total Wealth, Population, and Per Capita Wealth in 1995, 2000, and 2005

The following table shows estimates of total wealth and wealth per capita by economy for 1995, 2000, and 2005. Estimates are in 2005 U.S. dollars. The data in this table are summarized by grouping economies by geographic region and income group. The data in table B.2, summarized in chapters 1 and 2, are for the set of countries for which wealth accounts are available from 1995 to 2005.

TABLE B.1
Wealth and Wealth Per Capita by Economy

Economy/Group	Total Wealth (2005 US$ billions)			Population			Wealth Per Capita (2005 US$)		
	1995	2000	2005	1995	2000	2005	1995	2000	2005
Albania	–	106	166	–	3,061,775	3,129,678	–	34,462	53,096
Algeria	1,019	1,049	994	28,270,780	30,463,134	32,853,798	36,029	34,443	30,249
Angola	–	–	220	–	–	15,941,392	–	–	13,804
Argentina	2,610	2,707	2,761	34,834,902	36,895,712	38,747,148	74,917	73,373	71,252
Armenia	–	58	88	–	3,082,000	3,016,312	–	18,677	29,190
Australia	7,525	9,155	10,547	18,072,000	19,153,000	20,329,000	416,394	478,012	518,805
Austria	3,944	4,353	4,698	7,953,067	8,011,561	8,233,300	495,873	543,344	570,654
Azerbaijan	–	89	128	–	8,048,535	8,388,000	–	11,035	15,298
Bahrain	126	144	147	584,187	672,008	726,617	215,898	214,672	201,841
Bangladesh	642	787	1,008	116,454,619	128,915,876	141,822,276	5,517	6,104	7,109
Belarus	–	346	467	–	10,005,000	9,775,591	–	34,576	47,788
Belgium	4,757	5,345	5,893	10,136,800	10,252,000	10,478,650	469,275	521,329	562,363
Belize	11	15	19	216,500	249,800	291,800	50,116	59,956	64,527
Benin	54	69	80	6,200,647	7,196,955	8,438,853	8,680	9,647	9,524
Bhutan	5	8	10	507,032	558,565	637,013	10,473	14,159	16,423
Bolivia	122	143	138	7,481,694	8,316,648	9,182,015	16,334	17,175	15,068
Botswana	70	84	104	1,615,528	1,754,002	1,764,926	43,453	47,984	58,895
Brazil	11,669	13,264	14,752	161,375,961	173,857,672	186,404,913	72,307	76,293	79,142

Brunei Darussalam	105	103	87	294,975	333,463	373,819	356,457	308,598	232,275
Bulgaria	–	378	495	–	8,060,000	7,740,000	–	46,892	63,993
Burkina Faso	56	81	115	9,831,857	11,291,615	13,227,835	5,662	7,207	8,661
Burundi	16	14	17	6,159,060	6,486,071	7,547,515	2,519	2,152	2,191
Cameroon	191	232	281	13,302,275	14,856,343	16,321,863	14,334	15,604	17,238
Canada	13,329	15,451	17,399	29,354,000	30,769,700	32,299,000	454,068	502,141	538,697
Cape Verde	–	–	21	–	–	506,807	–	–	41,418
Central African Republic	23	27	27	3,414,404	3,777,405	4,037,747	6,844	7,175	6,706
Chad	50	62	49	7,033,631	8,215,517	9,748,931	7,177	7,503	4,994
Chile	1,195	1,526	1,660	14,394,935	15,411,830	16,295,102	82,990	99,004	101,901
China	11,861	18,069	25,091	1,204,855,000	1,262,645,000	1,304,500,000	9,845	14,310	19,234
Colombia	1,906	2,112	2,454	38,258,569	41,682,594	44,945,790	49,807	50,673	54,594
Comoros	7	7	9	486,193	540,327	600,490	13,541	13,721	14,530
Congo, Dem. Rep.	120	110	132	44,998,561	50,052,102	57,548,744	2,659	2,194	2,294
Congo, Rep.	25	22	24	2,915,594	3,437,797	3,998,904	8,553	6,456	6,017
Costa Rica	226	271	340	3,474,897	3,928,797	4,327,228	65,129	68,975	78,604
Côte d'Ivoire	224	251	263	14,755,305	16,734,951	18,153,867	15,213	15,005	14,463
Croatia	–	620	740	650,850	4,502,500	4,443,350	–	137,597	166,497
Cyprus	197	241	–	–	694,000	–	303,431	347,611	–
Czech Republic	–	1,571	1,851	–	10,273,300	10,234,092	–	152,942	180,820
Denmark	3,321	3,672	4,024	5,228,000	5,337,344	5,415,978	635,290	687,959	742,954
Dominica	5	5	5	73,000	71,326	72,000	62,790	71,186	76,084
Dominican Republic	371	499	638	8,013,383	8,743,983	9,469,601	46,317	57,059	67,354
Ecuador	443	482	577	11,396,394	12,305,544	13,228,423	38,888	39,179	43,634

(continued)

TABLE B.1 *(continued)*

Economy/Group	Total Wealth (2005 US$ billions)			Population			Wealth Per Capita (2005 US$)		
	1995	2000	2005	1995	2000	2005	1995	2000	2005
Egypt, Arab Rep.	1,051	1,340	1,579	61,224,735	67,285,498	74,032,884	17,167	19,916	21,328
El Salvador	257	307	364	5,668,606	6,280,482	6,880,951	45,399	48,843	52,947
Ethiopia	139	171	245	56,530,000	64,298,000	71,256,000	2,451	2,656	3,439
Fiji	38	39	36	767,936	810,736	847,706	49,055	47,646	43,003
Finland	2,128	2,494	2,992	5,108,000	5,176,198	5,246,100	416,680	481,870	570,256
France	28,649	31,897	35,699	57,844,000	58,895,517	60,873,000	495,275	541,594	586,448
Gabon	73	87	81	1,118,736	1,272,094	1,383,841	65,472	68,546	58,504
Gambia, The	6	7	9	1,115,216	1,315,884	1,517,079	5,346	5,210	5,831
Georgia	–	84	119	–	4,720,061	4,474,404	–	17,860	26,607
Germany	39,320	43,269	45,127	81,642,000	82,210,000	82,469,400	481,616	526,329	547,201
Ghana	128	162	210	17,725,205	19,866,984	22,112,805	7,220	8,157	9,475
Greece	3,208	3,732	4,362	10,634,000	10,917,500	11,104,000	301,632	341,860	392,815
Grenada	6	8	8	98,000	101,400	106,500	60,691	74,250	78,030
Guatemala	364	445	548	9,970,367	11,166,376	12,599,059	36,526	39,839	43,483
Guinea	39	49	56	7,323,222	8,202,628	9,002,656	5,280	5,996	6,271
Guinea-Bissau	7	6	6	1,189,331	1,365,650	1,586,344	6,005	4,753	3,740
Guyana	11	13	14	732,321	743,683	751,218	15,110	17,899	19,210
Haiti	81	82	90	7,391,265	7,938,791	8,527,777	11,019	10,340	10,512
Honduras	102	133	183	5,624,954	6,424,340	7,204,723	18,202	20,755	25,387
Hong Kong SAR, China	1,828	2,031	2,507	6,156,100	6,665,000	6,943,600	296,985	304,752	360,981

164

Hungary	1,206	1,373	1,745	10,328,965	10,210,971	10,087,050	116,792	134,456	173,007
Iceland	176	221	268	268,000	281,000	296,750	656,647	787,113	902,960
India	6,894	9,170	11,536	932,180,000	1,015,923,000	1,094,583,000	7,396	9,026	10,539
Indonesia	3,110	3,462	4,360	192,750,000	206,265,000	220,558,000	16,132	16,782	19,769
Iran, Islamic Rep.	1,548	1,461	2,282	58,954,000	63,664,000	68,251,085	26,255	22,950	33,437
Ireland	1,456	1,948	2,492	3,608,850	3,805,400	4,159,100	403,463	511,867	599,115
Israel	1,659	1,951	2,267	5,545,000	6,289,000	6,923,600	299,106	310,266	327,471
Italy	24,542	27,236	29,203	56,846,100	56,948,600	58,607,050	431,728	478,252	498,277
Jamaica	170	183	212	2,480,000	2,589,389	2,654,500	68,533	70,647	79,763
Japan	59,056	64,591	70,116	125,439,000	126,870,000	127,774,000	470,797	509,112	548,751
Jordan	151	197	278	4,195,000	4,797,500	5,411,500	35,959	41,103	51,454
Kenya	246	311	366	27,225,891	30,689,332	34,255,722	9,039	10,131	10,684
Korea, Rep.	7,169	9,188	11,986	45,093,000	47,008,111	48,294,143	158,985	195,448	248,180
Kuwait	739	832	827	1,802,000	2,190,000	2,535,446	410,166	379,842	326,320
Kyrgyz Republic	–	36	54	–	4,915,300	5,143,500	–	7,254	10,563
Lao PDR	–	–	46	–	–	5,663,910	–	–	8,068
Latvia	–	179	279	–	2,372,000	2,300,500	–	75,566	121,274
Lesotho	29	31	37	1,692,269	1,787,504	1,794,769	16,958	17,613	20,426
Liberia	–	11	11	–	3,065,441	3,283,267	–	3,431	3,368
Lithuania	–	327	454	–	3,499,527	3,414,300	–	93,437	132,915
Luxembourg	286	363	419	409,500	438,000	456,710	698,702	827,661	917,530
Macao SAR, China	63	72	87	412,832	443,537	460,162	151,472	163,005	189,948

(continued)

TABLE B.1 (continued)

Economy/Group	Total Wealth (2005 US$ billions)			Population			Wealth Per Capita (2005 US$)		
	1995	2000	2005	1995	2000	2005	1995	2000	2005
Macedonia, FYR	–	101	118	–	2,009,514	2,034,060	–	50,330	57,797
Madagascar	73	82	65	13,945,501	16,195,064	18,605,921	5,248	5,080	3,489
Malawi	42	50	45	10,110,516	11,512,454	12,883,935	4,148	4,343	3,471
Malaysia	1,059	1,209	1,642	20,362,330	22,997,185	25,347,368	52,026	52,557	64,767
Maldives	–	6	9	–	290,209	329,198	–	22,087	26,573
Mali	58	75	93	10,146,967	11,646,917	13,518,416	5,716	6,456	6,916
Malta	77	95	104	378,000	390,000	403,500	203,560	244,702	257,968
Mauritania	24	30	34	2,300,013	2,644,513	3,068,742	10,472	11,315	11,000
Mauritius	63	80	105	1,122,457	1,186,873	1,243,253	56,069	67,157	84,193
Mexico	10,130	12,323	13,544	91,145,000	97,966,000	103,089,133	111,142	125,788	131,385
Moldova	–	46	68	–	4,145,437	3,876,661	–	11,053	17,421
Mongolia	22	32	34	2,275,000	2,398,000	2,554,000	9,604	13,456	13,381
Morocco	710	774	955	26,434,672	28,465,720	30,142,709	26,869	27,185	31,677
Mozambique	56	79	108	15,853,741	17,910,521	19,792,295	3,511	4,395	5,476
Namibia	87	102	121	1,651,547	1,894,436	2,031,252	52,596	53,759	59,557
Nepal	99	122	152	21,682,060	24,430,617	27,132,629	4,543	5,012	5,584
Netherlands	7,444	8,857	9,687	15,460,000	15,925,431	16,319,850	481,476	556,176	593,547
New Zealand	1,238	1,445	1,697	3,673,400	3,857,800	4,098,900	337,137	374,676	414,113
Nicaragua	56	81	101	4,476,892	4,920,285	5,149,311	12,528	16,542	19,593
Niger	44	53	63	9,929,356	11,782,384	13,956,977	4,425	4,469	4,532

Nigeria	1,403	1,288	1,552	109,010,060	124,772,607	141,356,083	12,866	10,326	10,982
Norway	3,338	3,739	3,984	4,360,000	4,491,000	4,623,300	765,604	832,478	861,797
Oman	322	362	379	2,177,264	2,442,000	2,566,981	147,664	148,359	147,560
Pakistan	1,283	1,484	1,900	122,374,953	138,080,000	155,772,000	10,482	10,748	12,198
Panama	146	194	243	2,670,412	2,949,948	3,231,502	54,639	65,763	75,287
Papua New Guinea	65	64	53	4,687,236	5,298,867	5,887,138	13,928	12,123	8,989
Peru	910	1,076	1,256	23,836,863	25,952,191	27,968,244	38,179	41,443	44,912
Philippines	1,171	1,361	1,636	68,395,835	75,766,144	83,054,478	17,114	17,966	19,698
Poland	-	4,359	5,188	-	38,453,800	38,165,450	-	113,350	135,941
Portugal	2,541	3,004	3,226	10,027,000	10,225,803	10,549,450	253,372	293,743	305,832
Romania	-	1,383	1,750	-	22,443,000	21,634,350	-	61,643	80,906
Russian Federation	-	7,638	10,471	-	146,303,000	143,113,650	-	52,207	73,166
Rwanda	27	36	48	5,439,079	8,024,511	9,037,690	4,923	4,522	5,326
Saudi Arabia	2,938	3,241	3,378	18,508,698	20,660,703	23,118,994	158,730	156,886	146,105
Senegal	110	129	159	9,119,513	10,342,831	11,658,172	12,091	12,502	13,654
Seychelles	11	15	14	75,304	81,131	84,494	152,307	182,002	163,767
Sierra Leone	16	15	22	4,136,745	4,508,987	5,525,478	3,749	3,327	4,025
Singapore	770	1,051	1,307	3,526,000	4,017,700	4,341,800	218,461	261,663	300,975
Slovak Republic	-	606	767	-	5,388,741	5,387,000	-	112,471	142,373
South Africa	2,974	3,363	4,042	39,120,000	44,000,000	46,888,200	76,032	76,427	86,199
Spain	12,791	15,108	17,723	39,387,000	40,263,200	43,398,150	324,739	375,243	408,385
Sri Lanka	273	333	425	18,136,000	19,359,000	19,625,384	15,068	17,226	21,640

(continued)

167

TABLE B.1 (continued)

Economy/Group	Total Wealth (2005 US$ billions)			Population			Wealth Per Capita (2005 US$)		
	1995	2000	2005	1995	2000	2005	1995	2000	2005
St. Kitts and Nevis	5	6	6	41,000	44,286	48,000	111,618	130,608	132,194
St. Lucia	11	13	15	145,437	155,996	164,791	78,845	82,660	92,122
St. Vincent and the Grenadines	6	6	7	112,978	115,949	119,051	49,027	54,275	59,553
Sudan	284	348	440	29,352,022	32,902,415	36,232,945	9,671	10,570	12,148
Swaziland	36	42	46	900,000	1,045,000	1,131,000	39,692	40,460	40,393
Sweden	4,368	4,996	5,667	8,831,000	8,869,000	9,024,040	494,629	563,351	627,950
Switzerland	4,720	5,141	5,480	7,041,000	7,184,222	7,437,100	670,303	715,610	736,795
Syrian Arab Republic	302	345	388	14,754,705	16,812,824	19,043,382	20,441	20,536	20,369
Tajikistan	–	27	44	–	6,172,835	6,550,213	–	4,388	6,687
Thailand	1,649	1,817	2,426	58,335,951	61,438,314	64,232,758	28,272	29,571	37,765
Togo	29	36	41	4,512,159	5,363,751	6,145,004	6,459	6,758	6,616
Tonga	4	5	6	96,865	100,190	102,311	45,555	49,432	55,876
Trinidad and Tobago	111	143	152	1,259,324	1,284,700	1,305,236	87,752	111,208	116,119
Tunisia	293	369	475	8,957,500	9,563,500	10,029,000	32,660	38,621	47,389
Turkey	–	6,248	8,275	–	67,420,000	72,065,000	–	92,677	114,830
Uganda	89	124	172	20,892,272	24,308,745	28,816,229	4,272	5,106	5,957
Ukraine	–	968	1,380	–	49,175,848	47,075,295	–	19,693	29,322
United Arab Emirates	979	1,285	1,585	2,411,000	3,247,000	4,533,145	406,126	395,660	349,698
United Kingdom	29,265	34,411	39,908	58,250,000	59,742,980	60,226,500	502,395	575,979	662,624
United States	155,865	188,420	217,623	266,278,000	282,224,000	296,410,404	585,347	667,626	734,195

Uruguay	270	291	287	3,218,193	3,300,847	3,305,723	83,832	88,219	86,684
Uzbekistan	–	152	139	–	24,650,000	26,167,369	–	6,161	5,316
Vanuatu	–	6	6	–	191,457	211,367	–	33,371	28,900
Venezuela, RB	1,765	1,800	1,855	22,043,000	24,311,000	26,577,000	80,069	74,033	69,795
Vietnam	–	–	779	–	–	83,104,900	–	–	9,374
Zambia	91	102	113	9,559,420	10,702,114	11,668,457	9,539	9,533	9,678
Zimbabwe	76	81	65	11,819,622	12,595,084	13,009,534	6,435	6,467	4,988
World	504,745	615,707	707,726	4,884,435,862	5,679,671,767	6,128,328,330	103,337	108,405	115,484
Low income	2,447	3,187	4,670	462,526,066	560,925,206	715,963,412	5,290	5,681	6,523
Middle income	70,744	108,760	134,909	3,496,930,885	4,140,184,571	4,399,856,652	20,230	26,269	30,662
Lower middle income	33,950	45,490	60,228	2,996,609,737	3,297,080,219	3,519,642,686	11,330	13,797	17,112
Upper middle income	36,794	63,270	74,681	500,321,148	843,104,352	880,213,965	73,540	75,044	84,844
Low and middle income	73,191	111,947	139,579	3,959,456,950	4,701,109,778	5,115,820,063	18,485	23,813	27,284
East Asia and the Pacific	18,979	26,064	36,115	1,552,526,153	1,637,910,893	1,796,063,936	12,225	15,913	20,108
Europe and Central Asia	–	22,525	29,684	–	408,537,632	408,064,333	–	55,135	72,744
Latin America and the Caribbean	32,848	37,985	42,079	459,175,523	496,424,869	531,341,503	71,536	76,517	79,194
Middle East and North Africa	5,073	5,536	6,951	202,791,392	221,052,176	239,764,358	25,015	25,044	28,992
South Asia	9,197	11,911	15,040	1,211,334,664	1,327,557,267	1,439,901,500	7,592	8,972	10,445
Sub-Saharan Africa	7,094	7,926	9,709	533,629,219	609,626,940	700,684,434	13,295	13,002	13,857

(continued)

TABLE B.1 (continued)

Country/Group	Total Wealth (2005 US$ billions)			Population			Wealth Per Capita (2005 US$)		
	1995	2000	2005	1995	2000	2005	1995	2000	2005
High income	431,554	503,760	568,147	924,978,912	978,561,990	1,012,508,266	466,556	514,796	561,129
High income non-OECD	9,914	12,172	13,566	43,706,230	53,831,611	58,676,250	226,822	226,121	231,203
High income OECD	421,641	491,587	554,581	881,272,682	924,730,378	953,832,017	478,445	531,601	581,424

Source: Authors.
Note: — = not available.

TABLE B.2
Regional and Income Group Aggregates Using a Balanced Sample of 124 Countries

Group	Total Wealth (2005 US$ billions)			Population			Wealth Per Capita (2005 US$)		
	1995	2000	2005	1995	2000	2005	1995	2000	2005
World	504,548	590,121	673,593	4,883,785,012	5,246,728,488	5,591,158,713	103,311	112,474	120,475
Low income	2,447	2,962	3,597	462,526,066	522,121,630	586,050,253	5,290	5,672	6,138
Middle income	70,744	86,437	105,206	3,496,930,885	3,766,903,408	4,012,664,636	20,230	22,947	26,218
Lower middle income	33,950	44,127	58,023	2,996,609,737	3,224,364,897	3,432,693,572	11,330	13,686	16,903
Upper middle income	36,794	42,310	47,183	500,321,148	542,538,511	579,971,064	73,540	77,986	81,354
Low and middle income	73,191	89,399	108,803	3,959,456,950	4,289,025,039	4,598,714,889	18,485	20,844	23,659
East Asia and the Pacific	18,979	26,057	35,284	1,552,526,153	1,637,719,436	1,707,083,759	12,225	15,911	20,669
Europe and Central Asia	—	—	—	—	—	—	—	—	—
Latin America and the Caribbean	32,848	37,985	42,079	459,175,523	496,424,869	531,341,503	71,536	76,517	79,194
Middle East and North Africa	5,073	5,536	6,951	202,791,392	221,052,176	239,764,358	25,015	25,044	28,992
South Asia	9,197	11,905	15,031	1,211,334,664	1,327,267,058	1,439,572,302	7,592	8,970	10,441
Sub-Saharan Africa	7,094	7,916	9,457	533,629,219	606,561,499	680,952,968	13,295	13,050	13,888
High income	431,357	500,722	564,790	924,328,062	957,703,449	992,443,824	466,671	522,836	569,090
High income non-OECD	9,716	11,312	12,826	43,055,380	48,635,111	54,232,900	225,664	232,583	236,504
High income OECD	421,641	489,410	551,964	881,272,682	909,068,338	938,210,925	478,445	538,364	588,315

Source: Authors.
Note: – = not available.

171

Wealth Estimates in 2005

The following table shows estimates of total wealth and its subcomponents by economy for the year 2005. Estimates are in 2005 U.S. dollars per capita. The data in this table are summarized by grouping economies by geographic region and income category.

TABLE C.1
Wealth Estimates for 2005

Economy/Group	Population	Subsoil Assets	Timber	Nontimber Forest Resources	Protected Areas	Crop Land	Pasture Land	Natural Capital	Produced Capital + Urban Land	Net Foreign Assets	Intangible Capital	Total Wealth
Albania	3,129,678	1	62	626	574	1,444	2,360	5,068	6,975	−386	41,439	53,096
Algeria	32,853,798	13,293	188	25	384	903	1,022	15,815	11,046	1,135	2,254	30,249
Angola	15,941,392	11,052	392	872	80	632	279	13,307	2,897	−1,013	−1,387	13,804
Argentina	38,747,148	2,727	266	197	320	4,996	1,760	10,267	10,815	−211	50,381	71,252
Armenia	3,016,312	116	9	20	373	1,580	1,041	3,139	4,185	−489	22,356	29,190
Australia	20,329,000	20,328	804	3,590	2,932	6,138	6,186	39,979	111,671	−19,225	386,381	518,805
Austria	8,233,300	566	1,201	211	3,272	1,810	2,005	9,065	112,799	−8,033	456,824	570,654
Azerbaijan	8,388,000	9,194	1	27	212	1,345	904	11,684	4,535	−1,115	195	15,298
Bahrain	726,617	82,923	0	0	182	195	361	83,662	43,365	15,553	59,261	201,841
Bangladesh	141,822,276	190	28	24	16	640	495	1,394	1,007	−131	4,838	7,109
Belarus	9,775,591	773	106	243	560	2,890	1,400	5,972	9,812	−415	32,420	47,788
Belgium	10,478,650	..	248	29	222	2,480	1,954	4,933	98,822	11,095	447,515	562,363
Belize	291,800	0	2,027	1,356	6,468	13,618	257	23,726	9,258	−4,374	35,916	64,527
Benin	8,438,853	0	206	54	562	1,686	117	2,625	1,051	−194	6,042	9,524
Bhutan	637,013	0	8,431	1,234	2,407	1,129	805	14,005	6,319	−93	−3,808	16,423
Bolivia	9,182,015	2,191	951	1,466	443	2,563	691	8,305	2,000	−855	5,618	15,068
Botswana	1,764,926	982	414	1,487	888	357	1,294	5,420	20,988	4,541	27,947	58,895
Brazil	186,404,913	2,321	2,927	599	1,042	6,830	1,260	14,978	11,330	−1,735	54,569	79,142
Brunei Darussalam	373,819	172,958	991	323	8,337	181	227	183,018	73,831	121,649	−146,222	232,275
Bulgaria	7,740,000	556	133	127	938	1,834	1,971	5,560	10,079	−1,652	50,006	63,993

Burkina Faso	13,227,835	0	87	120	211	620	301	1,339	879	-112	6,554	8,661
Burundi	7,547,515	2	1,054	3	13	1,541	84	2,697	166	-145	-527	2,191
Cameroon	16,321,863	910	580	286	1,165	1,718	539	5,198	2,343	-412	10,110	17,238
Canada	32,299,000	12,644	3,980	4,302	11,293	2,603	2,103	36,924	89,811	-2,977	414,938	538,697
Cape Verde	506,807	0	0	41	17	451	409	919	5,797	-1,509	36,212	41,418
Central African Republic	4,037,747	..	724	1,337	2,007	1,151	642	5,861	515	-236	566	6,706
Chad	9,748,931	2,231	678	275	140	785	528	4,637	1,308	-494	-457	4,994
Chile	16,295,102	9,563	3,628	245	1,793	2,554	1,086	18,870	19,268	-2,007	65,770	101,901
China	1,304,500,000	804	231	45	107	2,501	325	4,013	6,017	284	8,921	19,234
Colombia	44,945,790	1,488	837	321	993	2,942	1,033	7,614	7,127	-853	40,706	54,594
Comoros	600,490	0	24	11	330	1,278	122	1,765	1,301	-251	11,714	14,530
Congo, Dem. Rep.	57,548,744	77	443	546	19	500	14	1,599	200	-183	678	2,294
Congo, Rep.	3,998,904	11,816	713	1,333	10	785	21	14,679	4,639	-2,032	-11,269	6,017
Costa Rica	4,327,228	..	2	133	1,026	6,903	1,371	9,437	10,703	-1,552	60,016	78,604
Côte d'Ivoire	18,153,867	464	584	138	39	2,668	93	3,987	1,473	-594	9,598	14,463
Croatia	4,443,350	1,923	351	119	445	1,580	1,141	5,559	25,231	-5,447	141,154	166,497
Czech Republic	10,234,092	332	513	433	924	1,542	852	4,595	44,254	-3,341	135,312	180,820
Denmark	5,415,978	8,536	217	587	2,463	2,808	5,005	19,616	130,827	1,288	591,224	742,954
Dominica	72,000	0	0	145	5,206	4,531	510	10,393	14,414	-4,312	55,588	76,084
Dominican Republic	9,469,601	418	217	35	1,028	1,997	1,055	4,750	8,041	-1,268	55,831	67,354

(continued)

175

TABLE C.1 (continued)

Economy/Group	Population	Subsoil Assets	Timber	Nontimber Forest Resources	Protected Areas	Crop Land	Pasture Land	Natural Capital	Produced Capital + Urban Land	Net Foreign Assets	Intangible Capital	Total Wealth
Ecuador	13,228,423	6,442	291	170	9,723	3,505	2,322	22,454	7,601	-1,843	15,422	43,634
Egypt, Arab Rep.	74,032,884	1,989	13	..	0	2,206	462	4,670	2,860	-63	13,860	21,328
El Salvador	6,880,951	0	40	9	18	1,780	2,094	3,941	5,201	-1,156	44,961	52,947
Ethiopia	71,256,000	2	8	48	261	522	281	1,123	324	-97	2,089	3,439
Fiji	847,706	384	1,131	282	333	8,302	1,183	11,616	8,693	-1,666	24,360	43,003
Finland	5,246,100	132	8,947	2,393	3,659	1,262	2,827	19,220	96,566	-5,642	460,111	570,256
France	60,873,000	71	251	125	2,646	2,995	2,522	8,609	93,619	2,561	481,658	586,448
Gabon	1,383,841	34,610	2,086	3,766	49	1,503	50	42,065	23,418	12	-6,991	58,504
Gambia, The	1,517,079	0	525	77	10	536	82	1,230	758	-554	4,396	5,831
Georgia	4,474,404	87	43	148	242	1,267	1,547	3,334	5,128	-930	19,076	26,607
Germany	82,469,400	535	205	97	1,935	1,391	1,552	5,716	98,285	6,219	436,981	547,201
Ghana	22,112,805	5	496	51	18	2,047	41	2,658	1,237	-257	5,838	9,475
Greece	11,104,000	405	205	157	458	4,319	2,435	7,980	74,237	-16,001	326,599	392,815
Grenada	106,500	0	0	9	66	1,915	94	2,083	23,375	-6,137	58,709	78,030
Guatemala	12,599,059	330	11,245	67	463	4,250	336	16,691	5,370	-370	21,792	43,483
Guinea	9,002,656	226	47	171	27	1,287	182	1,939	777	-357	3,911	6,271
Guinea-Bissau	1,586,344	0	304	299	85	1,164	226	2,078	604	-600	1,658	3,740
Guyana	751,218	649	5,854	4,813	160	10,000	406	21,882	4,106	-2,008	-4,770	19,210

Haiti	8,527,777	0	86	3	4	922	244	1,258	1,761	−165	7,657	10,512
Honduras	7,204,723	48	4,614	129	1,965	2,985	2,270	12,012	4,140	−590	9,825	25,387
Hong Kong SAR, China	6,943,600	0	10	0	0	0	0	10	77,653	63,268	220,051	360,981
Hungary	10,087,050	803	176	50	740	3,263	943	5,974	35,162	−9,425	141,296	173,007
Iceland	296,750	0	0	103	8,382	81	3,797	12,363	137,470	−45,995	799,123	902,960
India	1,094,583,000	353	195	17	145	1,391	602	2,704	1,980	−107	5,961	10,539
Indonesia	220,558,000	1,473	1,264	81	411	1,597	99	4,926	3,968	−523	11,398	19,769
Iran, Islamic Rep.	68,251,085	13,987	27	39	267	2,571	1,042	17,933	10,516	928	4,059	33,437
Ireland	4,159,100	290	380	80	304	1,123	9,013	11,189	112,374	−10,428	485,980	599,115
Israel	6,923,600	253	3	12	1,300	1,671	1,603	4,843	47,232	−3,495	278,892	327,471
Italy	58,607,050	525	323	81	2,158	3,012	1,403	7,502	89,860	−4,533	405,448	498,277
Jamaica	2,654,500	979	559	30	426	3,110	268	5,372	14,450	−2,840	62,781	79,763
Japan	127,774,000	47	135	92	128	652	1,041	2,094	135,866	11,920	398,870	548,751
Jordan	5,411,500	74	0	4	759	1,275	579	2,690	6,550	−3,750	45,963	51,454
Kenya	34,255,722	2	0	24	557	1,070	1,087	2,739	1,298	−83	6,729	10,684
Korea, Rep.	48,294,143	26	54	58	322	1,082	1,099	2,642	58,636	−3,252	190,155	248,180
Kuwait	2,535,446	212,013	0	1	222	369	507	213,112	58,115	62,476	−7,383	326,320
Kyrgyz Republic	5,143,500	69	18	42	96	1,514	1,254	2,992	1,210	−335	6,696	10,563
Lao PDR	5,663,910	..	1,370	653	554	1,739	128	4,444	1,208	−516	2,931	8,068
Latvia	2,300,500	0	0	317	3,444	1,560	2,025	7,346	23,260	−3,990	94,658	121,274

(continued)

TABLE C.1 (continued)

Economy/Group	Population	Subsoil Assets	Timber	Nontimber Forest Resources	Protected Areas	Crop Land	Pasture Land	Natural Capital	Produced Capital + Urban Land	Net Foreign Assets	Intangible Capital	Total Wealth
Lesotho	1,794,769	0	8	1	1	137	178	325	4,705	-1,295	16,691	20,426
Liberia	3,283,267	..	2,012	198	16	955	20	3,201	217	-1,709	1,659	3,368
Lithuania	3,414,300	347	499	168	958	2,080	1,962	6,014	21,265	-3,129	108,764	132,915
Luxembourg	456,710	0	255	85	1,413	718	3,621	6,092	213,425	99,449	598,563	917,530
Macao SAR, China	460,162	0	0	0	0	0	0	0	51,849	..	138,099	189,948
Macedonia, FYR	2,034,060	0	111	107	235	2,380	809	3,642	8,018	-1,266	47,404	57,797
Madagascar	18,605,921	0	486	161	41	693	537	1,918	551	-164	1,185	3,489
Malawi	12,883,935	0	279	58	60	716	57	1,170	528	-245	2,018	3,471
Malaysia	25,347,368	10,102	571	186	879	982	30	12,750	16,824	-750	35,943	64,767
Maldives	329,198	0	0	1	0	989	0	990	7,402	-726	18,907	26,573
Mali	13,518,416	0	84	208	64	704	846	1,907	990	-242	4,261	6,916
Malta	403,500	0	0	0	37	597	3,649	4,283	45,063	3,392	205,230	257,968
Mauritania	3,068,742	1,332	433	16	89	143	2,002	4,015	1,701	-1,241	6,525	11,000
Mauritius	1,243,253	0	8	343	288	8,592	148	9,379	14,841	419	59,555	84,193
Mexico	103,089,133	3,525	1	149	316	1,360	1,290	6,641	21,320	-3,085	106,508	131,385
Moldova	3,876,661	3	5	21	56	2,853	1,211	4,148	3,794	-439	9,919	17,421
Mongolia	2,554,000	1,186	154	897	443	168	2,629	5,477	3,675	-546	4,775	13,381
Morocco	30,142,709	71	81	35	18	1,559	683	2,448	5,984	-381	23,626	31,677
Mozambique	19,792,295	118	298	227	12	520	72	1,248	708	-309	3,830	5,476

Namibia	2,031,252	231	0	835	826	783	2,515	5,191	8,280	847	45,238	59,557
Nepal	27,132,629	0	351	28	433	1,117	534	2,463	828	-32	2,325	5,584
Netherlands	16,319,850	7,061	24	25	1,082	2,116	2,885	13,193	109,658	-1,676	472,371	593,547
New Zealand	4,098,900	3,675	1,707	988	19,395	2,210	25,005	52,979	76,281	-21,271	306,124	414,113
Nicaragua	5,149,311	21	738	216	549	2,307	898	4,730	3,127	-759	12,494	19,593
Niger	13,956,977	..	53	26	160	720	472	1,430	386	-144	2,859	4,532
Nigeria	141,356,083	3,940	95	14	17	1,859	116	6,042	1,698	-50	3,292	10,982
Norway	4,623,300	99,706	669	1,417	4,788	505	3,078	110,162	183,078	36,436	532,121	861,797
Oman	2,566,981	71,631	0	16	3,456	872	1,159	77,134	22,987	2,396	45,043	147,560
Pakistan	155,772,000	467	78	6	286	1,194	1,325	3,355	1,449	-205	7,600	12,198
Panama	3,231,502	0	1,424	315	2,611	2,338	1,255	7,944	11,672	-4,245	59,916	75,287
Papua New Guinea	5,887,138	2,618	1,361	1,146	319	3,112	13	8,569	2,547	-543	-1,584	8,989
Peru	27,968,244	1,047	1,028	583	603	1,988	568	5,818	7,160	-1,235	33,169	44,912
Philippines	83,054,478	139	355	17	302	2,582	72	3,468	2,745	-592	14,076	19,698
Poland	38,165,450	1,126	375	68	2,306	2,388	2,631	8,894	20,526	-3,414	109,935	135,941
Portugal	10,549,450	37	469	170	655	1,866	1,007	4,204	59,939	-12,359	254,047	305,832
Romania	21,634,350	2,353	486	70	297	2,444	3,408	9,058	14,292	-1,403	58,959	80,906
Russian Federation	143,113,650	24,238	326	1,353	2,380	1,665	1,356	31,317	17,712	-227	24,364	73,166
Rwanda	9,037,690	..	525	26	114	2,050	232	2,947	488	-112	2,003	5,326
Saudi Arabia	23,118,994	86,620	0	54	9,090	686	562	97,012	33,000	11,185	4,908	146,105

(continued)

179

TABLE C.1 *(continued)*

Economy/Group	Population	Subsoil Assets	Timber	Nontimber Forest Resources	Protected Areas	Crop Land	Pasture Land	Natural Capital	Produced Capital + Urban Land	Net Foreign Assets	Intangible Capital	Total Wealth
Senegal	11,658,172	6	496	175	102	584	258	1,621	1,520	−311	10,825	13,654
Seychelles	84,494	0	0	113	1,357	348	36	1,854	33,767	−12,804	140,950	163,767
Sierra Leone	5,525,478	0	201	112	8	991	51	1,363	251	−306	2,717	4,025
Singapore	4,341,800	0	0	..	2	..	0	2	81,405	54,719	164,849	300,975
Slovak Republic	5,387,000	102	146	121	2,190	1,491	929	4,979	31,954	−4,824	110,263	142,373
South Africa	46,888,200	2,595	89	47	93	1,915	985	5,723	11,087	−768	70,157	86,199
Spain	43,398,150	58	116	315	1,095	4,004	1,883	7,471	82,194	−11,999	330,718	408,385
Sri Lanka	19,625,384	..	58	21	640	1,185	170	2,075	3,371	−476	16,670	21,640
St. Kitts and Nevis	48,000	0	0	25	0	4,370	0	4,395	48,800	−17,047	96,045	132,194
St. Lucia	164,791	0	0	25	0	0	0	25	16,781	−6,176	81,493	92,122
St. Vincent and the Grenadines	119,051	0	0	24	599	2,298	144	3,065	12,183	−5,847	50,152	59,553
Sudan	36,232,945	1,554	381	722	295	1,082	2,878	6,911	1,495	−890	4,632	12,148
Swaziland	1,131,000	0	379	124	17	9,714	346	10,580	5,885	865	23,063	40,393
Sweden	9,024,040	366	3,508	1,728	7,284	1,109	1,679	15,673	92,488	−8,333	528,122	627,950
Switzerland	7,437,100	0	299	155	3,521	845	4,590	9,411	165,561	55,211	506,613	736,795
Syrian Arab Republic	19,043,382	4,657	5	7	63	1,709	1,468	7,909	3,709	625	8,126	20,369

Tajikistan	6,550,213	27	0	15	434	764	522	1,762	1,093	−219	4,052	6,687
Thailand	64,232,758	638	92	52	2,813	4,014	201	7,810	9,711	−905	21,150	37,765
Togo	6,145,004	5	200	11	39	796	60	1,110	794	−339	5,050	6,616
Tonga	102,311	0	..	9	28,471	4,322	113	32,916	5,440	−1,184	18,704	55,876
Trinidad and Tobago	1,305,236	44,486	64	77	238	332	81	45,278	24,826	−4,731	50,746	116,119
Tunisia	10,029,000	1,051	184	222	51	1,900	1,004	4,413	8,420	−2,912	37,467	47,389
Turkey	72,065,000	208	262	35	310	3,190	1,351	5,356	13,895	−2,414	97,993	114,830
Uganda	28,816,229	0	6	25	558	2,485	299	3,372	585	−165	2,165	5,957
Ukraine	47,075,295	1,970	58	49	266	2,699	1,856	6,899	7,250	−311	15,485	29,322
United Arab Emirates	4,533,145	118,111	0	31	600	1,846	401	120,989	72,873	46,914	108,922	349,698
United Kingdom	60,226,500	3,085	159	49	815	823	1,332	6,263	84,861	−7,290	578,791	662,624
United States	296,410,404	3,478	831	462	3,625	2,598	2,827	13,822	100,075	−6,947	627,246	734,195
Uruguay	3,305,723	0	2,193	123	19	2,372	3,581	8,288	9,743	−869	69,522	86,684
Uzbekistan	26,167,369	5,365	..	32	101	1,082	1,073	7,652	1,543	8	−3,887	5,316
Vanuatu	211,367	0	143	498	251	5,516	543	6,951	5,267	−853	17,535	28,900
Venezuela, RB	26,577,000	24,090	551	408	3,136	1,514	867	30,567	15,863	1,231	22,134	69,795
Vietnam	83,104,900	884	408	101	152	2,030	55	3,630	1,851	−303	4,196	9,374
Zambia	11,668,457	374	486	799	100	286	96	2,142	1,482	−907	6,961	9,678
Zimbabwe	13,009,534	75	247	280	79	1,049	235	1,965	827	−341	2,537	4,988
World	6,128,328,330	2,779	444	189	752	2,067	888	7,119	20,329	−325	88,361	115,484

(continued)

181

TABLE C.1 (continued)

Economy/Group	Population	Subsoil Assets	Timber	Nontimber Forest Resources	Protected Areas	Crop Land	Pasture Land	Natural Capital	Produced Capital + Urban Land	Net Foreign Assets	Intangible Capital	Total Wealth
Low income	715,963,412	393	231	133	166	1,031	362	2,316	945	−207	3,469	6,523
Middle income	4,399,856,652	2,388	444	138	422	2,232	684	6,307	6,166	−310	18,498	30,662
Lower middle income	3,519,642,686	1,207	318	57	254	1,998	523	4,357	4,130	−50	8,675	17,112
Upper middle income	880,213,965	7,107	949	461	1,094	3,166	1,327	14,104	14,309	−1,347	57,777	84,844
Low and middle income	5,115,820,063	2,108	414	137	386	2,064	639	5,749	5,436	−295	16,395	27,284
East Asia and the Pacific	1,796,063,936	988	379	60	268	2,404	267	4,365	5,677	52	10,013	20,108
Europe and Central Asia	408,064,333	9,563	239	519	1,241	2,146	1,624	15,330	13,357	−1,083	45,140	72,744
Latin America and the Caribbean	531,341,503	3,597	1,711	386	1,120	4,025	1,225	12,063	12,261	−1,555	56,425	79,194
Middle East and North Africa	239,764,358	6,842	56	29	155	1,977	837	9,895	6,937	196	11,964	28,992
South Asia	1,439,901,500	337	170	18	161	1,288	663	2,637	1,828	−123	6,104	10,445
Sub-Saharan Africa	700,684,434	1,530	248	207	179	1,280	457	3,901	1,929	−294	8,322	13,857

High income	1,012,508,266	6,167	593	452	2,597	2,086	2,147	14,043	95,580	−473	451,978	561,129
High income non-OECD	58,676,250	58,843	36	39	4,037	799	634	64,386	47,122	22,433	97,262	231,203
High income OECD	953,832,017	2,927	628	477	2,508	2,166	2,240	10,946	98,561	−1,882	473,799	581,424

Source: Authors.
Note: .. = negligible.

Calculating Adjusted Net Saving as a Percentage of Gross National Income, 2008

The following table shows the national accounting flows used to estimate adjusted net saving by economy for the year 2008. Adjusted net saving is equal to gross savings minus consumption of fixed capital, plus education expenditure, minus energy depletion, mineral depletion, net forest depletion, carbon dioxide damages, and particulate matter (PM)damages. Estimates are expressed as a percentage of GNI. Refer to *World Development Indicators 2010* for the calculation of adjusted net saving by geographic region and income category.

TABLE D.1
National Saving Flows for 2008

Economy/Group	Gross National Savings	Consumption of Fixed Capital	Net National Savings	Education Expenditure	Energy Depletion	Mineral Depletion	Net Forest Depletion	CO_2 Damage	PM Damage	Adjusted Net Savings
Afghanistan	–	7.0	–	–	0	0	3.4	0.1	0.2	–
Albania	18.0	10.1	7.9	2.8	1.7	0	0	0.3	0.2	8.5
Algeria	58.8	10.9	47.9	4.5	29.9	0.2	0.1	0.6	0.2	21.4
Andorra	–	–	–	2.2	–	–	–	–	–	–
Angola	24.1	12.9	11.2	2.3	54.6	0	0	0.2	1.3	–42.6
Antigua and Barbuda	47.8	13.1	34.7	1.6	0	0	–	0.3	–	–
Argentina	25.5	11.8	13.8	4.5	8.6	0.4	0	0.5	1.1	7.7
Armenia	28.1	10.0	18.1	2.2	0	0.8	0	0.3	1.2	18.1
Aruba	–	–	–	4.3	–	–	–	–	–	–
Australia	32.9	14.7	18.1	5.1	4.1	3.8	0	0.3	..	15.0
Austria	27.2	14.3	12.9	5.3	0.2	..	..	0.1	0.1	17.6
Azerbaijan	63.0	12.3	50.7	2.0	51.4	0	..	1.2	0.3	–0.1
Bahamas, The	–	–	–	3.8	–	–	–	–	–	–
Bahrain	45.4	6.7	38.7	4.4	26.4	0	0	0.8	0.2	15.6
Bangladesh	33.9	6.8	27.1	2.0	4.0	0	0.6	0.4	0.4	23.7
Barbados	–	–	–	6.4	–	–	–	–	..	–
Belarus	28.4	11.2	17.2	4.9	1.3	0	0	1.1	0	19.8
Belgium	–	13.9	–	5.8	0	0	..	0.2	0.1	–
Belize	15.7	11.9	3.8	5.6	0	0	0	0.5	0	8.8

Country										
Benin	–	8.1	–	3.3	0	0	1.0	0.3	0.3	–
Bermuda	–	–	–	2.0	–	–	–	–	–	–
Bhutan	60.7	9.2	51.5	3.4	0	0	4.1	0.3	0.1	50.4
Bolivia	29.9	9.5	20.4	4.7	27.6	0.8	0	0.5	0.9	–4.7
Bosnia and Herzegovina	41.0	10.4	30.6	–	2.0	0	–	1.2	0.1	–
Botswana	46.3	11.5	34.8	6.6	0.5	3.2	0	0.3	0.2	37.2
Brazil	17.5	11.8	5.8	4.8	2.7	2.3	0	0.2	0.1	5.2
Brunei	–	–	–	3.6	–	–	–	–	0.1	–
Bulgaria	14.1	11.6	2.5	4.1	1.1	0.8	0	0.9	0.9	2.9
Burkina Faso	–	7.5	–	3.3	0	0	1.2	0.1	0.6	–
Burundi	–	5.6	–	5.1	0	0.6	10.9	0.1	0.1	–
Cambodia	–	8.3	–	1.7	0	0	0.2	0.4	0.3	–
Cameroon	–	8.8	–	2.6	7.8	..	0	0.1	0.4	–
Canada	23.4	14.0	9.4	4.8	5.5	0.6	0	0.3	0.1	7.6
Cape Verde	26.0	10.5	15.5	5.0	0	0	0	0.2	–	–
Central African Republic	1.8	7.4	–5.6	1.3	0	0	0	0.1	0.2	–4.6
Chad	3.7	10.0	–6.4	1.2	43.7	0	0	..	1.0	–49.9
Chile	24.2	12.9	11.4	3.6	0.3	14.3	0	0.3	0.4	–0.4
China	53.9	10.1	43.8	1.8	6.7	1.7	0	1.3	0.8	35.1
Colombia	20.2	11.4	8.8	3.6	10.0	0.6	0	0.2	0.1	1.5
Comoros	11.2	8.1	3.1	4.2	0	0	0.1	0.1	..	7.0
Congo, Dem. Rep.	9.4	6.7	2.7	0.9	3.1	2.3	0	0.2	0.6	–2.5
Congo, Rep.	26.7	14.1	12.6	2.3	71.2	..	0	0.2	0.6	–57.1

(continued)

TABLE D.1 (continued)

Economy/Group	Gross National Savings	Consumption of Fixed Capital	Net National Savings	Education Expenditure	Energy Depletion	Mineral Depletion	Net Forest Depletion	CO_2 Damage	PM Damage	Adjusted Net Savings
Costa Rica	15.9	11.5	4.5	5.0	0	..	0.1	0.2	0.1	9.1
Côte d'Ivoire	12.7	9.0	3.8	4.7	6.2	0	0	0.2	0.3	1.7
Croatia	21.8	12.9	8.9	4.3	1.3	0	0.2	0.3	0.2	11.3
Cuba	–	–	–	13.2	–	–	–	–	0.1	–
Cyprus	5.6	14.4	−8.8	6.5	0	0	0	0.3	0.3	−2.8
Czech Republic	24.2	13.8	10.4	4.4	0.7	0	..	0.5	..	13.4
Denmark	23.6	14.2	9.4	7.4	3.0	0	..	0.1	..	13.7
Djibouti	–	7.8	–	3.6	0	0	0	0.4	1.2	–
Dominica	4.2	11.3	−7.1	3.9	0	0	..	0.3	–	–
Dominican Republic	9.0	11.1	−2.1	3.5	0	1.3	0	0.4	..	−0.3
Ecuador	31.8	10.8	21.0	1.4	21.1	0.4	0	0.5	0.1	0.4
Egypt, Arab Rep.	23.5	9.3	14.2	4.4	14.5	0.5	0.2	0.9	0.5	2.1
El Salvador	7.9	10.5	−2.6	3.3	0	0	0.4	0.2	0.1	−0.1
Equatorial Guinea	55.8	20.7	35.1	1.1	74.2	0	0	0.4	0	−38.4
Eritrea	–	6.9	–	1.9	0	0	0.8	0.3	0.3	–
Estonia	20.1	13.5	6.6	4.6	1.5	0	0	0.7	0	9.0
Ethiopia	17.3	6.7	10.6	3.7	0	0.3	4.7	0.2	0.2	8.9
Fiji	−1.2	10.6	−11.8	6.0	0	0.9	0	0.3	0.1	−7.1
Finland	24.8	14.1	10.7	5.6	0	0.1	0	0.2	..	16.0

Country										
France	18.7	13.9	4.9	5.1	..	..	0	0.1	..	9.8
Gabon	48.8	13.9	34.9	3.1	34.3	..	0	0.1	0	3.6
Gambia, The	11.1	7.9	3.2	2.0	0	0	0.6	0.4	0.4	3.9
Georgia	8.3	10.1	−1.8	2.8	0.2	0	0	0.3	0.7	−0.3
Germany	–	13.8	–	4.3	0.3	..	0	0.2	..	–
Ghana	7.3	8.8	−1.5	4.7	0	6.5	2.8	0.5	0.1	−6.5
Greece	7.4	13.9	−6.5	2.8	0.3	0.1	0	0.2	0.3	−4.8
Grenada	−13.3	11.7	−25.0	5.1	0	0	–	0.3	–	–
Guatemala	14.4	10.1	4.3	2.9	0.8	0	0.7	0.3	0.1	5.3
Guinea	2.9	7.7	−4.8	2.0	0	5.2	2.6	0.3	0.5	−11.3
Guinea-Bissau	22.4	6.7	15.7	2.3	0	0	0	0.5	0.8	16.6
Guyana	33.2	9.1	24.0	5.7	0	14.1	0	1.1	0.2	14.4
Haiti	–	–	–	1.5	–	–	–	–	0.4	–
Honduras	21.2	9.5	11.7	3.5	0	1.4	0	0.5	0.2	13.1
Hong Kong SAR, China	29.7	13.4	16.3	3.0	0	0	0	0.2	–	–
Hungary	15.9	15.1	0.8	5.3	0.8	..	0	0.3	..	5.0
Iceland	–	20.7	–	7.3	0	0	0	0.2	0	–
India	38.2	8.5	29.7	3.2	4.9	1.4	0.8	1.2	0.5	24.2
Indonesia	22.2	10.7	11.6	1.1	12.6	1.4	0	0.6	0.5	−2.4
Iran, Islamic Rep.	–	–	–	4.2	–	–	–	–	0.4	–
Ireland	19.7	17.1	2.5	5.2	..	..	0	0.1	0	7.5
Israel	19.8	13.5	6.3	5.9	0.2	0.3	0	0.3	0.1	11.3

(continued)

TABLE D.1 *(continued)*

Economy/Group	Gross National Savings	Consumption of Fixed Capital	Net National Savings	Education Expenditure	Energy Depletion	Mineral Depletion	Net Forest Depletion	CO_2 Damage	PM Damage	Adjusted Net Savings
Italy	18.5	14.0	4.5	4.5	0.2	..	0	0.2	0.1	8.5
Jamaica	–	11.4	–	5.3	0	1.3	0	0.6	0.2	–
Japan	25.9	13.3	12.6	3.2	..	..	0	0.2	0.3	15.3
Jordan	13.7	9.8	3.8	5.6	0.2	4.5	..	0.8	0.2	3.6
Kazakhstan	46.2	13.5	32.8	4.4	31.3	1.8	0	1.4	0.1	2.5
Kenya	13.1	8.0	5.0	6.6	0	0.1	1.0	0.3	0.1	10.2
Kiribati	–	6.0	–	–	0	0	–	0.1	–	–
Korea, Rep.	30.5	12.6	17.9	3.9	..	..	0	0.4	0.3	21.1
Kuwait	58.7	13.3	45.3	3.0	38.0	0	0	0.4	0.3	9.7
Kyrgyz Republic	14.9	8.5	6.4	5.8	0.7	0	0	1.0	0.2	10.4
Lao PDR	25.2	8.6	16.6	1.2	0	0	0	0.2	0.5	17.1
Latvia	22.3	12.6	9.6	5.6	0	0	0.2	0.2	..	14.8
Lebanon	10.2	11.3	–1.1	1.8	0	0	0	0.5	0.1	0.1
Lesotho	17.8	6.4	11.4	9.4	0	0	1.3	0	0.1	19.4
Liberia	–2.7	7.8	–10.5	–	0	..	7.7	0.9	0.3	–
Libya	66.8	12.3	54.5	–	38.8	0	..	0.5	1.0	–
Lithuania	15.2	12.7	2.5	4.6	0.1	0	0.1	0.3	0.1	6.6
Luxembourg	–	18.7	–	3.7	0	0	0	0.2	0	–
Macao SAR, China	–	–	–	2.2	–	–	–	–	–	–

Macedonia, FYR	16.1	10.8	5.3	4.9	0	0	0.1	1.0	0.1	9.0
Madagascar	14.7	7.4	7.2	2.6	0	0	2.5	0.3	0.1	7.0
Malawi	29.3	6.5	22.8	3.5	0	0	0.9	0.2	0.1	25.1
Malaysia	–	11.9	–	4.0	13.1	0.1	..	0.7	..	–
Maldives	–	11.1	–	6.5	0	0	0	0.6	0.1	–
Mali	–	8.1	–	3.6	0	0	0	0.1	1.1	–
Malta	–	–	–	4.6	–	–	–	–	–	–
Marshall Islands	–	8.0	–	6.6	0	0	–	0.3	–	–
Mauritania	–	–	–	2.8	–	–	–	–	0.5	–
Mauritius	16.5	11.1	5.4	3.4	0	0	..	0.3	..	8.5
Mexico	25.3	12.0	13.3	4.8	8.2	0.3	0	0.3	0.3	9.0
Micronesia, Fed. Sts.	–	9.1	–	–	0	0	–	0	–	–
Moldova	20.8	8.3	12.5	6.5	..	0	0.1	1.0	0.5	17.3
Mongolia	26.5	9.7	16.8	4.6	5.9	9.2	0	1.7	1.6	3.0
Morocco	31.4	10.1	21.3	5.2	..	6.1	0	0.4	0.1	19.8
Mozambique	7.4	7.9	–0.5	3.8	7.0	..	0.5	0.2	0.1	–4.6
Myanmar	–	–	–	0.8	–	–	–	–	0.4	–
Namibia	17.1	12.1	5.0	7.3	0	2.1	0	0.3	..	9.9
Nepal	37.5	7.1	30.4	3.4	0	0	3.1	0.2	..	30.5
Netherlands	10.3	13.9	–3.6	4.8	2.0	0	0	0.2	0.2	–1.2
New Zealand	–	14.5	–	6.6	2.3	0.2	0	0.2	..	–
Nicaragua	–	8.9	–	3.0	0	0.6	..	0.6	..	–

(continued)

TABLE D.1 *(continued)*

Economy/Group	Gross National Savings	Consumption of Fixed Capital	Net National Savings	Education Expenditure	Energy Depletion	Mineral Depletion	Net Forest Depletion	CO$_2$ Damage	PM Damage	Adjusted Net Savings
Niger	–	2.6	–	2.6	0	0	2.3	0.2	1.1	–
Nigeria	–	1.2	–	0.9	23.8	..	0.2	0.5	0.5	–
Norway	41.2	15.0	26.2	6.0	15.9	..	0	0.1	..	16.2
Oman	–	–	–	3.9	–	–	0	–	..	–
Pakistan	19.3	8.2	11.1	2.1	4.9	..	0.7	0.7	0.8	6.1
Palau	–	11.5	–	–	0	0	–	0.5	–	–
Panama	25.9	11.1	14.8	4.4	0	0	0	0.3	0.1	18.8
Papua New Guinea	30.8	9.4	21.4	6.3	0	24.1	0	0.5	..	3.1
Paraguay	16.1	9.9	6.2	3.9	0	0	0	0.2	0.8	9.0
Peru	24.1	11.4	12.7	2.5	1.4	6.2	0	0.3	0.3	7.0
Philippines	30.3	8.4	21.9	2.2	0.5	0.8	0.1	0.3	0.1	22.3
Poland	19.1	12.7	6.4	5.4	1.5	0.3	0.1	0.5	0.2	9.2
Portugal	12.6	13.6	–1.0	5.3	0	0.1	0	0.2	..	4.1
Romania	25.0	11.7	13.3	3.4	2.4	0.1	0	0.4	..	13.7
Russian Federation	32.8	12.4	20.4	3.5	20.5	1.0	0	0.9	0.1	1.5
Rwanda	25.4	6.7	18.7	4.6	0	..	3.0	0.2	0.1	20.1
Samoa	–	10.3	–	4.0	0	0	0.3	0.2	–	–
São Tomé and Principe	–	8.4	–	–	0	0	0	0.5	0.2	–
Saudi Arabia	48.3	12.5	35.9	7.2	43.5	0	0	0.6	0.7	–1.8

Senegal	18.0	8.6	9.4	4.5	..	0.9	0	0.3	0.5	12.2
Seychelles	3.0	12.8	−9.8	5.8	0	0	0	0.8	-	-
Sierra Leone	5.5	7.0	−1.6	3.9	0	0.5	1.5	0.4	0.8	−1.0
Singapore	47.0	14.1	32.9	2.7	0	0	0	0.3	0.6	34.7
Slovak Republic	-	13.1	-	3.7	0.1	0	0.4	0.4	..	-
Slovenia	27.0	13.6	13.4	5.3	0.1	0	0.2	0.2	0.1	18.1
Solomon Islands	81.2	10.4	70.8	3.8	0	0	19.4	0.4	0.1	54.7
South Africa	16.1	13.9	2.2	5.1	6.4	2.6	0.5	1.3	0.1	−3.4
Spain	20.6	14.0	6.6	3.9	..	..	0	0.2	0.2	10.1
Sri Lanka	18.4	9.7	8.8	2.6	0	..	0.4	0.3	0.2	10.4
St. Kitts and Nevis	11.9	12.7	−0.7	4.1	0	0	-	0.2	-	-
St. Lucia	−5.7	12.0	−17.7	5.5	0	0	-	0.3	..	-
St. Vincent and the Grenadines	13.6	11.5	2.1	5.8	0	0	0	0.3	0.1	7.6
Sudan	15.9	9.9	6.0	0.9	19.1	0.1	0	0.2	0.5	−13.1
Suriname	-	12.2	-	3.4	0	1.5	0	0.7	0.2	-
Swaziland	10.7	9.6	1.1	6.4	0	0	..	0.3	..	7.1
Sweden	27.1	12.5	14.6	6.4	0	0.4	0	0.1	0	20.5
Switzerland	-	13.3	-	4.7	0	0	0	0.1	0.1	-
Syrian Arab Republic	12.6	10.1	2.6	2.6	17.6	1.1	0	1.1	0.7	−15.2
Taiwan, China	-	12.2	-	-	0	0	-	0.5	-	-
Tajikistan	25.5	8.2	17.3	3.2	0.4	0	0	1.1	0.3	18.8

(continued)

TABLE D.1 *(continued)*

Economy/Group	Gross National Savings	Consumption of Fixed Capital	Net National Savings	Education Expenditure	Energy Depletion	Mineral Depletion	Net Forest Depletion	CO_2 Damage	PM Damage	Adjusted Net Savings
Tanzania	–	7.6	–	2.4	0.7	5.0	0	0.2	0.1	–
Thailand	30.7	10.9	19.8	4.8	5.3	..	0.2	0.8	0.2	18.0
Timor-Leste	–	1.2	–	0.9	0	0	–	0.1	–	–
Togo	–	7.3	–	3.7	0	5.2	2.5	0.4	0.1	–
Tonga	1.5	9.5	–8.1	3.8	0	0	..	0.3	–	–
Trinidad and Tobago	41.8	13.1	28.7	4.0	50.5	0	0	1.2	0.2	–19.2
Tunisia	22.6	11.1	11.5	6.7	5.8	4.7	0.1	0.5	0.1	7.0
Turkey	17.7	11.8	5.9	3.7	0.3	0.1	0	0.3	0.6	8.3
Turkmenistan	32.1	10.9	21.2	–	133.3	0	–	3.1	0.6	–
Uganda	12.6	7.4	5.2	3.3	0	0	5.1	0.1	0	3.3
Ukraine	20.2	10.5	9.7	5.9	5.3	0	0	1.6	0.2	8.5
United Kingdom	14.8	13.7	1.2	5.1	2.1	0	0	0.2	..	3.9
United States	12.6	14.0	–1.4	4.8	1.9	0.1	0	0.3	0.1	0.9
Uruguay	18.2	11.9	6.3	2.6	0	0	0.4	0.2	1.1	7.2
Uzbekistan	40.5	8.5	32.0	9.4	51.1	0	0	4.0	0.4	–14.1
Vanuatu	–	–	–	5.9	–	–	–	–	..	–
Venezuela, RB	34.6	11.9	22.7	3.5	18.6	0.6	0	0.5	0	6.5
Vietnam	30.4	8.8	21.6	2.8	12.9	0.3	0.2	1.0	0.3	9.7
Yemen, Rep.	–	9.4	–	–	22.3	0	0	0.7	–	–

Zambia	21.4	9.5	11.9	1.3	0.1	13.4	0	0.2	0.3	-0.7
Zimbabwe	–	–	–	6.9	–	–	–	–	0.1	–
World	20.9	13.0	7.9	4.2	3.9	0.5	..	0.4	0.2	7.2
Low income	25.9	7.9	18.0	3.4	7.8	1.0	1.0	0.7	0.3	10.7
Middle income	31.6	10.9	20.7	3.3	8.8	1.3	0.1	0.8	0.4	12.6
Lower middle income	41.1	9.6	31.4	2.3	8.1	1.4	0.2	1.1	0.6	22.4
Upper middle income	23.8	12.1	11.8	4.2	9.4	1.3	..	0.5	0.2	4.6
Low and middle income	31.4	10.8	20.6	3.3	8.7	1.3	0.1	0.8	0.4	12.5
East Asia and the Pacific	47.3	10.1	37.1	2.0	7.2	1.5	..	1.1	0.7	28.6
Europe and Central Asia	24.8	12.1	12.7	4.1	12.1	0.6	..	0.8	0.2	3.2
Latin America and the Caribbean	22.4	11.8	10.6	4.4	6.3	1.8	..	0.3	0.3	6.3
Middle East and North Africa	–	10.5	–	4.4	18.6	1.5	0.1	0.7	0.4	–
South Asia	35.3	8.4	26.9	3.0	4.6	1.1	0.8	1.0	0.5	21.8
Sub-Saharan Africa	16.5	9.0	7.6	3.3	14.2	1.3	0.6	0.6	0.4	-6.2
High income	18.5	13.8	4.7	4.6	2.0	0.2	..	0.2	0.1	6.8
High income: non-OECD	–	12.9	–	5.0	16.0	..	..	0.4	0.5	–
High income: OECD	18.0	13.8	4.1	4.6	1.4	0.2	..	0.2	0.1	6.8

Source: Authors.
Note: – = not available; .. = negligible.

Effect of Population Growth on Savings and Changes in Wealth Per Capita, 2005

The following table shows how population growth affects measures of savings and changes in wealth per capita. The first column shows GNI per capita. This is used just for reference. The second column shows the rate of population growth. The third and fourth columns show two alternative measures of capital accumulation that take into account population: adjusted net saving per capita and change in wealth per capita. The difference between the two columns is driven by the "Malthusian term" referred to in chapter 2. The fifth column shows how much extra savings (as a percentage of GNI) would be needed to obtain a zero change in wealth per capita. Data are for 2005.

TABLE E.1
Effect of Population Growth on Savings and Changes in Wealth Per Capita, 2005

Economy	GNI Per Capita (US$)	Population Growth Rate (%)	Adjusted Net Saving Per Capita (US$)	Change in Wealth Per Capita (US$)	Adjusted Net Saving Gap (% GNI)
Albania	2,729	0.6	158	91	n.a.
Algeria	2,960	1.5	361	−69	2.3
Angola	1,669	2.9	−553	−996	59.7
Argentina	4,557	1.0	164	−40	0.9
Armenia	1,669	−0.3	262	284	n.a.
Australia	31,962	1.2	2,217	655	n.a.
Austria	36,676	0.7	3,100	2,284	n.a.
Azerbaijan	1,382	1.0	−111	−260	18.8
Bahamas, The	19,745	1.3	2,091	2,061	n.a.
Bahrain	17,956	1.5	1,193	−957	5.3
Bangladesh	447	1.9	86	43	n.a.
Belarus	3,091	−0.5	567	643	n.a.
Belgium	36,037	0.6	2,917	2,283	n.a.
Belize	3,429	3.3	−211	−1,142	33.3
Benin	505	3.2	8	−104	20.5
Bhutan	1,184	2.2	343	−110	9.3
Bolivia	1,196	1.9	39	−142	11.9
Botswana	5,476	−0.2	2,269	2,342	n.a.
Brazil	4,616	1.4	170	−163	3.5
Brunei Darussalam	25,497	2.2	−2,419	−10,836	42.5
Bulgaria	3,523	−0.5	17	90	n.a.
Burkina Faso	409	3.2	−1	−67	16.5
Burundi	103	3.6	−13	−112	108.7
Cambodia	429	2.0	30	−19	4.4
Cameroon	988	1.8	29	−98	9.9
Canada	34,505	1.0	2,081	881	n.a.
Cape Verde	1,905	2.3	388	266	n.a.
Central African Republic	334	1.3	−15	−95	28.4
Chad	455	3.2	−169	−343	75.4
Chile	6,615	1.1	255	−129	1.9
China	1,722	0.6	636	570	n.a.
Colombia	3,095	1.4	−17	−214	6.9
Comoros	640	2.1	−12	−72	11.3

(continued)

TABLE E.1 *(continued)*

Economy	GNI Per Capita (US$)	Population Growth Rate (%)	Adjusted Net Saving Per Capita (US$)	Change in Wealth Per Capita (US$)	Adjusted Net Saving Gap (% GNI)
Congo, Dem. Rep.	117	3.0	−4	−53	45.4
Congo, Rep.	1,010	3.0	−611	−1,128	111.7
Costa Rica	4,431	1.7	460	136	n.a.
Côte d'Ivoire	862	1.6	−23	−100	11.6
Croatia	9,727	0	738	735	n.a.
Cyprus	21,497	2.4	1,780	128	n.a.
Czech Republic	11,624	0.3	703	582	n.a.
Denmark	48,330	0.3	2,891	2,475	n.a.
Djibouti	978	1.8	180	166	n.a.
Dominica	3,754	0.7	−297	−449	12.0
Dominican Republic	3,390	1.6	75	−104	3.1
Ecuador	2,664	1.4	−15	−423	15.9
Egypt, Arab Rep.	1,209	1.9	−12	−155	12.9
El Salvador	2,398	1.8	27	−113	4.7
Equatorial Guinea	8,288	2.3	−6,263	−8,195	98.9
Eritrea	262	4.0	−9	−27	10.5
Estonia	9,821	−0.2	1,152	1,187	n.a.
Ethiopia	172	1.9	1	−24	13.8
Fiji	3,546	0.8	−12	−165	4.6
Finland	37,503	0.3	3,586	3,207	n.a.
France	35,491	0.6	2,083	1,473	n.a.
Gabon	5,570	1.6	393	−641	11.5
Gambia, The	275	2.7	7	−31	11.4
Georgia	1,447	−1.0	187	260	n.a.
Germany	34,156	−0.1	2,808	2,871	n.a.
Ghana	479	2.1	48	−27	5.7
Greece	21,798	0.4	217	−35	0.2
Guatemala	2,133	2.5	98	−439	20.6
Guinea	296	1.9	19	−26	8.9
Guinea-Bissau	183	3.0	36	−27	15.0
Guyana	1,071	0.1	32	1	n.a.
Honduras	1,278	2.2	242	−104	8.1

(continued)

TABLE E.1 *(continued)*

Economy	GNI Per Capita (US$)	Population Growth Rate (%)	Adjusted Net Saving Per Capita (US$)	Change in Wealth Per Capita (US$)	Adjusted Net Saving Gap (% GNI)
Hong Kong SAR, China	25,633	0.9	4,806	3,557	n.a.
Hungary	10,345	−0.2	329	392	n.a.
Iceland	52,951	1.6	−1,091	−2,745	5.2
India	735	1.4	147	84	n.a.
Indonesia	1,143	1.4	0	−114	10.0
Iran, Islamic Rep.	2,762	1.4	−31	−440	15.9
Ireland	41,123	2.2	6,847	4,327	n.a.
Israel	19,190	1.8	1,763	905	n.a.
Italy	30,214	0.7	1,241	552	n.a.
Jamaica	3,946	0.5	221	141	n.a.
Japan	36,468	0	2,265	2,252	n.a.
Jordan	2,409	2.3	156	30	n.a.
Kazakhstan	3,395	0.9	−571	−785	23.1
Kenya	547	2.4	34	−59	10.9
Korea, Rep.	17,478	0.4	3,300	3,045	n.a.
Kuwait	34,700	3.1	3,733	−6,566	18.9
Kyrgyz Republic	461	1.0	6	−33	7.1
Lao PDR	456	1.6	42	−42	9.1
Latvia	6,893	−0.5	282	423	n.a.
Lebanon	5,404	1.2	−336	−379	7.0
Lesotho	936	−0.2	59	65	n.a.
Lithuania	7,421	−0.6	269	419	n.a.
Luxembourg	68,097	0.8	13,885	11,484	n.a.
Macedonia, FYR	2,830	0.2	298	280	n.a.
Madagascar	267	2.7	12	−50	18.9
Malawi	218	2.2	−6	−37	17.2
Malaysia	5,193	1.8	586	62	n.a.
Maldives	2,205	2.5	566	375	n.a.
Mali	377	3.0	16	−64	16.8
Mauritania	620	3.0	−186	−319	51.5
Mauritius	5,048	0.8	334	137	n.a.
Mexico	8,084	1.0	418	164	n.a.
Moldova	863	−1.2	103	196	n.a.
Mongolia	883	1.6	214	79	n.a.

(continued)

TABLE E.1 *(continued)*

Economy	GNI Per Capita (US$)	Population Growth Rate (%)	Adjusted Net Saving Per Capita (US$)	Change in Wealth Per Capita (US$)	Adjusted Net Saving Gap (% GNI)
Morocco	1,949	1.0	423	341	n.a.
Mozambique	314	1.9	−14	−45	14.3
Namibia	3,520	1.1	545	389	n.a.
Nepal	300	2.0	65	−1	0.4
Netherlands	39,028	0.2	3,825	3,541	n.a.
New Zealand	24,549	0.9	496	−501	2.0
Nicaragua	918	0.5	62	25	n.a.
Niger	243	3.4	37	−19	8.0
Nigeriaa	700	2.4	−94	−280	40.1
Norway	65,776	0.7	5,504	3,254	n.a.
Oman	11,662	1.3	−1,656	−2,997	25.7
Pakistan	718	2.4	88	−24	3.4
Panama	4,438	1.8	587	315	n.a.
Papua New Guinea	769	2.0	−2	−213	27.7
Paraguay	1,269	1.9	124	14	n.a.
Peru	2,657	1.5	176	3	n.a.
Philippines	1,288	1.8	208	109	n.a.
Poland	7,788	0	317	329	n.a.
Portugal	17,238	0.5	−577	−811	4.7
Romania	4,530	−0.2	91	142	n.a.
Russian Federation	5,209	−0.5	−13	236	n.a.
Rwanda	261	1.7	28	−30	11.6
Saudi Arabia	13,904	2.6	−54	−3,750	27.0
Seychelles	9,985	1.0	−1,018	−1,250	12.5
Sierra Leone	213	3.5	4	−42	19.9
Singapore	26,554	2.4	8,265	5,007	n.a.
Slovenia	17,691	0.2	2,264	2,256	n.a.
Solomon Islands	617	2.6	171	−30	4.9
South Africa	5,073	1.1	−63	−245	4.8
Spain	25,668	1.7	1,869	584	n.a.
Sri Lanka	1,228	0.8	230	189	n.a.
St. Vincent and the Grenadines	3,514	0.5	−40	−90	2.6
Sudan	701	2.0	−62	−212	30.3

(continued)

TABLE E.1 *(continued)*

Economy	GNI Per Capita (US$)	Population Growth Rate (%)	Adjusted Net Saving Per Capita (US$)	Change in Wealth Per Capita (US$)	Adjusted Net Saving Gap (% GNI)
Suriname	3,881	0.6	−90	−357	9.2
Swaziland	2,389	1.0	280	108	n.a.
Sweden	40,498	0.4	4,540	4,184	n.a.
Switzerland	54,782	0.6	8,291	6,811	n.a.
Syrian Arab Republic	1,436	2.5	−181	−485	33.8
Tajikistan	341	1.3	−11	−45	13.1
Tanzania	364	2.6	14	−43	11.8
Thailand	2,612	0.8	363	222	n.a.
Togo	337	2.6	−4	−45	13.3
Tonga	2,080	0.3	−48	−168	8.1
Trinidad and Tobago	10,977	0.3	−61	−258	2.3
Tunisia	2,723	1.0	215	118	n.a.
Turkey	6,641	1.3	288	71	n.a.
Uganda	304	3.6	28	−107	35.3
Ukraine	1,809	−0.8	154	261	n.a.
United Kingdom	38,048	0.7	1,162	613	n.a.
United States	41,966	0.9	182	−821	2.0
Uruguay	5,101	0.1	345	324	n.a.
Uzbekistan	546	1.2	−168	−276	50.5
Vanuatu	1,626	1.9	54	−167	10.3
Venezuela, RB	5,390	1.7	208	−613	11.4
Vietnam	623	1.3	99	32	n.a.
Zambia	579	1.7	19	−26	4.6
Zimbabwe	248	0.6	−31	−45	18.3

Source: Authors.
Note: Countries with savings gap are those with negative change in wealth per capita. n.a. = not applicable.
a. Nigeria's gross savings data are from the UN System of National Accounts 1993.

Decomposition Analysis as a Percentage of Change in Total Wealth, by Economy, 1995-2005

The following table shows the contribution of the change in the value of different assets to changes in total wealth between 1995 and 2005 (for Europe and Central Asia countries the period of analysis is 2000–05). For natural assets, the table also shows the relative contribution of changes in quantities, prices, and depletion time. All contributions are expressed as a percentage of the change in total wealth, shown in the third column of the table.

TABLE F.1
Decomposition Analysis as a Percentage of Change in Total Wealth, 1995–2005

Economy	Period	Change in Wealth (2005 US$ billions)	Produced Capital	Intangible Capital	Net Foreign Assets	Natural Capital	Land Production	Land Real Prices	Forest Production	Forest Real Prices	Forest Depletion Time	Subsoil Assets Production	Subsoil Assets Real Unit Rents	Subsoil Assets Depletion Time
Albania	2000-05	61	7	104	..	-11	1	-11	-1	-2	..	..	..	..
Algeria	1995-2005	-25	-146	1744	-349	-1149	-111	93	-4	-12	12	-494	-703	68
Argentina	1995-2005	151	22	-62	11	128	37	34	1	8	-5	14	52	-12
Armenia	2000-05	30	5	99	1	-5	7	-13	..	..	..	1	..	0
Australia	1995-2005	3,022	21	73	-4	10	2	-2	2	-1	0	4	4	..
Austria	1995-2005	755	22	83	-4	-1	..	-2	..	..	0	..	..	..
Azerbaijan	2000-05	40	45	-72	-9	136	15	-13	..	..	..	30	56	48
Bahrain	1995-2005	21	5	-47	9	134	..	-2	0	0	0	28	107	0
Bangladesh	1995-2005	366	20	62	-1	19	9	3	..	1	..	3	3	..
Belarus	2000-05	121	7	127	..	-34	4	-37	-1	-2	..	..	3	..
Belgium	1995-2005	1,136	16	77	6	1	3	-2	..	..	0	..	..	..
Belize	1995-2005	8	13	74	-13	26	14	7	-1	6	0	0	0	0
Benin	1995-2005	27	13	93	1	-8	24	-19	-15	4	0	..	-1	..
Bhutan	1995-2005	5	45	55	-2	3	1	-66	11	57	..	..	..	..
Bolivia	1995-2005	16	25	2	-19	93	55	-1	16	-70	0	46	62	-16
Botswana	1995-2005	34	62	24	16	-2	..	-6	-1	2	0	..	4	..
Brazil	1995-2005	3,084	7	65	-7	35	15	-4	1	13	..	6	4	-1
Brunei Darussalam	1995-2005	-18	-48	285	9	-146	..	7	..	..	0	-48	-122	17

Bulgaria	2000-05	117	-1	136	-4	-31	-7	-19	..	-6	0	..	1	..
Burkina Faso	1995-2005	59	7	100	-1	-6	7	-11	1	1	-3	0	0	0
Burundi	1995-2005	1	-35	-893	-63	1091	45	328	81	268	367	..	1	0
Cameroon	1995-2005	91	1	70	5	24	16	4	..	-1	0	-6	11	-1
Canada	1995-2005	4,071	16	73	6	5	2	-3	1	-1	0	2	5	..
Central African Republic	1995-2005	4	-3	119	-5	-12	46	-43	-59	45	0	..	..	0
Chad	1995-2005	-2	-561	1,238	180	-758	-239	700	-90	84	0	-303	-606	-303
Chile	1995-2005	466	30	41	-2	31	5	-1	3	7	0	14	4	..
China	1995-2005	13,230	36	48	3	12	12	-5	..	1	0	2	2	..
Colombia	1995-2005	548	11	85	-3	7	6	-6	1	2	0	3	5	-5
Comoros	1995-2005	2	-17	109	3	5	7	-3	..	..	..	0	0	0
Congo, Dem. Rep.	1995-2005	12	-36	138	38	-41	-31	-53	96	-52	0	-17	18	-1
Congo, Rep.	1995-2005	-1	-157	2,660	-588	-1,815	-168	329	-93	656	0	-1,043	-1,415	-81
Costa Rica	1995-2005	114	15	85	-3	3	7	..	..	..	-4	..	5	..
Côte d'Ivoire	1995-2005	38	-9	3	20	86	80	-20	1	4	0	16	2	..
Croatia	2000-05	120	31	96	-12	-14	-3	-9	..	-5	..	..	..	..
Cyprus	1995-2000	44	8	94	-6	4	..	4	..	..	0	..	1	0
Czech Republic	2000-05	279	19	101	-9	-12	-1	-9	-1	-3	..	..	3	..
Denmark	1995-2005	703	21	67	9	3	..	-1	..	..	..	3	3	-1
Dominica	1995-2005	1	17	90	-12	5	3	2	0	..	0	0	0	0
Dominican Republic	1995-2005	267	10	91	-1	..	..	-1	..	..	0	1	..	..

(continued)

TABLE F.1 (continued)

Economy	Period	Change in Wealth (2005 US$ billions)	Produced Capital	Intangible Capital	Net Foreign Assets	Natural Capital	Land Production	Land Real Prices	Forest Production	Forest Real Prices	Forest Depletion Time	Subsoil Assets Production	Subsoil Assets Real Unit Rents	Subsoil Assets Depletion Time
Ecuador	1995–2005	134	20	–11	–2	93	57	19	–2	2	–12	12	15	1
Egypt, Arab Rep.	1995–2005	528	8	62	3	27	12	–2	..	..	..	3	11	2
El Salvador	1995–2005	107	8	97	–5	..	2	1	..	..	–3	0	0	0
Ethiopia	1995–2005	106	8	103	..	–12	13	–11	1	4	–19	..	..	0
Fiji	1995–2005	–1	–118	–142	66	295	156	95	19	23	0	..	–1	0
Finland	1995–2005	863	5	91	3	1	..	–1	1	..	0	..	..	..
France	1995–2005	7,050	12	85	3	..	..	..	..	..	..	..	..	..
Gabon	1995–2005	8	–9	–266	76	299	–2	–14	32	–42	0	–157	238	244
Gambia, The	1995–2005	3	12	74	–21	35	9	–3	5	6	18	0	0	0
Georgia	2000–05	35	..	105	–4	–1	3	–5	..	..	..	..	..	..
Germany	1995–2005	5,807	13	80	7	1	..	..	..	..	..	..	1	..
Ghana	1995–2005	82	20	60	–1	21	21	4	2	18	–24	..	..	..
Greece	1995–2005	1,154	13	102	–14	–1	..	–1	..	..	0	..	..	..
Grenada	1995–2005	2	47	75	–20	–2	–2	..	0	..	0	0	0	0
Guatemala	1995–2005	184	13	33	–1	56	10	–15	9	71	–22	1	..	..
Guinea	1995–2005	18	11	82	–8	15	11	20	2	12	–24	–1	–4	0
Guinea-Bissau	1995–2005	–1	16	101	–12	–5	–54	46	3	..	0	0	0	0
Guyana	1995–2005	3	3	44	20	33	–5	–22	–20	86	0	..	–6	0

Haiti	1995–2005	8	48	115	–5	–58	–11	–56	1	1	6	0	0	0
Honduras	1995–2005	81	14	2	3	81	31	11	1	38	..	..	..	0
Hong Kong SAR, China	1995–2005	678	24	26	50	..	0	0	..	..	0	0	0	0
Hungary	1995–2005	539	7	107	–10	–5	..	–5	..	..	0	–1	1	..
Iceland	1995–2005	92	12	98	–9	–1	..	–1	..	..	..	0	0	0
India	1995–2005	4,642	23	81	..	–4	10	–21	..	2	..	2	2	..
Indonesia	1995–2005	1,251	19	45	2	35	4	–2	–5	20	0	2	14	1
Iran, Islamic Rep.	1995–2005	734	38	–24	10	75	13	–8	..	..	0	18	53	0
Ireland	1995–2005	1,036	24	79	–2	–2	..	–1	..	..	0	..	..	..
Israel	1995–2005	609	15	85	–1	1	..	..	..	..	0	..	..	0
Italy	1995–2005	4,660	13	91	–3	–1	1	–2	..	..	0	..	..	..
Jamaica	1995–2005	42	28	106	–4	–30	–4	–12	1	–2	–3	2	–12	0
Japan	1995–2005	11,060	12	81	8	–1	..	–1	..	..	0	..	..	..
Jordan	1995–2005	128	5	103	–11	2	2	1	..	..	..	..	..	..
Kenya	1995–2005	120	4	102	6	–12	13	–25	..	–1	..	..	..	0
Korea, Rep.	1995–2005	4,817	24	78	–3	..	..	..	..	..	0	..	..	..
Kuwait	1995–2005	88	32	–330	71	327	2	–1	..	..	0	174	153	0
Kyrgyz Republic	2000–05	19	–1	106	5	–11	13	–24	..	..	..	..	1	..
Latvia	2000–05	100	7	104	–6	–5	..	..	–1	–2	–1	0	0	0
Lesotho	1995–2005	8	30	105	–20	–15	–4	–12	..	..	..	0	0	0
Liberia	2000–05	1	57	–408	–28	479	24	–147	322	324	0	–11	–23	–11

(continued)

TABLE F.1 (continued)

Economy	Period	Change in Wealth (2005 US$ billions)	Produced Capital	Intangible Capital	Net Foreign Assets	Natural Capital	Land Production	Land Real Prices	Forest Production	Forest Real Prices	Forest Depletion Time	Subsoil Assets Production	Subsoil Assets Real Unit Rents	Subsoil Assets Depletion Time
Lithuania	2000–05	127	5	108	-3	-9	-1	-8	..	-1	..	..	..	..
Luxembourg	1995–2005	133	28	42	32	-2	..	-1	..	..	..	0	0	0
Macao SAR, China	1995–2005	25	9	91	..	..	0	0	0	0	0	0	0	0
Macedonia, FYR	2000–05	16	10	118	-5	-22	-1	-17	..	-3	0	0	0	0
Madagascar	1995–2005	-8	-49	57	-18	110	29	119	-8	-30	0	..	..	..
Malawi	1995–2005	3	27	488	6	-421	159	-583	2	2	0	0	0	0
Malaysia	1995–2005	582	26	40	5	29	..	1	-2	..	0	10	20	0
Maldives	2000–05	2	30	73	-4	2	1	1	0	..	0	0	0	0
Mali	1995–2005	35	15	87	-1	-1	24	-21	1	2	-8	0	0	0
Malta	1995–2005	27	13	83	1	3	1	2	0	0	0	0	0	0
Mauritania	1995–2005	10	12	36	-16	68	12	15	1	6	3	13	19	0
Mauritius	1995–2005	42	16	84	2	-3	-1	-2	1	-1	..	0	0	0
Mexico	1995–2005	3,414	16	95	..	-10	-2	-6	..	..	-1	2	4	-7
Moldova	2000–05	22	-12	139	3	-30	-5	-25	..	..	0	..	..	..
Mongolia	1995–2005	12	-14	239	-8	-117	9	-131	1	1	0	5	-2	..
Morocco	1995–2005	245	24	65	4	7	8	-1	-2	1	0	..	..	..
Mozambique	1995–2005	53	14	97	2	-13	8	-12	2	3	-19	4	..	0
Namibia	1995–2005	34	20	77	3	..	5	-2	-3	..	0	..	..	0

Country	Period											
Nepal	1995–2005	53	18	45	1	35	33	−4	1	15	−10	0	0
Netherlands	1995–2005	2,243	18	81	1	:	:	−2	:	:	:	3	−1
New Zealand	1995–2005	459	15	83	−1	3	11	−8	1	−1	1	:	:
Nicaragua	1995–2005	45	12	80	14	−6	18	−10	:	−14	0	:	0
Niger	1995–2005	19	4	94	:	2	10	−7	−1	1	:	:	0
Nigeria	1995–2005	150	52	94	54	−100	41	−211	3	−37	−24	86	43
Norway	1995–2005	646	21	17	25	38	:	−3	:	−1	:	22	24
Oman	1995–2005	57	29	−136	13	194	4	−3	:	:	:	68	104
Pakistan	1995–2005	617	11	81	1	7	18	−22	:	1	1	3	0
Panama	1995–2005	97	12	97	−6	−2	2	−6	:	2	0	0	0
Papua New Guinea	1995–2005	−12	−27	215	3	−90	−21	−17	22	−40	0	34	−75
Peru	1995–2005	346	7	75	−1	19	9	1	1	4	0	1	3
Philippines	1995–2005	465	6	75	−4	22	8	9	1	3	0	2	−1
Poland	2000–05	830	12	108	−5	−14	−3	−14	:	−1	:	:	3
Portugal	1995–2005	686	21	97	−16	−2	:	−3	:	:	0	:	:
Romania	2000–05	367	3	114	−4	−13	4	−15	:	−2	0	−2	−3
Russian Federation	2000–05	2,833	−7	111	−4	:	2	−43	:	−8	0	15	37
Rwanda	1995–2005	21	5	21	−2	75	35	20	5	12	3	:	0
Saudi Arabia	1995–2005	440	8	−111	38	165	2	−2	:	:	0	26	139
Senegal	1995–2005	49	15	92	1	−8	2	−14	1	3	:	:	:
Seychelles	1995–2005	2	38	92	−30	:	:	:	:	:	0	0	0
Sierra Leone	1995–2005	7	−5	94	−10	21	44	−10	8	1	−17	−1	−2

(continued)

TABLE F.1 (continued)

Economy	Period	Change in Wealth (2005 US$ billions)	Produced Capital	Intangible Capital	Net Foreign Assets	Natural Capital	Land Production	Land Real Prices	Forest Production	Forest Real Prices	Forest Depletion Time	Subsoil Assets Production	Subsoil Assets Real Unit Rents	Subsoil Assets Depletion Time
Singapore	1995–2005	536	20	46	34	..	..	..	..	..	0	0	0	0
Slovak Republic	2000–05	161	10	113	-12	-12	..	-9	..	-1	-1	..	..	..
South Africa	1995–2005	1,067	1	124	-1	-25	3	-32	..	..	-1	3	3	..
Spain	1995–2005	4,933	24	83	-8	1	1	..	..	..	..	..	..	..
Sri Lanka	1995–2005	151	16	98	-1	-12	-2	-10	..	..	..	..	..	0
St. Kitts and Nevis	1995–2005	2	55	93	-31	-18	-13	-5	..	..	0	0	0	0
St. Lucia	1995–2005	4	26	84	-11	..	0	0	..	..	0	0	0	0
St. Vincent and the Grenadines	1995–2005	2	33	102	-33	-2	-5	3	0	..	0	0	0	0
Sudan	1995–2005	156	16	116	..	-32	62	-120	10	-20	..	9	18	9
Swaziland	1995–2005	10	13	106	7	-26	34	-59	-2	-2	3	..	..	..
Sweden	1995–2005	1,299	6	93	2	..	1	-1	1	-1	0	..	..	..
Switzerland	1995–2005	760	6	78	20	-4	1	-5	..	..	..	..	..	..
Syrian Arab Republic	1995–2005	86	18	..	37	45	22	-30	..	..	0	5	28	21
Tajikistan	2000–05	17	-10	107	2	1	20	-19	..	..	0	..	..	..
Thailand	1995–2005	776	23	50	2	25	10	11	..	1	-1	2	3	-1
Togo	1995–2005	12	4	124	-4	-24	4	-14	..	7	-22	..	..	..

Country	Period													
Tonga	1995–2005	1	4	156	–5	–55	–2	–53	..	..	..	0	0	*0
Trinidad and Tobago	1995–2005	41	15	–10	5	89	–5	–5	–1	0	..	63	48	–11
Tunisia	1995–2005	183	14	82	–5	9	5	1	1	..	..	–1	3	2
Turkey	2000–05	2,027	8	102	–1	–9	..	–9	..	..	..	..	..	..
Uganda	1995–2005	82	13	44	–3	46	20	43	–5	–5	–13	0	0	0
Ukraine	2000–05	412	–11	116	3	–8	5	–23	–1	–1	..	1	10	..
United Arab Emirates	1995–2005	606	16	43	6	36	2	–1	..	..	0	8	27	0
United Kingdom	1995–2005	10,643	9	95	–4	..	..	–1	..	..	..	..	1	..
United States	1995–2005	61,758	13	89	–2	..	..	..	..	..	0	..	1	..
Uruguay	1995–2005	17	15	21	1	63	29	18	15	..	0	0	0	0
Uzbekistan	2000–05	–13	–28	1,092	–21	–942	–75	–90	–2	..	..	–49	–714	–11
Vanuatu	2000–05	..	–8	–283	–61	452	171	257	29	–4	0	0	0	0
Venezuela, RB	1995–2005	90	66	–120	38	116	11	–48	–4	4	0	59	95	..
Zambia	1995–2005	22	19	114	6	–39	–8	–37	12	..	–5	–2	2	0
Zimbabwe	1995–2005	–11	–3	141	19	–57	–15	–42	–18	–30	24	43	–30	10

Source: Authors.
Note: Values for Europe and Central Asia, Liberia, Maldives, and Vanuatu show change between 2000 and 2005; values for Cyprus show change between 1995 and 2000.
.. = negligible value.

INDEX

Boxes, figures, notes, and tables are indicated with b, f, n, and t following the page numbers.

Dynamic Integrated Model of Climate and
the Economy (DICE) 2007 model,
88, 89*n*4

E

Earth System Research Laboratory, 87
East Asia and Pacific. *See also specific countries*
adjusted net saving in, 39
agricultural land resources in, 9, 12
land and subsoil assets in, 55–56*f*, 58–59
produced capital investments in, 51
Economic performance measures, 18–20*b*
Economics of climate change, 77–80, 78*t*, 80*f*
Economics of Climate Change (Stern), 75
Ecosystem services
future research needs for, 17
natural capital and, 8
valuation of, 22–23, 49*n*3
wetlands, 22
Educational attainment
adjusted net saving and, 19*b*
in China, 14, 106, 107–9, 110*f*, 111–12
in intangible capital accounting, 13, 98, 98*t*
urban-rural gap in, 110, 110*f*
wealth changes and, 6
Egalitarianism, 84
Egypt, land and subsoil assets in, 58
EITI. *See* Extractive Industries Transparency
Initiative
EITI++, 122, 123–24, 126, 127*n*7
El-Serafy method, 133
Energy resources
country experiences with accounting for,
133–34, 134*t*, 135
valuation methodology, 145–46
Environmental debt, 84
Equipment valuation methodology, 143–44
Equity issues for climate change accounting,
84–85
Etheridge, D. M., 87
Ethiopia
per capita wealth changes in, 9
wealth changes in, 33
Europe and Central Asia. *See also specific
countries*
carbon stocks and flows in, 13, 83, 83*t*, 85
intangible capital in, 51
land and subsoil assets in, 9, 35, 53,
55–56*f*, 57
wealth changes in, 33, 34*f*, 35
European Union, carbon stocks and flows for,
79, 80, 81*f*

Eurostat, 105, 129, 148
Exhaustion time, 53
Expected lifetime earnings of individuals, 115
External Wealth of Nations Mark II database,
150
Extractive Industries Transparency Initiative
(EITI), 15, 122, 123.
See also EITI++

F

Fankhauser, Samuel, 78
FDI (foreign direct investment), 150
Ferreira, S., 24*n*1
Fisher, Irving, 93
Fisheries
country experiences with accounting for,
135
future research needs for, 16
resources missing from accounts, 21
Fitoussi, Jean-Paul, 16, 20*b*, 23, 129, 137
Fixed effects model, 99
Food and Agriculture Organization (FAO),
147, 149
Foreign direct investment (FDI), 150
Forest resources
in decomposition analysis, 12, 57
valuation methodology, 146–48
wealth changes and, 35
Fortech (Forestry Technical Services), 148
Fossil fuel combustion, 80
France, human capital in, 105
Fraumeni, Barbara M., 114. *See also* Jorgenson-
Fraumeni lifetime income approach
Free rider problem, 89*n*2
Fuelwood prices, 148

G

Gabon, adjusted net saving gap in, 41
GDP (gross domestic product), 4
Gender differences in human capital, 14,
109–12, 111*t*, 113
Genuine savings. *See* Adjusted net savings
(ANS)
Germany, carbon stocks and flows in, 81
Ghana
natural capital management in, 120
per capita wealth changes in, 9
wealth changes in, 33
Global Assessment of Energy Accounts, 134
Global Forest Resources Assessments (FAO), 147
Global Trade Analysis Project (GTAP), 149
Global Witness, 148

per capita wealth changes in, 9
wealth changes in, 33
Mungatana, E., 138n1

N

Namibia
economic growth in, 126f
fisheries accounting in, 21, 135
National Oceanic and Atmospheric
Administration (NOAA, U.S.), 87
National statistical offices, 16
Natural capital, 51–71
in decomposition analysis, 61
defined, 4
development and, 9–11, 10f
land values in, 53–59, 54–55f
resources missing from accounts, 21–22
subsoil assets in, 54f, 56f
wealth changes and, 6, 29, 29f, 30t, 37
Natural gas
prices, 57
reserves, 158n8
Natural pollinators, 17, 22
Net foreign assets valuation methodology, 150
Netherlands
human capital in, 105
renewable energy accounting in, 135
Net national income (NNI), 20b
Net present value (NPV), 133
Net price method, 133
New Zealand
adjusted net saving gap in, 41, 43
fisheries accounting in, 21, 135
human capital in, 105
water resources accounting in, 135
Nigeria
land and subsoil assets in, 55, 57
per capita wealth in, 9, 43
wealth changes in, 33, 35
Nitrous oxide, 76
NNI (net national income), 20b
Nongovernmental organizations (NGOs), 16,
129, 132
Nordhaus, William, 88, 89n4
Norway
adjusted net national income in, 20b
balance sheet use in, 136
energy resource accounting in, 134
fisheries accounting in, 135
human capital in, 105, 112, 135
hydropower accounting in, 21, 135
natural capital in, 15

natural capital management in, 120
wealth accounting by, 130
NPV (net present value), 133

O

OECD countries
composition of wealth changes in, 29f,
30t, 31
human capital in, 13–14
intangible capital in, 51, 101
machinery, equipment, and structures
valuation in, 143–44
per capita wealth in, 31, 32f, 32t
wealth changes in, 5, 28, 28t
Oil
prices, 57
reserves, 158n8
One-child policy, 106
Organisation for Economic Co-operation and
Development (OECD). *See also*
OECD countries
consortium to develop human capital
accounts, 105–6, 135
wealth accounting initiatives of, 129

P

Pareto compensation, 85
Pasquier, J., 132
Pasture land resources, 56, 59, 149
Patrinos, H., 97
Perpetual Inventory Method (PIM), 143
Persistence of CO2, 77–78
Peru, natural capital in, 10
Poland
carbon stocks and flows in, 82, 83
human capital in, 105
Population dilution effect, 31
Population growth
adjusted net saving gap and, 41–42, 42f
in China, 107–9, 109f
wealth changes and, 41–42, 42f, 198–202t
Positive economics, 76
Poverty reduction, 126
PPP (purchasing power parity), 24n5
Preindustrial levels of CO2, 79, 87
Price, Colin, 148
Price effect, 12, 59–60
Produced capital
defined, 4
intangible capital and, 94
investments in, 51
wealth changes and, 29, 29f, 30t

Weil, David N., 97
Weisbach, David, 84
Weitzman, Martin L., 24n1
Wetland ecosystem services, 22
Where Is the Wealth of Nations? (World Bank),
    4, 9, 13, 94, 96–97
Whiteman, Adrian, 148
World Conservation Monitoring
        Centre, 150
World Database on Protected Areas, 150

World Development Indicators (World Bank),
    96, 97, 130
World Development Report 2010 (World Bank),
    13, 75, 77
World Summit on Sustainable Development
    (2002), 122

Z

Zimbabwe, wealth changes in, 33